BIBLE DICTIONARY

Aar'on. Brother and spokesman of Moses, first high priest (Ex. 4:14-16, 27);
> Aaron's rod (Ex., ch. 5; 7:7-9:35; 17:1-10)
> descendants set apart as priests (Ex., chs. 28-30; 40:12-15)
> makes golden calf (Ex., ch. 32)
> Aaron and sons anointed (Lev., chs. 8-10)
> sacrifices scapegoat (Lev., ch. 16)
> speaks against Moses (Num., ch. 12)
> rebellion of Korah (Num., ch. 16)
> Aaron's rod buds (Num., ch. 17)
> Levites appointed assistants (Num. 18:1-8)
> Aaron excluded from Promised Land; dies; priesthood handed to Eleazar (Num. 20:12-29)
> descendants of (I Chron. 6:49).
> See also HIGH PRIEST; LEVITES.

Ab'ba. The word for father in Aramaic, the language Jesus spoke. It was the usual form of address used by a child when speaking to his father. Jesus used it to address God (Mark 14:36).

A·bed'ne·go. With Shadrach and Meshach, saved from the fiery furnace (Dan. 1:7; ch. 3).

A'bel. Adam's second son; his offering to God accepted, he is slain by his brother Cain in jealous anger (Gen., ch. 4; I John 3:12).

A·bi'a·thar. A priest who escaped Saul (I Sam. 22:20); later deposed for disloyalty to Solomon, ending the priesthood of the house of Eli (I Chron. 15:11-14; I Kings 1:7; 2:12-27). See HIGH PRIEST; ZADOK.

Ab'i·gail. 1. Wife of Nabal, later of David (I Sam., ch. 25; 27:3). 2. Half-sister of David (I Chron. 2:16).

A·bi'hu. Second son of Aaron, he offers "strange fire" and dies (Ex. 6:23; Lev. 10:1-2; Num. 3:2-4).

A·bi'jah. Among others of this name: 1. King of Judah, also called Abijam, who continued the war begun under his father, Rehoboam, against Jeroboam, with great slaughter of the men of Israel (I Kings 15:1-7; II Chron., ch. 13; cf. II Sam. 24:9). See KINGS, TABLE OF. 2. A son of Jeroboam, his death foretold by the prophet Ahijah (I Kings 14:1-18).

A·bi'jam. See ABIJAH (1).

A·bim'e·lech. 1. King of Gerar; rebukes Abraham (Gen., ch. 20). 2. King of the Philistines; rebukes Isaac (Gen., ch. 26). 3. Son of Gideon; murders his brothers and becomes king of Shechem (Judg., ch. 9). 4. At I Chron. 18:16, probably an error for Ahimelech.

A·bin'a·dab. Ark kept in his house 20 years, until its return to David (I Sam. 7:1; II Sam. 6:3; I Chron. 13:7).

A·bi'ram. See KORAH.

Ab'i·shag. Attends David; causes breach between Adonijah and Solomon (I Kings 1:1-4; 2:12-25).

A·bish'a·i. Brother of Joab; slays 300 men (I Sam. 26:6-9; II Sam. 23:18).

Ab'ner. Commander of Saul's army; makes Ish-bosheth king but later goes over to David and is slain by Joab (I Sam. 14:50; 26:5; II Sam. 2:8-11; 3:8-27).

a·bom'i·na'tion. Something that excites disgust and hatred, esp. something offensive to God. The term is applied to heathen gods, idolatry and various pagan or immoral practices (Deut. 7:25-26; 17:2-5; 27:15; I Kings 11:5-7; Ezek. 8:9-13).

a·bom'i·na'tion of des'o·la'tion. A phrase appearing in Matt. 24:15; Mark 13:14 (see also Dan. 11:31; 12:11), it means an evil, odious, hateful thing or act that lays waste something good or holy. An example was the stopping of the daily sacrifice in the Temple by a Syrian king in 168 B.C. and the performing there, instead, of sacrifices to a Greek god. This made the altar unclean, unusable, "desolate."

A'bra·ham, A'bram. Founder of the Hebrew people;

called Abram (Gen. 11:26)

removes to Egypt (Gen., ch. 12)

returns, parts from Lot, later rescues him (Gen., chs. 13-14)

Ishmael is born (Gen., chs. 15-16)

Abram now called Abraham, another son promised (Gen., chs. 17-18)

Isaac is born, Hagar and Ishmael cast out (Gen., chs. 20-21)

as test of faith, Abraham offers Isaac as sacrifice (Gen., ch. 22)

death of Sarah (Gen., ch. 23)

Abraham marries Keturah, dies (Gen., ch. 25).

N.T. references: Rom., ch. 4; Heb., chs. 7; 11; James 2:23. See also COVENANT; CHOSEN PEOPLE.

Abraham's bos'om. The Jews fondly thought of being, welcomed to paradise by Abraham, Isaac and Jacob, and even of resting in comfort on Abraham's breast (Luke 16:22).

Ab'sa·lom. A son of David (II Sam. 3:3), the story of his conspiracy and death is told in II Sam., chs. 15-18.

a·byss'. The bottomless pit; the place of the dead (Rom. 10:7).

a·ca'cia. See SHITTAH TREE.

ac·curse'. To call down evil upon (Gal. 1:8); sometimes (Josh. 7:1) to devote to God. See OATH.

A·cel'da·ma, A·kel'da·ma. This name, which in Greek means "field of blood," was given to the plot of ground bought by the priests with Judas' ill-gotten 30 pieces of silver for use as a burial place for strangers (Matt. 27:7; Acts 1:18-19). Also known as the potters' field, as it furnished clay for makers of pottery. It was probably located on the s. side of the Valley of Hinnom.

A'chan. A man stoned to death for sin (Josh., ch. 7).

A'chish. King of Gath; gives David refuge (I Sam., chs. 21, 27-29; I Kings 2:39).

a'cre. See MEASURES.

Ad'am. The first human being;
     created in God's image, blessed (Gen. 1:27-28)
     names every living creature (Gen. 2:19)
     with Eve, disobeys God; expelled from Garden of Eden (Gen., ch. 3)
     birth of Cain, Abel and Seth (Gen., ch. 4)
     Adam's death (Gen. 5:5).
     Paul calls our Lord the "last Adam" (I Cor. 15:22, 45).

ad'a·mant. An extremely hard metal or mineral, esp. the diamond (Ezek. 3:9).

ad'der. See ASP.

ad·jure'. To bind by oath (Matt. 26:63).

Ad'o·ni'jah. The most important of those mentioned in the O.T. is the son of David (II Sam. 3:4), who attempts to seize the throne and is put to death by Solomon (I Kings, ch. 1; 2:13-25).

a·dop'tion. The act of taking a stranger to be one's own child, as with Moses (Ex. 2:10) and Esther (Esth. 2:7). In the N.T. the word is used to denote: 1. the choice by God of Israel to be His special people (Rom. 9:4); and 2. the reception of all true Christians to be in a special sense the sons of God (Gal. 4:5; Eph. 1:5). The spirit of adoption enables us to feel to God as children do to a loving father. See also SONS OF GOD.

Ad'vent, Sec'ond. See SECOND COMING.

Ag'a·bus. A prophet who foretold Paul's sufferings (Acts 11:28; 21:10).

A'gar. See HAGAR.

ag'ate. See CHALCEDONY.

A·grip'pa. See HEROD.

a'gue. A fever. "Burning ague" (Lev. 26:16) may have been malaria.

A'hab. 1. King of Israel, son of Omri, husband

of Jezebel;
    his Baal worship (I Kings 16:29-33)
    and Elijah (I Kings, ch. 18)
    defeats Ben-hadad (I Kings, ch. 20)
    takes Naboth's vineyard (I Kings
        21:1-16)
    dies as prophesied (I Kings 22:20-40).
    See ASSYRIA; BAAL; KINGS, TABLE OF.
    2. An evil prophet (Jer. 29:21).
A·has'u·e'rus. 1. The father of Darius the
    Mede (Dan. 9:1). See DARIUS. 2. The Per-
    sian king Xerxes; orders destruction of the
    Jews but is dissuaded by Esther (Esth., chs.
    1-10).
A'haz. A young king of Judah, son of Jotham,
    who rejected Isaiah's advice to rely on the
    Lord; instead he made a treaty with Tig-
    lath-pileser of Assyria that cost him much
    of the treasure of the Temple (II Kings, ch.
    16; II Chron., ch. 28; Isa., ch. 7). See IM-
    MANUEL; KINGS, TABLE OF.
A'ha·zi'ah. 1. King of Israel, son of Ahab;
    death prophesied by Elijah (I Kings
    22:40-II Kings 1:17). 2. King of Judah, son
    of Jehoram; killed by Jehu (II Kings
    8:25-9:29). Also called Jehoahaz and Azari-
    ah (II Chron. 21:17; 22:6). See KINGS, TA-
    BLE OF.
A·hi'jah. A common name in the O.T.; best
    known is the prophet of Shiloh who pre-
    dicted that Jeroboam would be king and
    foretold his son Abijah's death (I Kings
    11:29-39; 14:1-18).
A·him'e·lech. 1. Chief priest at Nob; slain at
    Saul's command for his treachery (I Sam.,
    ch. 21; 22). 2. His grandson, likewise a
    priest (II Sam. 8:17). 3. A follower of David
    (I Sam. 26:6).
A·hith'o·phel. A disloyal counselor of David
    (II Sam. 15:12, 31-34; 16:15, 23; 17:23).
A·kel'da·ma. See ACELDAMA.
al'a·bas'ter. A soft stone, creamy white in col-
    or and delicately shaded or veined. It was
    most often used in perfume flasks and orna-
    mental vases. The best such objects were

imported from Egypt, but the Jordan Valley area yielded a useful, less expensive type of alabaster.

ALABASTER

Al'a·moth. A musical term (I Chron. 15:20; Ps. 46, title), uncertain in meaning; it may refer to soprano voices.

a'leph. The first letter of the Hebrew alphabet. The Greek *alpha* and the English *a* are derived from it, but *aleph* is a consonant and has no English equivalent. It stands at the head of the first section of Psalm 119, since in the original each verse of the section begins with this letter.

al'gum. See ALMUG.

al'mond. A tree and its fruit (Gen. 43:11; Eccl. 12:5). It is the first tree to blossom in the spring. In Palestine it is found in Lebanon, Hermon and in most of the region beyond the Jordan. There are two varieties: the bitter and the sweet; the former has white flowers, the latter roseate. The cups on the branches of the golden lampstand were modeled after almond blossoms (Ex. 25:33–34).

alms. Money, food, clothing, etc., given voluntarily to poor and needy people (Luke 11:41). An almsdeed was an act of charity (Acts 9:36).

al'mug, al'gum (II Chron.). A timber brought in abundance by sea from Ophir during the reign of Solomon. It was used to make pillars or balustrades, also harps and psalteries

(I Kings 10:11-12; II Chron. 9:10-11). We do not know exactly what wood this was. It was the botanist Celsius (1670-1756) who suggested the identification with Indian sandalwood. It had a sweet scent and took a high polish.

al'oes. Aloes in Palestine was known only as an aromatic substance and not as a tree (Ps. 45:8; Prov. 7:17; S. of Sol. 4:14). Both incense and perfume came from the essential oil of a tree native to s.e. Asia. It is the "lign aloes" of Num. 24:6 (KJV) as well as the "aloes" of John 19:39.

al'pha and o·me'ga. The first and last letters of the Greek alphabet. Rev. 1:8 means "I am the first and last" of beings; that is, all things begin and end in God, who Himself is without beginning or end.

al'tar. An elevated structure on which incense was burned or sacrifice offered to the deity. It might be a mound of earth; or a huge stone, or a platform built of several stones, dressed or undressed; or an object of similar shape made of metal. In the times of the patriarchs, worshipers built altars wherever they pitched their tents or had special occasion to sacrifice to God (Gen. 8:20; 12:7; 22:9; 35:1, 7; Ex. 17:15; 24:4). The fundamental law of the Hebrew altar called for the erection of an altar wherever God should appear or speak. The Tabernacle

ALTAR

had two altars: one was the bronze altar or altar of burnt offering, which stood in the outer court; the second was the golden altar or altar of incense, which stood in the Holy Place. On this altar incense was burned morning and evening. This arrangement was transferred from the movable Tabernacle to the permanent Temple built by Solomon. New bronze and golden altars were built, and these now became the only *permanent* altars on which sacrifices could be acceptably offered (Deut. 12:2–7). When the 10 northern tribes revolted, pious Israelites among them who were now debarred from making an annual pilgrimage to the Temple in Jerusalem either had to give up worshiping God by sacrifice or else erect local altars. They often chose the latter (I Kings 18:30, 32; 19:10). This situation caused much trouble, religious and political (I Kings 12:26–33). See also SACRIFICE; TABERNACLE; TEMPLE.

Am'a·lek. Son of Eliphaz, Esau's son, by his concubine Timna (Gen. 36:12). The name of the ancestor is also used collectively for the Amalekites (e.g. Ex. 17:8; Num. 24:20; Judg. 5:14).

Am'a·lek·ites. Descendants of Esau (Gen. 36:12). For a long time they were centered about Kadesh-barnea, where they were dwelling at the time of the Exodus (Num. 13:24; 14:25). From this center these desert people roamed and their camps radiated. Because of their hostility to Israel, their destruction was authorized (Ex. 17:8–16; Deut. 25:17–19). They suffered crushing defeat from Saul and from David (I Sam., chs. 15; 30) and seem never to have recovered.

Am'a·sa. 1. David's nephew; joins Absalom in revolt; is made commander-in-chief and is slain by Joab (II Sam. 17:25; 20:8–12). 2. A prince of Ephraim (II Chron. 28:12).

Am'a·zi'ah. 1. King of Judah, son of Jehoash (Joash); defeats Edomites in battle; taken prisoner by another Jehoash (Joash), king of Israel; flees to Lachish and is finally murdered (II Kings 14:1–20; II Chron., ch. 25). See KINGS, TABLE OF. 2. A priest who tried to silence the prophet Amos (Amos 7:10–17).

a·men'. An interjection "So be it," "May it be so!" added to whatever has been asked, said, promised or threatened (Matt. 6:13; Deut. 27:16–26; Neh. 8:6; Ps. 106:48; Rom. 11:36; II Cor. 1:20).

Am'mon. Same as Ben-ammi, Lot's younger son, ancestor of the Ammonites (Gen. 19:38).

Am'mon·ites. A people descended from Ben-ammi, Lot's second son. They moved into the territory between the Arnon and Jabbok rivers on the e. side of the Jordan River valley (Deut. 2:20–21; 3:11), but were in turn driven out by the Amorites and compelled to keep on the border of the desert farther e. (Num. 21:24; Judg. 11:13, 22). Later they re-entered the region and became inveterate enemies of Israel, and as such were denounced by the prophets (Jer. 49:1–6; Ezek. 21:20; 25:1–7; Amos 1:13–15; Zeph. 2:8–11). Their chief deity was Milcom, another name for Molech (I Kings 11:7, 33). In the time of Jephthah they were worshiping Chemosh, the Moabite god (Judg. 11:24).

A'mon. 1. Governor of Samaria (I Kings 22:10, 26). 2. King of Judah, son of Manasseh; after reigning but 2 years, murdered by his servants, who placed his young son Josiah on the throne (II Kings 21:19–26; II Chron. 33:21–25). See KINGS, TABLE OF.

Am'o·rites. The early history of the Amorites is obscure, but during the third millennium B.C. Palestine was called by Babylonians "the land of the Amorites." Later their territory included Babylonia, whose great king Hammurabi was an Amorite. At the time of Abraham they dwelt on the w. shore of the

Dead Sea (Gen. 14:7, 13) and they were the most powerful people in the hill country of

Palestine. At the time of the Exodus, their power had further increased, notably e. of the Jordan, from the Arnon River n. to Mt. Hermon, under Og, king of Bashan, an Amorite. A strong remnant remained in the land after the Conquest (Judg. 1:35; 3:5), with whom in Samuel's day there was peace (I Sam. 7:14), and who, with the survivors of other earlier resident races, were made bondservants by Solomon (I Kings 9:20-21).

A′mos. A shepherd in Tekoa, moved to preach by the disturbing conditions of his time. Very little is known about his life.

An′a·ni′as. 1. An early Christian; his lie and death (Acts 5:1-6). 2. A disciple; restores Saul's sight (9:10-18). 3. A high priest; judges Paul (23:2; 24:1).

a·nath′e·ma. In the N.T., a person or thing devoted to destruction, accursed.

A·nath′e·ma Mar′a·nath′a. The second word here (see I Cor. 16:22) is now regarded as a 2-word Aramaic expression (*Marana tha*) that should be put into a sentence by itself. The phrase would then read, "Let him be accursed. Our Lord, come!"

An′cient of days. This expression is found 3 times in Dan. 7:9-22. The Aramaic phrase means literally "advanced in days" and simply signifies "old man." Here the Deity is represented as an old person, and the term is applied to God in His capacity as judge of the world. The phrase itself has no mystical significance.

An′drew. A brother of Simon Peter, of Bethsaida on the Sea of Galilee (John 1:44). He was a follower of John the Baptist, but became one of the 12 apostles (Matt. 4:18; Mark 1:29; 13:3; Acts 1:13; etc.). According to John 1:40-42, he then introduced his brother Peter to Jesus. Tradition says that he was crucified on a cross shaped like the letter X, since called St. Andrew's Cross.

an′gel. The Greek word *angelos* means a messenger. Angels are the agents by means of

which God communicates with men, since
it was believed (Ex. 33:20) that no man
could see God Himself and live. On some
special occasions God sent "angels of the
Lord," who, because of the significance of
the message they bore, seemed to lose their
identity and take on human form (Ex. 3:2;
Judg. 13:3). At other times an angel's presence was equivalent to God's presence (Ex.
32:34; 33:14; Isa. 63:9). In the later books
differences among angels in rank and dignity appear, for there are archangels (chief
angels) as well as ordinary angels (I Thess.
4:16; Jude 9).

an'ise. Probably to be identified with dill, a
parsley-like plant somewhat like caraway
in appearance, cultivated in the East for its
seeds, which are used as a seasoning and for
the relief of intestinal disturbances. In Matt.
23:23 (where the RSV uses "dill"), Jesus is
criticizing the Pharisees' tithing of trifles.

An'na. An aged prophetess who witnessed the
dedication of the infant Jesus (Luke
2:36-38).

An'nas. A high priest at Jerusalem (Luke 3:2),
probably c. A.D. 26; Jesus is brought before
him (John 18:13, 24); he examines Peter
and John (Acts 4:6-21).

An·nun'ci·a'tion. The announcement by the
angel Gabriel to the Virgin Mary that she
was to give birth to the Son of God (Luke
1:26-38).

a·noint'. To pour oil upon the head, or in any
other way apply it to a person or to a thing
such as an altar vessel. Ordinary anointing
was simply a matter of the toilet and
grooming (Ruth 3:3; II Sam. 12:20). It was
also a courtesy extended to guests (Luke
7:46), and used medically to treat a sore or
wound (Isa. 1:6). Dead bodies were
anointed, probably as a gesture of respect
(Mark 14:8; Luke 23:56). Anointing was
also part of the official religious ceremony
of consecrating a prophet, priest or king
(Ex. 28:41; I Kings 19:16). "Anoint" came

to mean to provide a person with a particular quality or talent, esp. a God-given quality, as God anointed Jesus (Acts 10:38), and Israel was spoken of as God's anointed.

ant. In the Bible the ant is held up as an example of industry and forethought in connection with the provision and storage of food (Prov. 6:6-8; 30:24-25). Ants are social insects, living in well-ordered colonies.

an'te·lope. See CHAMOIS; DEER; PYGARG; OX, WILD.

An'ti·christ. This word may mean an enemy of Christ or a usurper of Christ's name and rights. From I John we learn that the early Christians had been taught that "antichrist" would appear in "the last time," i.e., before the Second Advent. While not denying that Antichrist would be a single person, John lays stress on the spirit to be embodied in him. The substance of the antichristian spirit, he says, is a denial that Jesus is the Christ or the real incarnation of the Son of God, and an antagonism to Christ's claims on men.

an'ti·mo'ny. Probably a hard dark mortar for setting off precious stones (I Chron. 29:2). See also PAINT.

An'ti·och. 1. A metropolis of Syria in the period between its founding in c. 300 B.C. until first destroyed in A.D. 538 by the Persians. It was situated about 15 miles from the mouth of the Orontes River; its seaport, Seleucia Pieria, was one of the principal harbors of the e. Mediterranean. Though basically Greek, its population was mixed, with not a few Jews. Numerous Christians fled here from Jerusalem to escape persecution after the death of Stephen. Antioch became the birthplace of foreign missions; it was here that the disciples were first called Christians. From Antioch Paul and Barnabas were sent on a missionary journey (Acts 13:1–14:26). Paul's second missionary journey also started from Antioch (15:35–36). In apostolic days it was a city of over

500,000 inhabitants and was known as "Antioch the Beautiful," "The Queen of the East," etc. The place, still called Antākiyeh, is now unimportant. 2. Another town in Asia Minor of the same name and, like the above Antioch, founded by Seleucus Nicator and named after his father, Antiochus. Situated in Phrygia, near the borders of Pisidia, it was accordingly designated "Antioch toward Pisidia" and "Pisidian Antioch" to distinguish it from Antioch in Syria. Paul and Barnabas visited it on their first missionary journey (Acts 13:14-52).

An'ti·pas. 1. A Christian martyr (Rev. 2:13). 2. Son of Herod the Great (see HEROD).

ape. If the animals that were brought to Palestine by ships that went to Ophir for gold (I Kings 10:22; II Chron. 9:21) came from India, they were a species of tailed monkey and not the true ape, which is without a tail.

A·poc'ry·pha. This Greek word means "hidden things." The adjective, apocryphal, is used by Bible scholars for: 1. matters secret or mysterious; 2. writings of unknown origin, forged, spurious; 3. writings unrecognized, uncanonical. The noun Apocrypha is the name given generally to the following 16 books: I and II Esdras, Tobit, Judith, The Additions to Esther, The Wisdom of Solomon, Ecclesiasticus, Baruch with The Letter of Jeremiah, The Prayer of Azariah and the Song of the Three Young Men, Susanna, Bel and the Dragon, The Prayer of Manasseh and I, II, III and IV Maccabees. Sometimes the last 2 are omitted. Unlike the books of the O.T., which are almost entirely in Hebrew, the apocryphal books are in Greek. The Jewish authorities considered them uninspired, and they are not found in the Hebrew canon. They were never quoted by Jesus. The early churches permitted them to be read for edification and recommended them to young pupils for study, but rejected them from the canon.

The Apocrypha, as a group between the Testaments, were introduced into the English version by Myles Coverdale in 1535. The Catholic Church declared most of them to be canonical in 1546. These books were again included and placed between the Testaments in the King James Version, but began to be omitted as early as 1629.

To sum up, the books of the Apocrypha may be regarded as writings which have, at times at least, had some claim to be regarded as holy Scripture and to be accepted into the canon of our Bible, but which, among Protestants, have failed to get acceptance.

A·pol'los. A Jew who became a disciple of John the Baptist and preached at Corinth (Acts 18:24-19:7; I Cor. 3:6; Titus 3:13). Many scholars have thought Apollos to be the writer of the Epistle to the Hebrews.

a·pos'tle. The Greek word *apostolos* means one sent forth, a messenger, an ambassador. An apostle was one of the men selected by Jesus to be eyewitnesses of the events of his life, to see him after his Resurrection and to testify to mankind concerning him (Matt. 10:2-42; Acts 1:21-22; I Cor. 9:1). They were often called disciples or pupils (Matt. 11:1; 14:26; 20:17; John 20:2). The original 12 were Andrew, Bartholomew (or Nathanael), James the younger (son of Alphaeus), James the elder and John (sons of Zebedee), Judas (or Thaddaeus, not to be confused with Judas Iscariot), Philip, Simon the Zealot or Canaanite, Simon called Peter, Judas Iscariot, Matthew (or Levi) and Thomas. Matthias was chosen to replace Judas Iscariot. Paul possessed the qualifications for an apostle of having seen Jesus after the Resurrection, in a vision while on his way to Damascus. Where the several apostles labored, how they lived and how they died is in most cases known only by the doubtful evidence of tradition.

ap'ple. A tree and its fruit (Prov. 25:11; S. of

Sol. 2:3; 8:5). The one referred to in the
O.T. is probably the variety *Pyrus malus*,
which has been found growing well at As-
kelon in the Philistine country. Some authorities believe that the apricot is meant,
while others argue for the quince. In their
favor is the fact that the fruit from apple
trees in Bible lands is of poor quality and
hardly matches the graphic Bible imagery.

ap'ple of the eye. The pupil of the eye, thus
something highly cherished (Ps. 17:8).

a'pri·cot. See APPLE.

Aq'ui·la. A Jew who, with his wife Priscilla,
worked at Corinth at tent-making, where
Paul, a weaver, joined them. They became
Christians and continued Paul's teachings
(Acts, ch. 18).

A·ra'bi·ans. Among the Hebrews the name
"Arabians" denoted the nomadic peoples of
the desert portions of n. Arabia (a very
large peninsula) with whom they early
came in contact, as distinct from the well-
settled inhabitants of S. Arabia. Among
these usually hostile Arabian peoples were
the Ishmaelites, Amalekites, Midianites,
Dedanites and Sabeans.

Ar'a·me'ans. Persons from the region known
as Aram (Gen. 25:20; 28:5). They were
Semites, i.e., descended from Shem (Gen.
10:22-23). They probably were one of the
nomadic groups that were a part of the
mass migration out of the Syrian desert into
fertile lands about 3000 B.C., and then
moved both s. toward Egypt and e. across
the Euphrates River and n. to the Taurus
Mountains. In the ultimate possession of
these lands they succeeded the Amorites.
The contact between Hebrews and Arameans goes back to the period of the patriarchs
(Gen. 31:47). The maternal ancestry of Jacob's children is Aramean. Politically the
Arameans formed several district-states under kings: e.g. Aram-naharaim, in which
Padan-aram was situated, and Aram-maa-
cah, near Mt. Hermon. Damascus became

the center of Aramean influence w. of the Euphrates and waged intermittent war with the Northern Kingdom, until both fell to the Assyrians.

A·rau'nah. A Jebusite who sold David a site for the Temple (II Sam. 24:16-25). In Chronicles he is called Ornan.

Ar'che·la'us. Successor of Herod the Great; feared by Joseph (Matt. 2:22; cf. Luke 19:12-14). See HEROD.

Ar·e·op'a·gus. Same as Mars Hill (Acts 17:19, 22). Areopagus also came to mean the court of justice of the city of Athens, which met there. On the Areopagus Paul addressed an informal gathering of philosophers. See also ATHENS.

Ar'i·el. The meaning of the Hebrew word, used by Isaiah (29:1, 2, 7) as a symbolic name for Jerusalem, is uncertain, perhaps "altar hearth."

Ar'is·tar'chus. A companion and fellow prisoner of Paul (Acts 19:29-20:6; 27:2; Col. 4:10; Philemon 24).

ark. A chest, box or covered receptacle, as the vessel constructed by Noah (Gen. 6:14-8:19); the basket made for the infant Moses (Ex. 2:3-6); the Ark of the Covenant (Ex. 25:10 ff.).

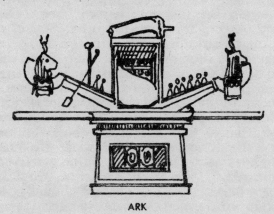

ARK

Ark of the Cov'e·nant. A chest 2½ cubits long, 1½ cubits broad and the same in

depth, made of acacia wood overlaid inside
and out with pure gold, it was the central
object of the Tabernacle. The lid was called
the mercy seat. The Ark, in symbolizing the
presence of God with His people, also indicates the impossibility of representing God
in the form of an animal or of a human
being. It was made especially to hold the
testimony written on the tables of stone (the
Ten Commandments). It accompanied the
Hebrews on their wanderings, was carried
into battle, was captured by the Philistines
and later sent back. In Solomon's Temple it
was placed in the Holy of Holies. It disappeared forever when Jerusalem was destroyed by Nebuchadnezzar. See TABERNA-
CLE.

Ar·ma·ged'don. A symbolic battlefield where
the last battle between the forces of good
and evil will be fought. "Har Megiddo" is
"Mount of Megiddo" in Hebrew, and Megiddo was next to the plain where many important battles took place throughout history. See JEZREEL.

ar'mor. See BREASTPLATE; BUCKLER.

ar'my. The army of Israel consisted originally
of infantry only: spearmen, slingers and
archers (Num. 11:21; I Sam. 4:10; 15:4). It
included all able-bodied men 20 years old
and upward. For military operations of no
great magnitude, each tribe furnished its
quota of warriors (Num. 31:4; Josh. 7:3;
Judg. 20:10). In time of national peril messengers were sent throughout the land to
summon the men of war (Judg. 6:34-35; I
Sam. 11:7). The militia was organized on
the basis of the political divisions. The unit
was the thousand, a term apparently interchangeable with father's house, family or
clan (Ex. 12:37; Num. 1:2-3, 16, 46; Judg.
6:15; I Sam. 10:19, 21). Each of these divisions was under its own officer (Num.
31:14; Judg. 20:10; I Sam. 8:12; II Kings 1:9;
11:4). The commander-in-chief and the officers formed a council of war (I Chron.

13:1). The first traces of a standing army in
Israel are found in the reign of Saul (I Sam.
13:2; 14:52). David increased the army
vastly (I Chron., ch. 27) and Solomon
added a large force of chariots and horse-
men which he distributed in key military
centers throughout his kingdom (I Kings
9:19; 10:26; II Chron. 9:25).

Ar'tax·erx'es. Son of Xerxes and his successor
to the Persian throne, ruling 465-424 B.C.
(Ezra-Neh.).

Ar'te·mis. See DIANA.

A'sa. King of Judah, son of Abijah; rules well,
abolishes idols, but later makes league with
Ben-hadad against King Baasha of Israel
instead of trusting in the Lord. His story is
told in I Kings 15:9-24 and II Chron., chs.
14-16. See KINGS, TABLE OF.

As'a·hel. A brother of Joab, slain by Abner (II
Sam. 2:18-23).

A'saph. Among others of the same name, a
singer and cymbal-player, leader of David's
choir (II Chron. 5:12; 29:30; 35:15; Neh.
12:46). 12 Psalms (50; 73-83) are attributed
to his family.

A·scen'sion. The bodily ascent of the risen
Christ, a disappearance by upward move-
ment into the sky, on the fortieth day after
his Resurrection (Acts 1:9). At the Ascension he entered a higher sphere, which the
Christians call heaven, where God is, and
whence in human form he had come to the
earth in humility.

A'ser. See ASHER.

Ash'er. 1. Eighth son of Jacob, his second by
Zilpah (Gen. 30:12-13; 35:23; see also
46:17). 2. The tribe of Asher (Aser, Luke
2:36) and the territory assigned to them,
which lay to the n.w. of Palestine; the Ash-
erites failed to drive out the Canaanites
from the cities along the Mediterranean
coast, but "dwelt among them" (Josh.
19:24-31; Judg. 1:31-32). 3. Possibly a town
(Josh. 17:7).

A·she'rah. The Hebrew form of the name of

an Amorite or Canaanite goddess. When
not the name of a deity, Asherah refers to a
wooden pole or mast that stood at Canaanite places of worship (Ex. 34:13, where it is
mistakenly translated "groves"; originally it
was, perhaps, the trunk of a tree with the
branches chopped off) and was regarded as
the wooden symbol of the goddess Asherah,
who, like Ashtoreth, was a goddess of fertility. See also GROVE, HIGH PLACE.

Ash'ta·roth. This is the plural form of the
name of the Canaanite goddess Ashtoreth.
But "Ashtaroth" is used as a general designation for all the female divinities of the
Canaanite religion.

Ash'to·reth. A goddess of the Phoenicians and
Canaanites; also called Astarte, and in
Babylonia, Ishtar. She was the goddess of
sexual love, maternity and fertility. Her
worship was early established at Sidon and
was popular e. of the Jordan in the days of
Abraham (Gen. 14:5). As early as the times
of the Judges it had spread to the Hebrews
(Judg. 2:13; 10:6). Solomon in his old age
gave it support (I Kings 11:5; II Kings
23:13). Prophets strove earnestly and constantly to wipe out the worship of her,
which suggests that she had much appeal to
peoples dependent on the fertility of soil
and flocks. See also ASHTAROTH.

A'shur·ban'i·pal. Known also as Asnapper or
Osnappar (Ezra 4:10), he was the son and
successor of Esarhaddon to the Assyrian
throne. He carried on his forebears' policy
of conquest and resettlement, but eventually lost Egypt, which his father had taken.
He collected a great library in Nineveh,
from the discovery of which we owe much
of our information about the Assyrian empire. See ASSYRIA.

As·nap'per. See ASHURBANIPAL.

asp. A species of venomous snake (Deut.
32:33), dwelling in holes (Isa. 11:8), found
in Egypt and Palestine. It is the snake used

by snake-charmers in their performances. The Hebrew word for "asp" is also translated as "adder" in Ps. 58:4, 91:13. See also VIPER.

ADDER

ass. The ass genus belongs to the horse family. The wild variety is described in Job 24:5; 39:5-8; Dan. 5:21; also in Ps. 104:11; Isa. 32:14; Jer. 14:6, where, however, "zebra" may be meant. The domestic ass descended from a wild ass of the Sahara and Arabia. Abraham rode on asses and so did Jacob (Gen. 12:16; 22:3; 30:43). They were also used for burden-bearing (Gen. 49:14; Isa. 30:6) and for plowing, etc. (Deut. 22:10). Jesus rode upon an ass in his triumphal entry into Jerusalem (Zech. 9:9; Matt. 21:5). Balaam's ass spoke when it saw the angel of the Lord (Num. 22:28-30; II Peter 2:15-16). White or tawny asses were deemed fit for persons of rank (Judg. 5:10).

As'shur. See ASSYRIA.

as·suage', as·swage'. To lessen, cause to subside (Gen. 8:1).

As·syr'i·a. The country of the Assyrians lay immediately e. of the Tigris River in its middle stretches. The only town w. of the Tigris was the old capital Asshur, from which the whole land takes its name. Roughly speaking, Assyria lay directly n. of Babylonia. This district, compassed on the

n. by the mountains of Armenia, on the e.
by the ranges of Media, on the s. by the
Lower Zab River, is the Assyria proper of
history. The name is often applied to the
extensive empire conquered and ruled by
the Assyrians.

The origins of the Assyrians are still
wrapped in mystery. Undoubtedly they
were an amalgam of many stocks, among
which the Hurrians are of special importance, but ultimately the Semitic element
prevailed. Later Assyria became a part of
the Akkadian Empire. The language of Asshur is closely related to that of Akkad and
both are written in cuneiform. The Assyrian culture was deeply indebted to that of
the Babylonians, the Hittites and the Hurrians. The Assyrian religion was borrowed
from Babylon, except that Asshur, the pre-
siding god of the city named for him, became the chief deity of Assyria. It was ani-
mistic nature worship. Every object and
phenomenon in nature was believed to be
animated by a spirit. The great gods, after
Asshur, were the prominent objects of nature.

The first Assyrian king to come into contact with the Israelites was Shalmaneser III
(ruled 859–824 B.C.). He captured Carchemish in 857 and in 853 fought at Qarqar a
coalition of Ben-hadad of Damascus, Ahab
of Israel and their allies. In 842 he defeated
Hazael of Damascus, but did not take the
city. In that year he received tribute from
Tyre and Sidon and from Jehu of Israel.
Other great Assyrian kings were Tiglath-pileser III (745–727 B.C.); Shalmaneser V
(727–722); Sargon II (722–705); Sennacherib (705–681); Esarhaddon (681–669);
Ashurbanipal (669–c. 627). Sennacherib
made Nineveh the capital. The spoils of the
conquered cities and nations were brought
to Nineveh to embellish it. About 650 B.C.
Ashurbanipal gathered a great library
there, discovered in modern times.

In 625 B.C. the Assyrian Empire began to decline in vigor. Nabopolassar, governor of Babylon, declared himself independent, and in 612 the Medes, allies of Nabopolassar, and the Babylonians captured and destroyed Nineveh. They were aided by a sudden rise of the Tigris River, which washed away part of the city and made it indefensible. So complete was the desolation that in Greek and Roman times Nineveh became almost like a myth. The search for its site began in 1820 and ended in 1851. Excavations have gone on almost continuously since. The site is a roughly rectangular area containing several city mounds and surrounded by a wall 8 miles in circumference. See also BABYLONIANS.

a·strol′o·ger. Ancient stargazers and astrologers divided the heavens into eight concentric spheres or "mansions," with the view of tracing the course of the planets through each of them, in hopes of being able to tell fortunes and predict events. Though their failure was complete, their careful study of the heavens led to the gradual growth of the science of astronomy.

A·sup′pim. A building for storing Temple goods, a storehouse (I Chron. 26:15, 17).

Ath′a·li′ah. Daughter of Ahab and Jezebel; wife of King Jehoram (Joram) of Judah and later queen (II Kings 8:26; ch. 11; II Chron., chs. 22:23). See KINGS, TABLE OF.

Ath′ens. The capital of Attica, one of the Greek states. The city, named after the patron goddess Athene, became the center of enlightenment in science, literature and art for the ancient world. Four great schools of philosophy flourished here and attracted students from around the Greek and (later) the Roman world. The Areopagus, where Paul discoursed with Athenians (Acts 17:15-18:1), was a short distance w. of the Acropolis, a rocky hill that was the highest point in the city, and on which stood outstandingly beautiful temples.

a·tone′ment. A "setting at one" of those who before were at variance. As applied to the relation between God and man, it was effected through the death of Jesus Christ upon the cross. The word is also used for the act which produces this reconciliation, as well as the satisfaction or payment given for wrongdoing, injury (II Sam. 21:3), etc., as by sacrifices (Ex. 30:16; Lev. 4:20, 26, 31, 35), by prayer, suffering or repentance. See also PROPITIATION; RECONCILIATION.

A·tone′ment, Day of. Yom Kippur, a Jewish holy day, the annual day of humiliation and expiation for the sins of the nation. In the O.T. it was celebrated by the high priest offering sacrifices as an atonement—for the sanctuary, the priests and the people (Lev., ch. 16; 23:26-32; Num. 29:7-11). It was and still is observed on the tenth day of the month of Tishri by abstinence from labor, by a holy convocation and by fasting.

au′gur. One reputed to foretell events by omens; a soothsayer.

au′gu·ry. 1. The art of foretelling events by omens. 2. An indication of the future; foreboding. See DIVINATION.

aul, awl. A small pointed tool for making holes in wood or leather (Ex. 21:6).

a·ven′ger, avenger of blood. The Semitic nations, like the ancient Greeks, Germans and Slavs, acted to a large extent on the system of each injured man being his own avenger. When murder took place, the nearest relative of the victim was expected to avenge the murdered man's death, and was called the avenger of blood. He then would slay the murderer without any preliminary trial to settle the facts of the case. The Mosaic legislation introduced modifications into the system that destroyed its worst features. Cities of refuge were established, and anyone killing a man and fleeing to one of these cities was granted a fair trial and not put to death unless he had committed proven murder (Num. 35:12; Deut. 19:6; II Sam.

14:11). See BLOODGUILTINESS.

Az'a·ri'ah. In the O.T., 21 men bear this name,
one of them a king of Judah (see UZZIAH).
It was the original name of Abednego and
was probably used in error in II Chron.
22:6 for Ahaziah.

B

Ba'al. Baal worship apparently had its origin
in the belief that every tract of ground owed
its productivity to a supernatural being, or
baal, that dwelt there. The farmers probably
thought that from the baals, or fertility
gods, of various regions came the increase
of crops, fruits and cattle. It was common to
use the word Baal as part of place names,
such as Baal-hermon (Judg. 3:3) and Baal-
peor (Deut. 4:3). Eventually the worship of
these local deities became focused in the
worship of a common Baal god. Baal was

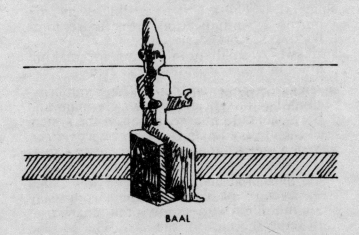

BAAL

worshiped on high places in Moab as early
as the days of Balaam and Balak (Num.
22:41). In the time of the Judges there were
altars to him in Palestine (Judg. 2:13;
6:28-32), and when Ahab married Jezebel,
the princess of Sidon, the worship of Baal

almost supplanted that of the Lord. The struggle between the two religions reached a climax on Mt. Carmel when Elijah met the priests of Baal (I Kings 16:31-32; 18:17-40). Baal worship in Judah was advanced by support from Queen Athaliah, Jezebel's daughter (II Chron. 21:6; 22:2), and despite temporary setbacks continued to attract Hebrew followers in both kingdoms (Hos. 2:8; II Chron. 28:2; II Kings 21:3; 23:4-5). Jeremiah (19:4-5) frequently denounced it. Baal seems to be the same as the Amorite storm-god Hadad, who also represented fertility, and was often associated with the goddess Ashtoreth (Judg. 2:13); in the vicinity of an altar to Baal there was often an Asherah (Judg. 6:30; I Kings 16:32-33). See also ASHERAH; MOLECH.

Ba'a·li. The word means "my lord," "my master." Because of the degrading influence of the god Baal, and the direct connection between the two words, Hosea proposes (2:16) that the synonym "Ishi" be used hereafter.

Ba'al·im. The plural form of Baal (Judg. 2:11; 3:7; I Sam. 7:4; 12:10).

Ba'al-ze'bub. See BEEL-ZEBUB.

Ba'a·sha. King of Israel, successor to Nadab, whom he murdered. His history is found in I Kings 15:16-16:7; II Chron. 16:1-6. See KINGS, TABLE OF.

Ba'bel. Another name for the city of Babylon, used only in Gen. 10:10 and 11:9. It was the site of a large temple tower (ziggurat), in the form of a terraced pyramid with each story smaller than the one below it. The traditional account of the building of this structure (Gen. 11:1-9) describes how the men of Babel attempted to build a tower to reach heaven; God punished them for their arrogance and prevented them from finishing it by causing them all suddenly to speak in different languages so that they could not understand one another. Since the people were then scattered about the earth, this story has been popularly looked upon as explaining how the various languages of the earth originated and became dispersed.

Bab'y·lo'ni·ans. Babylonia was a region of w. Asia at the e. end of the so-called Fertile Crescent which extends from Egypt to the Persian Gulf. Babylon was its capital. Babylonia was sometimes called Shinar (Gen. 10:10; 11:2; Isa. 11:11), and sometimes the land of the Chaldeans (Jer. 24:5; Ezek. 12:13). It lay mostly between the Tigris and Euphrates rivers and probably contained less than 8,000 square miles, roughly the size of New Jersey. The deep, rich alluvial soil, artificially irrigated, was of almost matchless fertility. The land originally consisted of 2 political divisions, Sumer in the s. and Akkad in the n., speaking different languages. Among the 8 or 9 principal cities of Akkad was Babylon. Ur was in Sumer, as were Nippur, Lagash, Larsa, Uruk (Erech) and Eridu. Most of these cities were on or near the Euphrates. At first (3000-2600 B.C.) these cities were independent kingdoms. Then a certain sense of unity under dynamic king-warriors developed first in Sumer, then in Akkad. Sargon I of Akkad (c. 2350) even conquered all the Sumerian cities, but Ur-Nammu of Ur 225 years later reversed the situation. From 1950 B.C. on, however, the Sumerians declined and lost their national identity. Babylon, which had been taken over by Amorites, now began a 3-cornered fight with Larsa and Isin for supremacy. Hammurabi, Babylon's great king, conqueror and law reformer (reigned c. 1728-1650 B.C.), carried Babylon to the leadership of all Mesopotamia. Hammurabi's dynasty came to an end in a raid by the Hittites from the n.w., and next Kassites from n.e. of Babylon dominated the "land between the rivers." With the fall of the Kassites, still another dynasty arose in Babylon, native

Babylonians, among them Nebuchadnezzar
I (1146-1123 B.C.). He defeated the Hittites
and Elamites but was stopped by the Assyrians, people of Asshur, a city-state with territories e. of the Tigris River and n. of
Babylonia. Assyria for 5 centuries interfered in Babylonian affairs. Tiglath-pileser
III of Babylon (under the name of Pul)
raised a standard against Assyria but later
Sennacherib in 689 B.C. sacked Babylon and
burned it to the ground. Though Sennacherib's son and successor, Esarhaddon, rebuilt Babylon, he was not able to solve the
problem of ruling Babylonia peaceably. In
652 another civil war followed and Babylon
was once more destroyed. A new era began
in Babylon in the year 626 B.C. when Nabopolassar became king of the Chaldeans, a
nation from north of the Persian gulf that
had worked its way into Babylonia among
the Aramean tribes. With his ally, Cyaxares
king of the Medes, Nabopolassar destroyed
Assyria's capital, Nineveh, in 612. His son,
the Nebuchadnezzar of the Bible, totally
defeated Pharaoh-nechoh of Egypt at Carchemish in 605, and the Chaldean-Babylo-
nians were now in control of the whole Fertile Crescent. Nebuchadnezzar (605-562)
had one of the longest and most brilliant
reigns of history. He took Jerusalem twice
(597 and 586) and destroyed it the second
time. The buildings and city walls of Babylon, admired by Greek historians, were
erected by him. His son, Evil-merodach
(562-560), who befriended the captive King
Jehoiachin of Judah (II Kings 25:27), was
assassinated, and thereafter the Babylonian
power waned. Nabonidus, who became
king in 556, appointed his son, Belshazzar,
as coregent; the latter appears in the Daniel
stories. In 539 a general under Cyrus, king
of Persia, took Babylon. One of the things
Cyrus did was to permit the Jews in exile in
Babylon to return to Jerusalem. The country remained under Persian rule to 332 B.C.,

when it fell to another great conqueror,
Alexander. After Rome's destruction of Jerusalem in A.D. 70, Babylon became and for
centuries remained a center of Jewish life
and esp. a seat of Jewish schools devoted to
the study and interpretation of Jewish law.

back'bite. To speak maliciously about a person (not present); to slander (Ps. 15:3; II
Cor. 12:20).

back'slid'ing. The word really means back-
turning, and by extension slipping or re-
gressing from good moral habits and become faithless toward the Lord. Backsliding
can mean merely forgetting the worship of
God, or a slipping back into worship of pagan deities or into various deceitful practices. The word was used esp. by Jeremiah
(3:6, 8, 11, 12) and Hosea (14:4).

bad'ger. In several verses in the KJV (e.g. Ex.
25:5; Num. 4:6), skins of badgers are said to
have been used for the outer covering of the
Tabernacle. But the meaning of the Hebrew
word is not certain. Some believe that goat-
skin was meant, others the hide of sea cows.
See also CONEY.

Ba'laam. Hired by King Balak of Moab to
curse the Israelites, he blesses them instead
and predicts their victory; later he gives the
Israelites evil counsel and is slain (Num.,
chs. 22-24; 31:8, 16; see also Deut. 23:4-5;
Josh. 24:9-10; Neh. 13:2; Micah 6:5; Jude
11; Rev. 2:14). The story of his ass who
spoke appears also in II Peter 2:15-16.

Ba'lak. A king of Moab, who hired Balaam to
curse Israel (Num., chs. 22-24).

bal'anc·es. An instrument for weighing, consisting of two matched pans hanging from
the ends of a rod or beam, supported exactly in the middle. It was used for weighing money or foodstuffs (Lev. 19:36; Jer.
32:10). A stone piece of known weight was
placed on one of the scales and the money,
metal or other medium of exchange was
placed on the other. There are many references in the Bible denouncing false or de-

ceitful balances and commending just ones.

bald lo'cust. A species of edible locust or grasshopper (Lev. 11:22). See LOCUST.

balm, balm of Gilead. A balm is an aromatic resin or gum of widespread therapeutic usage in antiquity, e.g. as an ointment for the healing of wounds (Jer. 51:8). Biblical references do not claim that balm trees grew in Gilead, and there is no known tree in the area that produces an aromatic resin or gum with medicinal properties of the kind attributed to balm. Perhaps "balm of Gilead" came to Palestine via traders who got it elsewhere.

bal'sam. See MULBERRY.

bap'tism. Baptism to Christians today is a sacred act (sacrament) by which one is admitted into the Christian Church. Among the Jews the rite of washing with water had been much practiced as a sign of religious purification and consecration (Ex. 29:4; 30:20; 40:12; Lev., ch. 15; Num. 19:8, etc.). Many believe that in Christ's time, as was certainly true later, proselytes to Judaism were baptized. John the Baptist administered baptism to those who accepted his message. His rite is called "a baptism of repentance for the remission (forgiveness) of sins" (Mark 1:4), and recipients of it thereby acknowledged their sins. Jesus allowed himself to be baptized by John (Mark 1:9) as an act of ceremonial righteousness. He commanded his disciples to baptize others (Matt. 28:19), making it the initiatory rite of his Church. St. Paul's view of baptism is set forth in Rom. 6:4-11. Christians have differed, even from early times, as to the mode of baptism, which Scriptures nowhere describe, much less prescribe. Nevertheless, Christians generally agree that baptism signifies and seals a believer's union with Christ through repentance and faith; the removal of one's sins by Christ's death and the Spirit's operation in him; and his intention to be the Lord's (Gal.

3:27; Col. 2:11-12; I Peter 3:21).

Bar. This Aramaic prefix means "son": e.g. Bar-jona (son of Jona), Matt. 16:17.

Bar·ab'bas. A prisoner released by Pilate instead of Jesus (Matt. 27:16-17).

Bar'ak. An Israelite who called together 10,000 men and defeated Sisera and the Canaanites (Judg. 4:6-5:12).

bar·bar'i·an. Anyone not a member of one's own national, religious or cultural group (Acts 28:4; I Cor. 14:11), esp. one who was not a Greek (Rom. 1:14). A foreigner. The word in the Bible is not derogatory, as it is today.

bar'bar·ous. Native (Acts 28:2).

Bar-Jo'na. See BAR.

bar'ley. A cereal grain widely cultivated in Palestine (Ruth 1:22), Egypt (Ex. 9:31) and the adjacent regions. It was made into cakes or loaves (Judg. 7:13; John 6:9).

BARLEY

Bar'na·bas. An early convert; sells his land, giving money to the apostles (Acts 4:36-37); preaches at Antioch and makes missionary journeys (Acts 11:22-30; 12:25-15:35); at Lystra the people take him for a god (14:12). His disagreement with Paul (15:36-39) is later reconciled (Gal. 2:1-13).

Bar'sa·bas, Bar'sab·bas. The surname of 2 early Christians, Joseph and Judas, possibly brothers (Acts 1:23; 15:22).

Bar·thol'o·mew. One of the 12 apostles (Matt. 10:3; Mark 3:18; Luke 6:14; Acts 1:13). Probably the surname of Nathanael (John 1:45). See NATHANAEL.

Bar'ti·mae'us. A blind man cured by Jesus at Jericho (Mark 10:46).

Bar'uch. Among others, a scribe who wrote from dictation the prophecies of Jeremiah and was taken captive with him into Egypt (Jer., chs. 32; 36; 43).

Bar·zil'la·i. An ally of David (II Sam. 17:27; 19:31; I Kings 2:7).

ba'son, ba'sin. A portable vessel for holding water for washing (John 13:5) and for other purposes. The "bason" of the Tabernacle and Temple was a large bowl, made of gold, silver or bronze, used to hold meal offerings (Num. 7:13) at the great altar and to receive the blood of sacrificed animals (Zech. 9:15; 14:20).

bat. The bat was ceremonially "unclean" (Lev. 11:13, 19; Deut. 14:11-12, 18).

BAT

Though listed with "unclean" birds, the bat is a mammal: it suckles its young. Also it has hair instead of feathers and teeth instead of a bill, and its "wings" are membranes that stretch out between its 4 legs. Bats are found in old buildings in Jerusa-

lem, in grottoes and caves of Galilee and in
the Dead Sea region, where they live in
great colonies. Their excrement gives off an
odious stench.

bath. A unit of liquid measure, equivalent to
9.8 U.S. gallons. See MEASURES.

Bath. A Hebrew prefix meaning daughter of:
e.g. Bath-sheba (daughter of Sheba).

Bath-she'ba. Wife of Uriah, whom David
sent to his death, later David's wife and the
mother of Solomon. In David's old age she
appealed to him to assure Solomon's accession to the throne over Adonijah (II Sam.
11:3-27; 12:24; I Kings 1:15-31; 2:13-25).

bdel'li·um. It is quite uncertain what this word
means. In Num. 11:7, manna is said to re-
semble bdellium. The ancient Greeks gave
the name *bdellion* to a transparent, waxy
fragrant gum obtained from a tree in Arabia, Babylonia, India and Media. Yet Gen.
2:12 suggests that it belongs to the mineral
kingdom.

bear. The Syrian bear once roamed over Palestine, but is today confined largely to
Lebanon. It is of a yellowish-brown color,
and unless pressed by necessity lives chiefly
on vegetable food. All bears are dangerous
when meddled with (Amos 5:19), esp. when
robbed of their cubs (II Sam. 17:8; Prov.
17:12; Hos. 13:8).

beard. The beard was cherished by the Hebrews as the badge of manly dignity. As a
mark of mourning it was customary to
pluck it out or cut it off (Ezra 9:3; Isa. 15:2;
Jer. 41:5). The king of the Ammonites offered grave insult to David's ambassadors
when he shaved off half their beards (II
Sam. 10:4-5). The ancient Egyptians, in
contrast, shaved the head and the face, but
often wore a false beard. In mourning they
let the hair and beard grow. Hence Joseph,
when released from prison, followed the
Egyptian custom and shaved his beard in
preparation for his appearance before Pha-

raoh (Gen. 41:14).

Be·at'i·tudes. The primary meaning of beatitude is blessedness. A derived meaning is that of a declaration about blessedness, about happiness in God's love. In this latter sense the term Beatitudes has been given to the sayings of Jesus which introduce the Sermon on the Mount (Matt. 5:3-12). It is generally held that there are 8 Beatitudes, counting Matt. 5:10-12 as one. (Luke 6:20-23 records 4, and adds 4 "woes.") All begin: "Blessed are . . ." They do not necessarily describe 8 different classes of people, but 8 different elements of excellence which may all be combined in the same individual. They offer a picture, then, of perfect spiritual well-being, and they correct the prevailing low and materialistic views of human happiness.

bee. An insect that makes honey (Judg. 14:8, 18). As Canaan was a land "flowing with milk and honey" (Ex. 3:8), bees must have been there in large numbers. Their nests were in rocks (Ps. 81:16) and in woods (I Sam. 14:25), esp. in Judah (Ezek. 27:17; Matt. 3:4). In Egypt bee-keeping was an ancient art, going back at least to 3000 B.C.

Be·el'ze·bub, Be·el'ze·bul. The word may mean "lord of the flies" or "lord of the dung." It could also mean "Prince Baal." In the Gospels it is a designation applied to the prince of the demons, whom Jesus identifies with Satan (Matt. 10:25; 12:24, 26; Mark 3:22-23; Luke 11:15, 18-19). In the O.T. it is spelled Baal-zebub.

Beer. A Hebrew prefix meaning "a well": e.g. Beer-elim (well of heroes), Isa. 15:8.

bee'tle. A "clean," edible insect (Lev. 11:22, KJV; RSV "cricket").

be·he'moth. A large amphibious animal described by Job (40:15-24); probably a fanciful name for the hippopotamus, once common in the Nile marshes.

be'ka, be'kah. See WEIGHTS.

Bel. The patron god of Babylon (Isa. 46:1; Jer.

50:2; 51:44). His proper name was Marduk, or as called by the Hebrews, Merodach. He was a sun-god, and was regarded as the son of Ea, god of the ocean and other terrestrial waters. His festival was celebrated in the spring, at the beginning of the Babylonian year.

Be'li·al. The word means worthlessness, wickedness. The phrase "sons of Belial" is an expression meaning vile scoundrels or ungodly men (Deut. 13:13; Judg. 19:22). Belial is personified in II Cor. 6:15.

Bel·shaz'zar. Ruler of Babylon, at whose profane feast the hand appeared, writing on the wall (Dan., ch. 5).

Bel'te·shaz'zar. See DANIEL.

Ben. A Hebrew prefix meaning "son of": e.g. Ben-hadad (son of Hadad), I Kings 20:1.

Be·na'iah. A common O.T. name. Chief among them is a follower of David who proclaimed Solomon king and at his command killed Adonijah, Joab and Shimei (II Sam. 23:20; I Chron. 11:22; I Kings 1:38; 2:25–46).

Ben'-am'mi. See AMMON.

Ben-ha'dad. 1. King of Syria; hired by Asa to invade Israel (I Kings 15:18–21; II Chron. 16:1–6); defeated by Ahab (I Kings 20:1–34; 22:1); besieges Samaria (II Kings 6:24–25); murdered by Hazael (8:9–15). 2. Son of Hazael; loses cities of Israel to Jehoash (Joash) (II Kings 13:3, 25; see also Jer. 49:27; Amos 1:4).

Ben'ja·min. 1. Twelfth and last son of Jacob and Rachel (Gen. 35:18, 24). For his journey to Egypt at Joseph's demand, see Gen., chs. 42–45. 2. The tribe formed by his descendants (46:21), whose fertile territory, also called Benjamin, lay n.w. of the Dead Sea and included Jerusalem (Jebusi), Jericho and other major cities (Josh. 18:11–28). The tribe was nearly exterminated for aiding the guilty inhabitants of Gibeah (Judg., chs. 19–21). King Saul was a Benjaminite; when the kingdom divided after Solomon's

death, most of the tribe remained loyal to
Judah (I Kings 12:21) and shared its for-
tunes to the end (Ezra 4:1). The apostle
Paul was also of this tribe (Phil. 3:5).

Ber·ni'ce. Daughter of Herod Agrippa I, she
believed in Paul's innocence (Acts, chs. 25;
26). See HEROD AGRIPPA II.

Be·ro'dach-bal'a·dan. See MERODACH-BALA-
DAN.

ber'yl. Three words are translated "beryl" in
the Bible. The 2 Hebrew words give no
clues as to the qualities of the stone. The
Greek word (Rev. 21:20) used for the
eighth jewel for the foundations of the walls
of the New Jerusalem signifies a silicate of
beryllium and aluminum. An emerald is a
superior type of beryl.

Beth. A Hebrew prefix meaning "house of":
e.g. Beth-el (house of God), Gen. 12:8.

be·troth'. To promise in marriage; see ES-
POUSE.

Beu'lah. The name given to Palestine when it
was restored to God's favor after the Exile
(Isa. 62:4).

Bil'dad. One of Job's 3 friends (Job 2:11; chs.
8; 18; 25; 42:9).

birth'right. A certain right or privilege considered to belong to the firstborn son in a family, and not shared by his younger brothers.
This right included succession to the father's position as head of the family, and a
double portion of his father's property, a
right guaranteed to the firstborn even when
his mother was the less loved of two wives
(Deut. 21:17). A birthright might be sold to
a younger brother (Gen. 25:29-34; Heb.
12:16). It might also be forfeited on account
of misconduct (I Chron. 5:1).

bish'op. The Greek word, *episkopos*, means an
overseer. Originally a bishop was but one
name for a person charged with responsibility for the care of the flock of God (Acts
20:28; I Peter 5:2), the others being called
"elders" and "presbyters." The terms seem
to be but different designations for the in-

cumbents of the same office in different communities. The distinction between bishops, elders and presbyters developed later and appears in the letters of Ignatius (died about A.D. 107). There is no trace in the N.T. of the apostles' appointing any man to succeed them. See also ELDER.

bish'op·rick. The office or position of an overseer, a bishop (Acts 1:20).

bit'ter herbs. One of the elements of the Passover meal commemorating the Exodus of the Jews from Egypt. The herbs were probably endive, lettuce, watercress and chicory. Their bitter taste symbolizes the bitter experiences of the fleeing and wandering Hebrews (Ex. 12:8; Num. 9:11).

bitter water. Holy water in an earthen vessel, mingled with dust from the floor of the sanctuary, apparently to give it divine potency (Num. 5:17), intended to reveal the innocence or guilt of a woman accused of adultery by her husband when there were no witnesses. The essential part of this procedure was the oath: the ritual was symbolical; the effect was left to God. It is probable that this ordeal was an old custom that the Mosaic law took up in order to regulate and elevate it. See also JEALOUSY OFFERING.

bit'tern. A long-necked, long-legged wading bird that frequents marshes and pools of water (Isa. 14:23, KJV). The RSV translates this word as "hedgehog" or "porcupine."

bi·tu'men. See SLIME.

blas'phe·my. The Greek word behind the English means abusive or scurrilous language. In English the word is specifically reserved for defamatory or other wicked language directed against God (Ps. 74:10-18; Isa. 52:5; Rev. 16:9, 11, 21). Under the Mosaic law it was punishable by stoning to death (Lev. 24:16). The charge of blasphemy was falsely brought against Naboth (I Kings 21:9-13), Stephen (Acts 6:11) and Jesus (Matt. 9:3; 26:65-66; John 10:36). Blasphemy against the Holy Spirit consisted in attributing the miracles of Christ, which were enabled by the Spirit of God, to satanic power (Matt. 12:22-23; Mark 3:22-30). This deliberate, willful rejection of God and of good in favor of evil is also called "the unpardonable sin."

blem'ish. A defect or imperfection, esp. one in an animal rendering it unfit for sacrifice. Any broken, diseased or malformed part was regarded as a blemish. See Lev. 22:19; Deut. 15:21. Priests were required to be without blemish (Lev. 21:16-24).

bless. 1. To bestow divine favor and confer divine benefits (Gen. 1:22; 2:3; 9:1-7). 2. To adore God for His goodness and return thanks (Ps. 103:1; Matt. 26:26). 3. To invoke God's favor on a person (Gen. 27:4, 27-29; I Chron. 16:2; Ps. 129:8), including salutations and even ordinary greetings (I Sam. 25:5-6, 14; II Kings 4:29).

bless'ed. 1. Having received the favor of God, hence enjoying great happiness (Ps. 84:4; Luke 11:28; Matt. 5:3-11). 2. Receiving praise and an expression of thanks, said of God (Job 1:21; Ps. 119:12).

bless'ing. 1. A favor or gift bestowed by God and bringing joy to the recipient (Ex. 32:29; Deut. 33:1, 7; Heb. 6:7). 2. Any gift or present (Josh. 15:19; II Kings 5:15). 3. A wish for prosperity, good health, success, etc. (I Peter 3:9).

blood. In the Bible, the life is in the blood (Lev. 17:11, 14), or the blood is the life (Deut. 12:23), though not exclusively (Ps. 104:29-30). The blood represented the life, and so sacred is life before God that the blood of murdered Abel could be described as crying to God for vengeance (Gen. 4:10). The loss of life is the penalty for sin, and a symbolical vicarious surrender of life was necessary to remission of sin (Heb. 9:22). And so, under the Mosaic law, the blood of animals was used in all offerings for sin. The "blood of Jesus Christ," or "blood of the Lamb," are figurative expressions for his atoning death (I Cor. 10:16; Eph. 2:13; Heb. 9:14; I Peter 1:2, 19; I John 1:7).

blood′guilt′i·ness. The state of being guilty of bloodshed or murder. Originally there was no distinction between accidental and premeditated killing (Gen. 9:6). The law of bloodguiltiness automatically required revenge upon a slayer (Num. 35:19, 21, 27). Later, cities of sanctuary were provided for refuge, if lack of intent could be shown (Deut. 19:5-6). See AVENGER; CITY OF REFUGE.

blood′y flux. Dysentery, a disease characterized by inflammation and ulceration of the lower parts of the intestines, with bleeding from the bowels (Acts 28:8).

Bo′a·ner′ges. A name meaning "sons of thunder" given by Jesus to James and John (Mark 3:17), perhaps because of their impetuosity (see Luke 9:54-55).

boar. The male of wild swine (Ps. 80:13). It is still found in swamps, marshes and thickets in Palestine.

BOAR (WILD)

Bo′az. 1. Ruth's second husband (Ruth, chs. 2-4). In Matt. 1:5 of the KJV the name is spelled Booz. 2. For Jachin and Boaz, see JACHIN AND BOAZ.

bo′dy of Christ. The church is the body of Christ, in Paul's figure of speech (I Cor.

12:12-26). Christian believers are members (parts) of the body of Christ. As the head, Christ rules over the body (Eph. 1:22-23; 4:12, 15-16).

bond'age. A word used to describe Israel's servitude in Egypt, which is called the house of bondage (Ex. 13:3, 14; 20:2; Deut. 5:6, etc.). It is also applied to the exile in Babylonia (Ezra 9:8-9). In the N.T. the term refers to a form of slavery which makes men subject to the law, which, while commanding what is right, gives man no power to fulfill it; in contrast to this are the freedom in Christ and the grace of God which can free man from the power of sin (Rom. 6:15-23; 7:13-25; Gal. 2:4; 4:3-9; 5:1). In an allegory, Paul expresses the difference between freedom and slavery (Gal. 4:21-31).

bond'man. A man or boy who is legally a slave (Gen. 44:33).

book. A written document or collection of writings (Job 31:35).

book of life. This figurative concept of a book is drawn from the custom of recording lists of names (e.g. Neh. 7:5, 64). In this sense there is a heavenly record of the righteous (Ps. 69:28; Rev. 3:5; 21:27) and of their sufferings (Ps. 56:8). In connection with divine judgment, the books are opened (Dan. 7:10; Rev. 20:12). In the N.T. those redeemed by Christ are in this book and are given a place in God's eternal kingdom.

book of the law. The book of Deuteronomy, esp. chs. 5-26, found during the reign of Josiah, in which the law of Moses is set down for the second time (Deut. 29:21; II Kings 22:8). This phrase is to be contrasted with the "book of the law of Moses" (Neh. 8:1), which consisted of the books of Genesis through Deuteronomy, the Pentateuch (= 5 books).

booth. A rude structure designed in most cases for a longer occupation than a tent, but not for permanence like a house. It was formed by poles and leafy tree branches. The keeper of a vineyard occupied a booth. Some were large enough to provide shelter for cattle, or summer homes for a farmer's family. For the "Feast of Booths" see TAB-ERNACLES, FEAST OF.

boss. The projecting center part or knob of a shield (Job 15:26), often ornamental. It also strengthened the shield.

bot'tle. The "bottles" of biblical times were either a hollow vessel of leather or the hollow hide of an animal, used for holding liquids (Matt. 9:17); or a small earthenware vessel, formed by potters (Jer. 19:1, 10-11) and easily broken and cheaply replaced.

BOTTLES

bow'man. An archer (Jer. 4:29).

box tree. A small evergreen tree about 20 feet high. The fir, pine and box trees were the "glory" of Lebanon (Isa. 60:13; cf. 41:19).

bram'ble. A sturdy plant with sharp spines and masses of tangled runners which, in Jotham's fable, was asked by the trees to "reign over us" (Judg. 9:8-20). This thorn is quite common in the warmer parts of Palestine. The tradition is that the crown of thorns placed on Christ's head was made from twigs of it.

bra'sen. We would say "bronze" today. Brass,

from which we get the archaic adjective "brasen," was not known in ancient times. Copper and tin, which they used, produced bronze; copper and zinc make brass.

bra'sen sea. A great basin of the Temple of Solomon in which the priests washed their hands and feet before ministering in the sanctuary or at the altar (I Kings 7:39; II Chron. 4:6). It stood upon 12 brasen oxen, in 4 groups of 3 each, facing the 4 quarters. Ahaz took it down from its oxen-legs, and when Nebuchadnezzar captured Jerusalem, he broke the basin into pieces (II Kings 25:13, 16; Jer. 27:19-22).

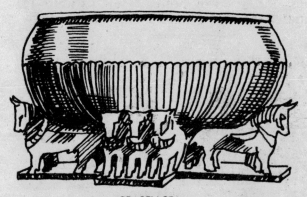

BRASEN SEA

bra'sen ser'pent. This was a figure of a serpent made of bronze and erected by Moses on a pole in the wilderness (Num. 21:4-9). In later years the Israelites began to use it as an idol or fetish, and so King Hezekiah had it broken into pieces (II Kings 18:4).

bray. 1. To make a loud, harsh sound, as a donkey (Job 6:5). 2. To pound or grind into a powder (Prov. 27:22).

bread. The bread in use among the Israelites consisted normally of small flat cakes of wheat flour or, among the poor, of barley flour. The grain was ground daily and fresh-baked every day. When this bread was to be eaten at once, it was often unleavened

(Gen. 19:3; I Sam. 28:24), but the art of making leavened bread, achieved today by use of yeast, was also understood. In Luke 11:3 "bread" stands for all kinds of food. See also UNLEAVENED BREAD.

breast'plate. 1. A sacred article of dress worn by the high priest (Ex. 28:15-30, KJV; RSV translates "breastpiece"). 2. Armor designed to protect the body in battle (Rev. 9:9). "Harness" (I Kings 22:34) is the same. Figuratively, righteousness was likened to a breastplate (Isa. 59:17; Eph. 6:14). See also COAT OF MAIL.

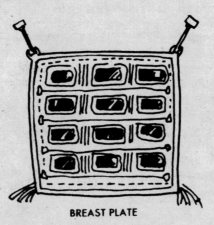

BREAST PLATE

breech'es. Part of the garb of priests (Ex. 28:42), these were short linen drawers, though possibly a double-apron garment that could be changed easily. The wearing of linen undergarments was taken from the Egyptians.

breth'ren of the Lord. Their names are given in the gospels as James, Joseph or Joses, Simon and Judas (Matt. 13:55; Mark 6:3). Other references to them are found in Matt. 12:47-50; Mark 3:31-35; Luke 8:19-21; John 2:12; 7:4-5; Acts 1:14; I Cor. 9:5. One of them, James (Gal. 1:19), became a distinguished leader of the Jerusalem church (Acts 12:17; 15:13; Gal. 2:9) and was author of the letter that goes by his name. In what sense they were Christ's "brethren" has been much disputed. In very early times they were regarded as the children of Joseph by a former marriage. Other theories have been proposed. That they were the children of Joseph and Mary is the natural view, and that Mary had other children is implied by Matt. 1:25 and Luke 2:7.

bride. A woman just married or about to be married. In both the O.T. and the N.T. the words and phrases describing marriage are used to express the spiritual relationship between God and His people (Isa. 62:5) and between Christ and his church (Eph. 5:25-33). The New Jerusalem, the city of the redeemed, i.e., the Church, is called the Bride of Christ (Rev. 21:9-10).

bride'cham'ber. The room prepared for a bride at the home of the groom or the groom's father. The "children (or sons) of the bridechamber" (Mark 2:19; Luke 5:34) were the friends of the bridegroom who would be his guest for a week to celebrate his marriage.

brig'an·dine. A coat of mail, composed of light, thin-jointed scales, or of thin, pliant plate armor, backed by leather or fabric tied below the arms (Jer. 46:4; 51:3).

brim'stone. Sulphur (Gen. 19:24; Deut. 29:23). Used figuratively, it suggests "destruction" or "punishment," as in Job 18:15; Rev. 9:17.

bronze. See BRASEN.

broom tree. See JUNIPER.

buck'ler. A small, usually round shield, normally carried in the left hand or strapped on the left arm (S. of Sol. 4:4). Solomon's ceremonial "shields" (I Kings 10:17) were really the smaller bucklers. Bucklers are used by writers figuratively in II Sam. 22:31; Ps. 18:2, 30; Prov. 2:7.

buf'fet. To strike or beat (I Cor. 4:11).

bull'ock. A young bull, often used by writers as a sign of youthful strength (Ex. 29:3). A "bullock without blemish" would be a young but uncastrated bull. They were much used in sacrifice.

bull, wild. The male of the species called by naturalists *Bos taurus* (Job 21:10; Ps. 68:30; Isa. 34:7). From such bulls came ultimately the domesticated cattle of the Bible. See ox. Figuratively the bull represented strength, virility, pride.

bul'rush. A plant also called papyrus that grows in marshy land, of which the tiny ark of Moses (Ex. 2:3) and also larger boats (Isa. 18:2) were made. The bulrush or papyrus plant is not a grass or a rush, but a giant sedge with a triangular stalk 8 or 10 feet high. The pith of the plant was transformed into writing materials as early as 2000 B.C.

bur'i·al. Interment in Bible lands followed speedily after death: the speed of decomposition of the body in that climate requires almost immediate burial (Gen. 23:3-4). When a death occurred, friends, especially women, hurried to the house and made loud lamentations (Mark 5:38). Sometimes mourners were hired (Jer. 9:17). The body was washed (Acts 9:37) and wrapped in a cloth or loosely bound in bands (Matt. 27:59; John 11:44). The wealthy added spices and perfumes (John 12:7; 19:39), or burned fragrant materials (Jer. 34:5). The body was carried on a bier to the grave (II Sam. 3:31; Luke 7:14). Burial was generally in a cave or in a sepulchre scooped horizontally in the soft Palestine rock (Gen. 25:9-10; Matt. 27:60). See SEPULCHRE.

burnt of'fer·ing. The burnt offering required the use of a male lamb, ram, goat or bullock. The blood of the freshly slain animal was sprinkled round about on the altar, and the entire animal was consumed by the fire on the altar. This was expressive of the entire self-dedication of the offerer to God. See also OFFERINGS.

bush, burn'ing. A thorny bush which Moses saw burning and from which Yahweh spoke (Ex. 3:2-3; Deut. 33:16; Mark 12:26), perhaps the Egyptian thorn. Often 12 feet high, it grows throughout a large part of Africa, in the Sinai Peninsula and on the shores of the Dead Sea. The identification, however, is not certain.

but'ler. See CUPBEARER.

by'word. An object of ridicule; a contemptible person or thing (II Chron. 7:20; Ps. 44:14).

C

cab. A unit of dry measure. See MEASURES.

Cae'sar. The family name of a branch of the Julian house or clan in Rome. Its most illustrious representative was Gaius Julius Caesar (100-44 B.C.), who became the dictator of Rome. The name Caesar was assumed by his grandnephew Octavianus (Octavian), later the emperor called Augustus. Tiberius, Caligula, Claudius and Nero, who followed in succession, were all entitled by relationship to the great dictator to bear the family name. Later emperors assumed the name as a title. The name "Caesar" to Jews and Christians became the type or symbol of the civil power in discussions of civil vs. ecclesiastical authority (Matt. 22:17, 21; Mark 12:14, 16-17; Luke 20:22, 24-25).

Cae'sar's house'hold. Some early converts to Christianity in Rome were slaves and freedmen working in the imperial palace (Phil. 4:22).

Ca'ia·phas. A Sadducee and high priest before whom Jesus was brought for trial, he proposed and was deeply responsible for our Lord's death (John 11:49-53; 18:14, 24). He also took part in the trial of Peter and John (Acts. 4:6). See SADDUCEES.

Cain. First son of Adam; his works being evil, his offering to the Lord is rejected and he kills Abel in jealous anger (Gen., ch. 4; I John 3:12).

cal'a·mus. A reed. The plant was sweet-smelling (S. of Sol. 4:14), a constituent of the holy anointing oil (Ex. 30:23, KJV; "aromatic cane," RSV) and used in connection with sacrifice ("sweet cane," Isa. 43:24; Jer. 6:20). The Tyrians obtained it apparently from Javan, the regions of w. Asia Minor and Greece (Ezek. 27:19).

Ca'leb. The name of several O.T. men, the best known being the son of Jephunneh (Deut. 1:36; Num., chs. 13; 14), sent by Moses to spy out the land of Canaan, for which he receives the towns of Hebron and Debir (Josh. 14:6-14; 15:13-20).

Cal'vary. A place close to Jerusalem, but outside the city walls, where Christ was crucified. The Latin form of this word means "skull." Where Calvary was exactly, nobody knows. The Hebrew and Greek word for the same site is translated "Golgotha" (Matt. 27:33), which also means "skull" in those languages.

cam'el. In the Bible the one-humped Arabian camel is meant. There are 2 distinct varieties of it: a slow-going draft camel (II Kings 8:9) and the dromedary, which is swift of foot and can cover 8-10 miles an hour and keep going 18 hours out of 24. More normal use of a dromedary is a day's journey of 60-75 miles per day. A transport camel can carry burdens of 400-500 pounds, but in the Sinai desert 250 is regarded as the maximum. The camel's foot is enveloped in a hardened skin, enclosing the cushionlike soles, which are adapted to walking over sand without sinking deeply. Another adaptation is that in the walls of the paunch, or first stomach, there are 2 collections of water cells on which the camel can draw when no other water is procurable. The camel can subsist on the poorest food. His hump is a storehouse of food, and becomes larger or smaller as the animal is in good or in bad condition. Perhaps e. Arabia is the region where he was domesticated. Camels apparently were used to some extent long before 1200 B.C. and commonly thereafter. The milk was used (Gen. 32:15), but the animal was ceremonially "unclean" for eating (Lev. 11:4). From its hair a coarse cloth was woven, which was sometimes made into clothing (Matt. 3:4) and used for tents. The burden was borne on the "bunch" or hump (Isa. 30:6).

cam'phire. A plant with fragrant yellow and white flowers, also known as henna. In Palestine it flourished in the virtually tropical region of Engedi (S. of Sol. 1:14; see also 4:13) and Jericho. The leaves and young twigs are made into a fine powder, converted into paste with hot water and used by wealthy Orientals to dye the finger- and toenails and soles of the feet a reddish-orange color.

Ca'naan. 1. Son of Ham and grandson of Noah. 2. The descendants of Ham, according to Gen. 9:18, 22; 10:6, who occupied Canaan and took their name from that country. See CANAANITES. 3. The old and native name of Palestine, extending from Sidon and Mt. Hermon on the n. to Kadesh-barnea in the s. and from the Mediterranean on the w. to the desert on the e. However, the Hebrews called "Canaan" only that portion of Palestine that lay w. of the Jordan; the land e. of the river they called "Gilead."

Ca'naan-ites. The inhabitants of Canaan. They were of Semitic stock. Canaan is called a son of Ham because the Egyptians (the country of the Hamites) long dominated Canaan before the arrival of the Hebrews. The Hebrews conquered the Canaanites under the leadership of Joshua, but the inhabitants were by no means exterminated. Important towns were left in possession of the Canaanite population (Josh. 11:13; 15:63; 16:10, etc.). Even where the destruction had been most complete, many Canaanites escaped by flight and hiding, to return and, when the army of Israel moved on, to rebuild towns and cultivate anew their wasted fields. In some cases they paid tribute (Judg. 1:27-36). Solomon made them perform forced labor (I Kings 9:20-21). The Canaanites eventually devoted themselves extensively to trade, and their name became synonymous with trader (Isa. 23:8).

Can'da·ce. A queen of Ethiopia (Acts 8:27)

can'dle. See LAMP.

can'dle·stick. The lampstand in the Tabernacle consisted of a base and a shaft with 6 branches; the shaft and branches supported 7 lamps (not candles) in a horizontal line. This candelabrum was perhaps deposited in the Temple (I Kings 8:4). Solomon made 10 of them (7:49). They were carried away to Babylon (Jer. 52:19).

CANDLESTICK

can'ker·worm'. As the cankerworm is mentioned in Joel and Nahum with the typical locust which it resembles and also in the numbers in which it appears, it is probably a locust of another species or the locust in the larva or pupa stage of development. See LOCUST.

cap·tiv'i·ty. 1. The state of being in bondage to enemies, esp. in a foreign land (Deut. 28:41). 2. Captives referred to collectively. 3. The enforced transplanting or carrying away by a conqueror of a whole population or of its leading people, a practice the Assyrians introduced and the Babylonians adopted. Captivity was a punishment of the vanquished as an extreme military policy when other means of pacifying a defeated country failed. Under the reign of Tiglathpileser, Assyrians began emptying the land of the 10 tribes of Israel of its inhabitants (II Kings 15:29; I Chron. 5:26). His successor, Shalmaneser V, deported a large number of residents of Samaria in 721 B.C. The word "captivity" most significantly applies, however, to the carrying off to Babylonia of thousands of the people of Judah by Nebuchadnezzar, first in 597 B.C., and then in larger numbers after the destruction of Jerusalem in 586 B.C. (II Kings 24:11-14), leaving only the poorest of the land to be plowmen and vinedressers (25:2-21). It is these captives in Babylonia, who sometimes flourished there, who were looked upon as forming a significant part of what became known as the Diaspora, or Dispersion.

car′bun·cle. The Hebrew word so translated means "shining like lightning." A gem is meant (Ezek. 28:13), one that stood third in the first row of the high priest's breastplate (Ex. 28:17; 39:10). Some think a ruby or garnet was meant.

cas′si·a. The aromatic bark of a tree resembling the cinnamon. Cassia was an ingredi-

CASSIA

ent of the anointing oil (Ex. 30:24); a product of trade with Tyre (Ezek. 27:19); a fragrance used on clothing (Ps. 45:8).

Cas'tor and Pol'lux. In Greek mythology these were the twin sons of Zeus and Leda, who, after their deaths, were placed in the heavens as the constellation Gemini (the Twins). They were regarded as the protectors of sailors; thus the ship on which Paul sailed (Acts 28:11) had a figurehead of them carried on its bow, thereby dedicating the ship to them.

cat. There are no references in the Bible to the domestic cat. It was first domesticated in Egypt. But some of the references to "wild beasts" (e.g. Isa. 13:21; Jer. 50:39) may refer to wildcats which almost certainly were common in the mountains or the desolate regions of Palestine.

cat'er·pil'lar. Probably a species of locust, or the common migratory locust in one stage of development. It is a destroyer of vegetation (I Kings 8:37; II Chron. 6:28; Ps. 78:46; Isa. 33:4; Joel 1:4; 2:25).

CEDAR OF LEBANON

ce'dar. A famous tree of Lebanon (I Kings 5:6), tall (often to 120 feet) and stately (Isa. 2:13; Ezek. 17:22; 31:3). It furnished a tim-

ber much prized in the construction of pal-
aces and temples (II Sam. 5:11; I Kings
5:5-6; 7:1-12; Ezra 3:7). From it masts were
made for ships (Ezek. 27:5). It still survives
in the mountains of Syria and flourishes in
the Taurus Mountains region of Turkey.

cen'ser. A vessel for holding incense while it
is being burned (Num. 16:6-7, 39). The cen-
sers of the Tabernacle were of bronze; those
of the Temple were of gold. See INCENSE.

cen·tu'ri·on. An officer in the Roman army in
command of 100 men.

Ce'phas. The name, meaning "rock" or
"stone," given by Jesus to Simon Peter
(John 1:42; I Cor. 1:12; Gal. 2:9).

chaff. Threshed or winnowed husks of wheat
or other grain, usually allowed to be blown
away by the wind. Chaff is used in figures of
speech as a symbol for something worthless
(Ps. 1:4; Isa. 41:15; Matt. 3:12). See THRESH-
INGFLOOR.

chal·ced'on·y. A precious stone, a variety of
quartz, though with a dull, waxy luster, and
containing much silica. It comes in white-
gray, brown and blue colors. Agate is a var-
iegated chalcedony.

Chal·de'ans. A people within the Babylonian
empire who dominated it in its last years of
glory, from about 626 B.C. to 539, when the
Persians captured Babylon. Chaldea was
the very s. portion of Babylonia, at the head
of the Persian Gulf. Ur, where Abraham
came from originally, was in Chaldea.
"Chaldees" (Gen. 11:31) is a variant form of
"Chaldeans."

cham'ber·lain. 1. A person in charge of the
household or the private chambers of a
ruler or lord (Acts 12:20). In the O.T., also
a person in charge of a king's harem (Esth.
1:10; 2:15). 2. A city treasurer (Rom. 16:23).

cha·me'le·on. A reptile that belongs to the
same order as lizards (Lev. 11:30). Chame-
leons are known for their ability to change
color. They live in trees and feed on insects
they capture by means of a long tongue

covered at the end with a viscous substance. The Palestinian varieties are 8-12 inches long.

cham'ois. A small, goat-like antelope found in the mountainous regions of Palestine.

chan'cel·lor. A commander, an officer in the Persian court (Ezra 4:8, 9, 17).

char'ger. 1. A large, flat dish or platter (Num. 7:13, 19, 25; Mark 6:25, KJV). 2. A horse trained to charge, or bear down upon, in battle (Nahum 2:3, RSV).

char'i·ot. A two-wheeled vehicle, drawn by horses, used for military, state and private purposes. Chariots were poorly adapted to the hills of Palestine, but they were used by the Canaanites in the valleys (Josh. 17:16; Judg. 4:3) and by the Egyptians (Isa. 31:1), Ethiopians (II Chron. 16:8), Syrians (II Kings 5:9), Hittites (II Kings 7:6) and Assyrians (Nahum 2:3-4; 3:2). The war chariots commonly carried a driver and occasionally a shield-bearer, besides the warrior himself, armed with bow and arrows and a supply of javelins. They were at times constructed of iron or covered with iron plates. The wheels were not clumsy, but consisted of rims, spokes and hubs, and were often of metal.

char'i·ty. 1. Alms-giving (Acts 9:36). 2. In 25 places "charity" was chosen to translate the Greek word *agape.* The best-known example of this is I Cor., ch. 13. Modern translations use "love" instead.

Che'bar. A river, or better, canal, s.e. of Babylon, on the banks of which some of the Jewish exiles were settled (Ezek. 1:1; 3:15, etc.).

check'er work. A crisscross or latticework design ornamenting the pillars of the Temple (I Kings 7:17).

Ched'or·la·o'mer. King of Elam; conquers valley of Siddim and takes Lot prisoner; Abraham's forces defeat him and rescue his captives (Gen. 14:1-16).

Che'mosh. The god of the Moabites (Num. 21:29; Jer. 48:46), worshiped in the same manner as Molech, god of the Ammonites, by the sacrifice of children as burnt offerings (II Kings 3:27). Solomon erected a high place in his honor (I Kings 11:7), possibly for political reasons, which was later destroyed by Josiah (II Kings 23:13). See also MOLECH.

Cher′eth·ites, Cher′e·thims. A nation or tribe inhabiting a southern portion of the Philistine country (I Sam. 30:14). Or they may be identical with the Philistines. Some of them were members of David's bodyguard (II Sam. 8:18; 15:18).

cher′ub, plural **cher′u·bim.** A winged, heavenly being (Ezek. 1:5-11); cherubim acted as guardians of sacred treasures (Gen. 3:24), symbols of God's presence (Lev. 16:2),

CHERUB

bearers of God (Ps. 18:10). Figures of cherubim were embroidered on the hangings of the Tabernacle (Ex. 26:1) and later were carved all around the walls of the Temple. For the Holy of Holies Solomon had two large cherubim made, about 15 feet high and with similar wingspread. Biblical writers represent the cherubim as animate beings with the intelligence of man, the strength of an ox, the courage of a lion and the free motion of an eagle through the air. The winged, man-headed bulls found in Assyrian and Babylonian art have at least an external resemblance to the cherubim described in Scriptures. See also MERCY SEAT.

ches'nut, chest'nut. A tree of uncertain identification, perhaps the Oriental plane tree which grows to 90 feet high, wild by the side of mountain streams, cultivated in places near water (Gen. 30:37; Ezek. 31:8).

chick'en. It is probable that the chicken was a common domesticated bird, at least by the time of Jesus. See Matt. 23:37; Luke 13:34; also Mark 13:35; Matt. 26:34. See COCK; FOWL.

chil'dren of God. Those persons who accept God as their father and seek to do His will (Matt. 5:9; Rom. 8:16). The relationship includes the unquestioned acceptance of the authority of God (the Father) as head of the household and the full rights of sonship by believers to inherit the graces obtained through the merits of the Son of God, Jesus Christ.

chil'dren of the east. Nomadic tribes from lands e. of Palestine, esp. the Syrian desert; they were considered to have superior wisdom (Judg. 6:3, 33; I Kings 4:30).

CINNAMON

cin'na·mon. A fragrant wood (S. of Sol. 4:14; Rev. 18:13), an ingredient in the sacred anointing oil (Ex. 30:23); used in later times to perfume beds (Prov. 7:17). Its source is the aromatic bark of a tree belonging to the laurel order native in Ceylon. The bark yields an oil which is used in perfumery.

Chin'ner-eth, Chin'ner-oth. A lake beside the town of Chinneroth. The name has also been applied to the region in Naphtali around the town. See GALILEE, SEA OF.

cho'sen peo'ple. A term applied to the Hebrews as the people to whom God made a special revelation and through whom He made His special purposes known to man (Deut. 14:2; I Kings 3:8; Isa. 41:8-9; Amos 3:2). The conception starts with the call of Abraham (Neh. 9:7-8; Acts 13:17). See ABRAHAM; ELECTION.

Christ. "The Anointed One," a title derived from a Greek word, *Christos*, corresponding to Hebrew and Aramaic "Messiah," which in later O.T. days meant the anticipated royal son of David. "Christ" is so constantly added to "Jesus," the distinctive personal name of our Lord, as virtually to constitute part of the proper name. But "the Christ," the more exact form, is found in Matt. 16:16; Mark 8:29; Luke 3:15; John 1:41, etc.; sometimes the word "the" being omitted (Matt. 26:68; John 4:25). See also MESSIAH.

chrys'o-lite, chrys'o-lyte. An olive- or yellowish-green semiprecious stone (Rev. 21:20).

chry-sop'ra-sus. An apple-green, chromium-colored variety of chalcedony (Rev. 21:20). The modern spelling is chrysoprase.

church. The church may be defined as the communion of saints, that is, of those who truly believe on Christ, in which the gospel is rightly preached and the sacraments properly administered. "Church" is a translation of Greek *ekklesia*, the word used in the N.T. for an organized community acknowledging the Lord Jesus Christ as its supreme ruler, and meeting statedly, or as opportunities offered, for religious worship. As followers of Jesus arose in many different cities, the plural "churches" began to be used, the Christian community in each separate locality being considered a church. Nowhere in the N.T. is the word "church" used for the building in which any particular Christian community met. Protestants generally hold that the church is both invisible and visible. The invisible church is composed of all who are really united to Christ (I Cor. 1:2; 12:12-13, 27-28; Col. 1:24; I Peter 2:9-10). The visible church consists of all who profess to be united to Christ.

cir·cum·ci'sion. Circumcision seems to have been a very ancient custom, for it is known to have been practiced in upper Syria nearly 3000 years B.C. The Egyptians and the Arabs practiced it, as well as the Hebrews. The act consists in removing the foreskin, and it was performed on the child by the father of the house or some other Israelite, or even by the mother (Ex. 4:25). The proper time to carry out the rite among the Hebrews was when the boy was 8 days old. Circumcision was the rite of initiation, instituted by God and enjoined upon Abraham, into the covenant privileges of the family of God represented by Abraham and his descendants through Isaac. It was also the token of the covenant (Gen. 17:1-10, 21). To "circumcise the heart" is so to regenerate it that its irreligious obstinacy will disappear (Deut. 10:16; Jer. 4:4; 9:25-26), so that it can love God with all its powers (Deut. 30:6; Rom. 2:28-29).

cit'y of ref'uge. A city designated to afford sanctuary to a person who had committed an accidental or justifiable manslaughter from the pursuit of the avenger of blood (Num. 35:9-14; Ex. 21:13). See AVENGER. No part of Palestine was far from a designated city of refuge. If a manslayer reached a city of refuge, he was received into it and obtained a fair trial. If guilty of willful murder, he was delivered to death. If innocent he could live there indefinitely in security, and upon the death of the high priest he was at liberty to return to his own home and enjoy the protection of the authorities (Num., ch. 35; Deut., ch. 19; Josh., ch. 20).

clean. God's people must be free from any pollution, physical, ceremonial, moral and spiritual, and accordingly a sharp distinction is made between clean and unclean (Lev. 10:10). Certain animals were declared "clean" for food and sacrifice, while others were forbidden as "unclean" (Lev., ch. 11; Deut. 14:1-21). In approaching God, both priests and laity had to be physically clean (Ex. 19:10-15; 30:18-21). Ultimately, however, cleanness is an inner state (Ps. 24:4; Matt. 15:1-20; Mark 7:1-23; I Cor. 6:12-20; II Cor. 7:1), and involves a personal relation to God (Ps. 51:7-10). See UNCLEAN ANIMALS; UNCLEANNESS.

cleave. To adhere closely; to cling (Deut. 10:20; Ps. 102:5).

Clem'ent. A "fellow laborer" of Paul (Phil. 4:3).

Cle'o·pas. One of 2 disciples who met, but did not recognize, Jesus on the road to Emmaus (Luke 24:18).

Cle'o·phas. The husband of one of the Marys present at the Crucifixion (John 19:25, KJV; the RSV spells this name "Clopas").

cloak, cloke. A loose-fitting outer garment, often decorated, and containing pockets for carrying articles. It was often used to sleep in; hence common law stated that, if borrowed, it must be returned by nightfall (Matt. 5:40; Luke 6:29).

Clo'pas. See CLEOPHAS.

coat of mail. A covering worn to protect a soldier's breast, back and shoulders against offensive weapons. It was made of leather, quilted cloth, linen, bronze or iron (I Sam. 17:5; Rev. 9:9). There were joints in it to provide flexibility (I Kings 22:34).

cock. The male of the well-known domestic

fowl (Matt. 26:34, 74-75). Cockcrow, as a portion of time, is the third watch of the night, just before dawn (Mark 13:35).

cock′a·trice. This is a 17th-century word for a snake-like monster (Isa. 14:29) with a deadly glance, said to be hatched by a serpent from a cock's egg. Like a "sea dragon" or "unicorn," such a beast existed only in fables and legends. Undoubtedly a venomous reptile which cannot now be identified was meant by the Hebrew word. See ASP.

cock·crow′ing. The third watch of the night, from midnight to 3 a.m. (Mark 13:35). The night, which went from sunset to sunrise, was divided by Romans into four parts or watches.

cock′le. A sturdy plant that is a pest in the grain fields of Palestine.

co′hort. A military unit consisting of 600 foot soldiers.

col′lege. A section of Jerusalem (II Kings 22:14; II Chron. 34:22); more correctly called the Second Quarter, possibly because it was an expansion (to the north) of the old city.

colt. The young of the horse, or of camels (Gen. 32:15), or of the ass (Gen. 49:11; Zech. 9:9; Mark 11:2).

Com′fort·er. A proper name given to the Holy Spirit in John 14:16, 26; 15:26; 16:7. Comfort conveys the meaning to make strong, to bolster, rather than to console. See also HOLY SPIRIT.

com′ing of the Lord. The expected return of Christ to earth, confidently anticipated among the early Christians at any moment (James 5:8). The time of this "Second Coming" was not revealed even to Christ, but he does discuss it and ways of recognizing it in Matt., ch. 24. See SECOND COMING.

com·mand′ment. A command or order, esp. by one who has authority and who could expect it to be obeyed (II Kings 18:36; Neh. 11:23). The Ten Commandments (Ex.

20:2-7) are the rules for moral conduct established by God. Jesus summed up these commandments in his commandments of love for God and for one's fellow man (Matt. 22:36-40; John 13:34).

com·mune′ with. To converse with (Ps. 4:4).

com·mun′ion. 1. A sharing of one's thoughts and emotions with another or others; comradeship (II Cor. 6:14; 13:14). 2. A sharing or partaking of something one has in common with another or others; participation, fellowship (I Cor. 10:16). See also HOLY COMMUNION.

com·mun′ion of saints. Christians are "saints," according to Paul (Phil. 1:1) by virtue of being "in Christ Jesus." Elsewhere (I Cor. 1:2) those called to be saints are "sanctified in Christ Jesus." Saints became naturally a term for members of the Christian Church. "Saints" and "Christians" are made the same thing also in Acts 9:13 and 26:10. The communion of saints, then, is the church of God's people within the Christian community.

com′pass. v. To go around; to make the circuit of (Josh. 6:11). n. The circumference (Ex. 27:5); a circuit (Acts 28:13).

con′cu·bine. A secondary wife under the system of polygamy, usually purchased as a slave or taken as a captive in war. A concubine could more easily be put away than a wife (Gen. 21:10-14), yet their rights were recognized and guarded by the Mosaic law (Ex. 21:7-11; Deut. 21:10-14). In O.T. Societies the practice of having more than one wife was a common and a legal one; it was the only way, in many instances, that a man could have the large family essential to raise crops or protect the animals.

con·demn′. 1. To declare (a person) to be guilty of wrongdoing (Deut. 25:1). 2. To pass final judgment on; to doom (John 3:17). 3. To express disapproval of; to criticize adversely (Matt. 12:7; I John 3:20). 4. To give a judicial decision against; to inflict a penalty upon (Luke 24:20).

con'dem·na'tion. A condemning or being condemned; esp. God's judgment against sin (Luke 23:40; John 5:24).

con'duit. A channel or tunnel, usually cut out of rock, for bringing water from a river, lake, etc. to a desired spot, as a city or garden; esp. the conduit built by Hezekiah to carry water inside the walls of Jerusalem (II Kings 18:17; 20:20; Isa. 36:2).

co'ney. The coney of England is the rabbit; that of the KJV is called the rock badger in the RSV. A small, wary Palestinian animal, living among the rocks (Ps. 104:18; Prov. 30:26), it is neither a rabbit nor a badger, but has a unique structure that makes it one of a kind. It was considered "unclean" (Lev. 11:5; Deut. 14:7).

con·fes'sion of Jesus. Paul expressed the ideas behind this expression in Rom. 10:9-10: "If thou shalt confess with thy mouth the Lord Jesus, and shalt believe in thine heart that God hath raised him from the dead, thou shalt be saved. For with the heart man believeth unto righteousness, and with the mouth confession is made unto salvation." The would-be follower has always been required to make this or a very similar "confession of Christ" in public (I Tim. 6:12). The Christian by his confession commits himself to loyal following of Jesus as God's Son, however risky the decision or hard the path.

con·fes'sion of sin. In the O.T., confession was rooted in the liturgical tradition of the nation. The typical ritual confession began with a proclamation of God's saving acts, such as freeing the people from Egyptian bondage, or delivering the nation or the individual from enemies. Secondly, confession spoke words of recognition of the power of sin, men's helplessness before it, and of God's power to rescue His people or His praying follower. Confessional Psalms praising God are: Ps. 22; 30; 34; 40; 51; 116.

To John the Baptist, confession was part of his baptismal rite readying the Jews for the appearance of the Messiah. Confession of sins plays a central part in Jesus' parables (Luke 15:18; 18:10-13) and in the Lord's Prayer, and he witnessed his own vocation. After Christ's death the N.T. emphasis veers sharply from focus on God's saving acts for Israel to Jesus Christ as God's redeeming act for all who will "confess Christ." See CONFESSION OF JESUS.

con'gre·ga'tion. In Scripture the word is used mainly for: 1. The body politic of Israel, including men, women and children (Ex. 12:3, etc.). 2. An assemblage of the people, esp. for religious purposes (Ps. 22:22, 25). 3. The "tabernacle of the congregation" was the appointed place where the Lord and His people met (Ex. 27:21, etc.).

Co·ni'ah. See JEHOIACHIN.

Con'quest, the. This term refers to the military conquest of the land of Canaan by the Israelites under Joshua, recorded in the book of Joshua.

con'se·crate. To set apart as holy; to devote to the service of God (Num. 6:12; I Chron. 29:5; Ezek. 43:26). Also to install (someone) in a sacred office by a religious ceremony (Ex. 29:9; Judg. 17:5).

con·ver'sion. The basic idea of conversion is "to turn." It signifies a turning away from sin and a returning to God. It is through the grace of God that a person can turn from evil to good, from sin to living under God (Jer. 31:18; Acts 3:26).

con·vert' (v.), con'vert (n.). v. To turn, to change—from one religion, doctrine, opinion or way of life to another. Often, to turn to the worship of the one true God (Isa. 6:10; Matt. 18:3; Mark 4:12). n. One who has been converted to the worship of God (Isa. 1:27). See also PROSELYTE.

con'vo·ca'tion, ho'ly convocation. The terms refer to a solemn assembly, a summons to the people of Israel to come together, set aside all work and fulfill sacred functions. These "holy convocations" were every Sabbath (Lev. 23:1-3) and on prescribed days of the major festivals.

cop'ing. Probably, but not certainly, the low wall, or parapet, on all sides of the flat roof of a house was meant (I Kings 7:9).

cor. A unit of liquid measure. See MEASURES.

Cor'ban. The bad practice arose of children's avoiding giving aid to parents needing their support, on the pretense that the money or service that would otherwise have been available for the parents had been dedicated to God and that it would be a sacrilege to divert it from this sacred purpose. "Corban" means, literally, "offering." The custom of dedicating something to God by saying of it "Corban," came to be abused, making it a way of evading a troublesome obligation, a duty or commitment. It is this abuse that Jesus denounces in Mark 7:11.

co'ri·an'der. A plant that grows wild in Egypt and Palestine. Its white seeds (Ex. 16:31; Num. 11:7) provide flavoring for breads and sweets, and have medicinal uses.

cor'mo·rant. A large swimming bird of the pelican family. In Palestine it lives on the Mediterranean coast and on the Sea of Galilee. It is a greedy bird and a very skillful diver after fish. It was held to be "unclean" (Lev. 11:17; Deut. 14:17). See also PELICAN.

corn. A word designating several cereal grasses cultivated in Palestine, whereas in the U.S. "corn" means Indian corn or maize. The chief grains meant by "corn" were wheat, barley, millet and spelt (Deut. 8:8; Isa. 28:25-28; Ezek. 4:9). In Gen. 27:28; Deut. 7:13, "corn and wine" (RSV, "grain and wine") stand figuratively for the entire vegetable and fruit produce of the fields. See also WHEAT.

Cor·nel'i·us. An Italian captain who received a vision and was later baptized by Peter (Acts, ch. 10).

cor'ner·stone. A stone placed at the angle
where two walls of a building meet, and
helping to bind them together. Any stone in
this position, from the foundation to the
roof, is a cornerstone. Figuratively, Christ
is the "chief cornerstone" at the foundation
(Eph. 2:20; I Peter 2:6), and also "head of
the corner" (Matt. 21:42; I Peter 2:7).

cor·net'. A musical instrument played by
blowing air through it, probably indicating
a trumpet (I Chron. 15:28) in some instances and a horn, the hollow horn of an
animal, in others (Dan. 3:5). Rather than
"cornet" in II Sam. 6:5, probably a percus-
sion instrument is meant. See also TRUMPET.

couch. As a verb, this may mean to crouch
(Gen. 49:9) or to hide (Deut. 33:13).

coun'cil. 1. The Sanhedrin, the Jewish governing body, which under the Roman prefects
(later called procurators) had extensive
powers. It was composed of 70 ordinary
members and the high priest, the official
president of the body. It was the highest
court in Judea, with power of life and death
(Matt. 26:3, 57; Acts 4:5-6; 5:21, etc.),
though apparently it had no recognized authority to execute its sentence of death, but
had to submit its action to the review of the
Roman authorities. The council also had
the general administration of the government and of justice, so far as this was not
exercised by the Roman governor or minor
officials (Acts 22:30). It had police at its
command and could make arrests on its
own authority (Matt. 26:47; Mark 14:43).
Jesus was tried before the council (Matt.
26:59, etc.). It was before the council that
Peter and other apostles were brought
(Acts, ch. 4), also Stephen (6:12) and Paul
(22:30). The Sanhedrin was swept out of existence at the destruction of Jerusalem in
A.D. 70. 2. Roman officials would sometimes appoint groups of advisors to assist
them in administering justice in their provinces. Such a body is called a council in

Acts 25:12. See also SADDUCEES.

cov'e·nant. A binding and solemn agreement between 2 or more parties, not necessarily equals, made out of loyalty to each other, to do or keep from doing a specific thing (Gen. 21:27; Josh. 24:25; I Sam. 18:3); specifically: 1. The agreement between God and man for man's continued life and welfare on condition of obedience to God's will (Ex. 34:28). 2. The agreement between God and Noah that there would not be another flood (Gen. 9:12-15). 3. The agreement between God and Abraham that Abraham's descendants would inherit the land of Canaan (Gen. 15:18). 4. A second agreement between God and man (called a "new covenant") in which man would receive righteousness and forgiveness of his sins through the intercession of Christ (Heb. 8:8, 13; 12:24). The Greeks had trouble finding a good word to use for the Hebrew word meaning "covenant." They selected a Greek word for their Bibles in Greek that means "will" or "testament." Hence we now speak of the Old Testament and New Testament, though Old Covenant and New Covenant could be said to be more accurate. See also TESTAMENT.

cov'ert. A covered or protected place; a shelter (II Kings 16:18; Job 38:40; Isa. 4:6).

cov'et. To desire (Ex. 20:17).

cow. Cows were domesticated early, and were kept in Egypt, Philistia and Palestine, wherever pasturage permitted. References to them include Gen. 12:16; 15:9; 32:15; 41:2; Lev. 3:1; Num. 19:2, 9 (compare Heb. 9:13); Deut. 21:1-9; I Sam. 6:7, 14; II Sam. 17:29.

craft. Handicraft, trade (Ex. 3:5).

crane. A long-legged wading bird, tall and elegant-looking, with a chattering cry (Isa. 38:14; Jer. 8:7).

creep'ing thing. Any animal that creeps (Gen. 1:24-25), whether a land or water reptile (Gen. 6:7; Ps. 104:25) and whether crawling on the belly or creeping on 4 or more feet (Lev. 11:41–42).

crib. A manger or a stall (Isa. 1:3).

crick'et. See BEETLE.

Cris'pus. At Corinth, the ruler of the synagogue, converted and baptized by Paul (Acts 18:8; I Cor. 1:14).

cro'cus. See ROSE.

cross. The cross on which Christ died was of wood and was heavy, but not too heavy to be borne by a strong man (Matt. 27:32, etc.). It was probably shaped in the form of a dagger, which more easily than the T-shape or X-shape crosses allowed the name, title or crime of the victim to be affixed to the upper part (Matt. 27:37, etc.). It was raised from the earth either before or after the victim was affixed to it. Until the death of Christ the cross was a name of horror and loathing (John 19:31; I Cor. 1:23, etc.), so that to bear the cross meant great reproach. But after the Crucifixion, zealous followers of Jesus reversed the popular conception. Paul gloried in the cross of Christ (Gal. 6:14), by which he meant the atonement resulting from Christ's Crucifixion (Eph. 2:16; Col. 1:20).

crow. See RAVEN.

crown. 1. An ornamental headdress worn as a badge of authority or dignity. Hebrew royal crowns were generally a circlet of gold, (Ps. 21:3), often studded with gems (II Sam. 12:30; Zech. 9:16). For the headdress of the high priest, see Ex. 29:6. 2. The wreath or garland placed on the head of a victor in a contest (I Cor. 9:25). 3. Anything resembling a crown, as the border or molding about the Ark, the table and the altar (Ex. 25:11, 24–25; 30:3–4). For "crown of life," see James 1:12; Rev. 2:10. For "crown of thorns," see Matt. 27:29; Mark 15:17; John 19:2, 5. For "crown of glory," see I Peter 5:4. For "crown of righteousness," see II Tim. 4:8.

crown of thorns. The crown that was plaited

by the Roman soldiers and placed on the head of Jesus to torture and insult him (Matt. 27:29; Mark 15:17; John 19:2, 5), generally supposed to have been made of the *Zizyphus spina Christi*. The flexible boughs are tough and well suited for shaping into a crown, and bear sharp thorns.

cru'ci·fix'ion. The act of fixing a victim to a cross for the purpose of capital punishment. Ropes bound the shoulders or torso to the wooden frame, and usually also nails were driven through hands or wrists and feet. Death came slowly, from fatigue, exposure to heat and cold, thirst and hunger. This method of punishment existed in many ancient nations; the Romans reserved it for slaves or non-Romans who had committed the greatest crimes. See CROSS.

cruse. A small jar or jug (I Kings 17:12). Those used for olive oil stood 4–6 inches high.

CRUSE

cu'bit. About 18 inches. See MEASURES.

cuck'oo, cuck'ow. The Palestinian cuckoo is not an eater of reptiles or carrion, as are the other "unclean" birds on the lists in Lev. 11:16 and Deut. 14:15. The RSV says "sea gull" here.

cu'cum·ber. The cucumber we know today is similar to the one raised in biblical times (Num. 11:5; Isa. 1:8).

cum'min. A cultivated plant, sown broadcast and, when ripe, beaten with a rod to detach its seeds (Isa. 28:25, 27), which were eaten as a spice or relish with food. As with anise (Matt. 23:23, RSV "dill"), Jesus criticizes the tithing of cummin as a trifle of which the Pharisees were particular, while neglecting more significant actions.

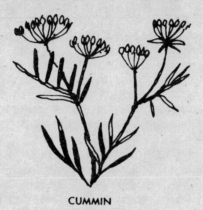

CUMMIN

cup·bear'er. The official who poured drink into the cup and gave it to the king (Gen. 40:9-14, where he is called "butler," and Neh. 1:11; 2:1-2). It was considered a position of great honor in an Oriental court and required trustworthiness in its occupant, lest he be bribed to offer poisoned wine to the king.

Cush. 1. A son of Ham and his descendants collectively (Gen. 10:6-8). 2. The land of the Cushites, usually designating Ethiopia (II Kings 19:9; Esth. 1:1; Ezek. 29:10).

cus·to'di·an. See SCHOOLMASTER.

cut'tings. The practice of making scratches or cuts in the skin, usually as a sign of mourning. This was looked upon as a heathen custom and was forbidden by Mosaic law. The phrase occurs only in Lev. 19:28; 21:5, but the practice is referred to elsewhere (Deut. 14:1; Jer. 48:37), so it was probably done at times by some Hebrews.

cy'press. The common cypress is an evergreen widespread in the Near East in 2 varieties, one a tall tree 60 feet high with erect branches, the other smaller, with spreading branches.

Cy'rus. Founder of the Persian empire, he lived from c. 600–529 B.C. In 539 B.C. he conquered Babylonia and issued a proclamation permitting the Jews in Babylon to return and rebuild the Temple at Jerusalem (II Chron. 36:22–Ezra 1:11; 5:13-15; 6:3-5). See EXILE; MEDES.

D

Da'gon. The national God of the Philistines. He had a temple at Gaza, at Beth-dagon, and esp. at Ashdod (Judg. 16:21, 23; I Sam. 5:1-7; I Chron. 10:10). He was thought to have been the god of agriculture. He was represented as having the head, arms and torso of a human, while the lower body tapered into the tail of a fish.

DAGON

dam·na'tion. This word and words related to it, as "damn" and "damnable," mean simply condemnation or condemn; they refer to the act of judging someone guilty.

Dan. 1. Fifth son of Jacob, first by Bilhah (Gen. 30:5-6; 35:25). 2. The tribe to which he gave origin, and the territory allotted to them between Jerusalem and the seaport of Joppa (present-day Jaffa) (Num. 1:12, 38-39; Josh. 19:40-48). Samson was a Danite (Judg., ch. 13). Restricted by the powerful Amorites to the hill country (Judg. 1:34), the Danites spied on and later seized the remote northern town of Laish (Leshem), which they rebuilt under the name of Dan (ch. 18). 3. The town of Dan, formerly called Laish, was at the extreme n. of Palestine, hence the phrase "from Dan even to Beer-sheba" (Judg. 20:1), meaning the entire length of the land. King Jeroboam placed one of the golden calves at Dan (I Kings 12:28-30). The town was later destroyed by Ben-hadad (15:20).

Dan'iel. A prophet, taken captive and later made ruler of Babylon by Nebuchadnezzar, who named him Belteshazzar; cast into a den of lions, he emerges unhurt because of his belief in God. See also Matt. 24:15; Mark 13:14.

dar'ic. See DRAM.

Da·ri'us. Two kings of this name appear in the Bible. 1. Darius the Mede (Dan. 5:31; 9:1), a historically shadowy figure who preceded Cyrus (6:28) as king of the Medes and Persians. 2. Darius Hystaspis, ruler of the Persian empire 521-486 B.C. This is the Darius mentioned in Ezra and Nehemiah; also in Haggai 1:1 and Zech. 1:1.

Da'than. See KORAH.

Da'vid. King and psalmist;
  anointed king (I Sam., ch. 16)
  slays Goliath (I Sam., ch. 17)
  covenants with Jonathan; escapes Saul's
    jealousy (I Sam., chs. 18-20)
  lives as outlaw (I Sam., chs. 21-26)
  Nabal and Abigail (I Sam. ch. 25) ·
  Philistines refuse him (I Sam., chs. 27-29)
  becomes king of Judah (I Sam. 31:1-II
    Sam. 2:11)
  death of Abner and Ish-bosheth (II Sam.,

chs. 3; 4)

made king of Israel (II Sam., ch. 5)

brings Ark to Jerusalem (II Sam., ch. 6)

kindness to Jonathan's son (II Sam., chs. 9; 21)

Uriah and Bath-sheba (II Sam., ch. 11; cf. I Kings 15:5)

birth of Solomon (II Sam., ch. 12)

Absalom's conspiracy and death (II Sam., chs. 15-18)

song of thanksgiving (II Sam., ch. 22)

mighty men (II Sam., ch. 23)

numbers the people (II Sam., ch. 24)

appoints Solomon his successor (I Kings, ch. 1)

death (I Kings, ch. 2; I Chron. 29:26-30).

David was considered the ideal king, the founder (rather than Saul) of the Hebrew monarchy and the type of the Messiah.

day of the Lord. See JUDGMENT, DAY OF; LORD'S DAY.

day star. The morning star (II Peter 1:19). See also LUCIFER.

dea'con, dea'con·ess. A Christian officer whose qualifications are laid down in I Tim. 3:8. It is justly assumed that the 7 men chosen to relieve the apostles of the secular care of widows and poor people were deacons (Acts 6:1). Our English word comes from a Greek word meaning "servant."

Dead Sea. See SALT SEA.

dearth. A scarcity or lack, esp. of the food supply (Neh. 5:3; Acts 11:28) or the water supply (Jer. 14:1).

Deb'o·rah. 1. Rebekah's nurse (Gen. 35:8). 2. A prophetess and judge (Judg., chs. 4-5), whose song of triumph after Barak's victory over the Canaanites is one of the oldest surviving examples of Hebrew poetry.

de·ci'sion, val'ley of. The name given in Joel 3:14 to the scene of Judgment Day, when God judges all people finally. It is thought by many to be the Kidron Valley, between Jerusalem and the Mount of Olives. Others regard it as a symbolic term.

deck. To dress with more than ordinary elegance; to adorn (Prov. 7:16).

ded'i·ca'tion. 1. The act of dedicating or setting apart for God's use (Ezra 6:16). 2. The ceremony at which something is consecrated to God, as the Tabernacle (Num. 7:84), the altar of Solomon's Temple (II Chron. 7:9), and the city wall (Neh. 12:27).

Dedication, Feast of. An annual festival instituted in 164 B.C. to celebrate the purification and renewal of the Temple after it had been desecrated by the Greek Syrian king Antiochus IV. The festival, also called Lights and Hanukkah, is celebrated for 8 days in the first half of December. See John 10:22.

deep, deeps. A vast expanse of water, the primeval ocean (Gen. 1:2). The "great deep" was the vast extent of water that lay under the flat earth and surrounded the foundations. In Noah's time it was from this source that the water was thought to rise and flood the earth (Gen. 7:11). In Ps. 148:7 "deeps" means all the waters on earth. In the Exodus story and later references to it the "deeps" refers to the waters God controlled to save Israel.

deer. In the KJV, the word occurs only in the

DEER (GAZELLE)

combination of "fallow deer" (Deut. 14:5; I
Kings 4:23). The European fallow deer is
small, standing only 3 feet tall at the shoulders. The RSV calls this animal a gazelle, a
small, swift-footed, graceful antelope which
is timid and flees a pursuer with great
bounds. Other words refer to other species
of deer. "Hart" refers to the adult male red
deer. "Hind" is the adult female red deer.
"Doe" is the name for a female deer of any
species other than red deer, and "buck" is
the male. "Roe" is the female of a third
type, roe deer, and "roebuck" the male.
Roe deer are among the smallest of deer,
only 26 inches tall. All 3 are now extinct in
Palestine.

de·file′. 1. To make ceremonially unclean
(Lev. 18:24; 22:8; Num. 19:13). 2. To make
filthy or foul; to pollute (Num. 35:34). 3. To
make morally unclean; to deprave, corrupt
(Matt. 15:18). 4. To rape or violate sexually
(Gen. 34:2).

de·gree′. Rank; station in life (I Tim. 3:13).

de·grees′. A word occurring in the titles of 15
Psalms (120–134), which are called Songs of
Degrees or Ascents. The common opinion
is that they were sung by the pilgrims during the ascent to Jerusalem at the time of
the great annual feasts.

De·li′lah. See SAMSON.

del′uge. An overflowing of the land by water
(Ezek. 13:11, RSV). See also FLOOD.

De·me′tri·us. 1. A silversmith at Ephesus, who
incited the riot against Paul (Acts
19:24-41). 2. A Christian commended by
John (III John 12).

de′mon. See DEVIL.

de·mo′ni·ac. One possessed and ruled by an
evil spirit. See DEVIL.

de·nar′i·us. See PENNY.

dep′u·ty. 1. A person appointed by someone
of higher authority to act for him in governing a country or province (I Kings 22:47;
Esth. 8:9; 9:3). 2. A Roman officer who

commanded an army in one or more provinces and often acted as a provincial governor or proconsul (Acts 13:7; 19:38).

de·sire' of all nations. The treasures or precious gifts of all the nations (Hag. 2:7), as for example the gold and silver of the next verse. Some have seen here a Messianic prophecy.

dev'il. 1. An evil spirit (Mark 1:34; Luke 4:33; 8:29). The Greek N.T. distinguished between a demon and the devil, but this distinction is lost in some English Bibles. Demons take possession of wicked men and are subject to the devil (Matt. 4:24; 12:24). 2. The evil one, Satan, the greatest of all the fallen spirits (Matt. 4:8-11; 13:38-39; 25:41; Rev. 12:9). Sinful, unrighteous men are figuratively called children of the devil (John 8:44; I John 3:8, 10). See also SATAN. 3. A word applied to a heathen god (Deut. 32:17; Ps. 106:37).

de·vot'ed thing. Anything devoted or dedicated to God, esp. objects captured in war. According to Semitic custom, captured booty had to be entirely or in part sacrificed or dedicated to God; violators of this custom were condemned (Lev. 27:28; see also Josh. 6:18-19; ch. 7).

di'a·dem. An ornamental cloth headband worn by Eastern kings, esp. those of Persia. It was, therefore, a symbol of royalty and kingly power (Isa. 28:5; 62:3). It is also used as another name for the high priest's miter (Ezek. 21:26).

di'al, sun dial. An instrument consisting of a surface which is marked off into hour lines and furnished with a projecting pointer to cast a shadow as the sun advances on its daily course, and thus indicate the hours. King Ahaz had one (II Kings 20:11; Isa. 38:8).

Di·an'a. The Diana of the Ephesians (Acts 19:24-35) was a very ancient fertility goddess, and had no connection with the Roman Diana, goddess of the moon, or the corresponding Greek Artemis, goddess of nature. The temple to Diana at Ephesus was one of the 7 Wonders of the World.

DIANA

Did′y·mus. See THOMAS.

dill. See ANISE; FITCH.

Di′nah. Daughter of Jacob and Leah (Gen. 30:21; ch. 34).

Di·ot′re·phes. A trouble-making member of the early church (III John 9, 10).

dirge. A song of mournful character, expressive of grief. See also LAMENTATION.

dis·cern′ing of spir′its. A spiritual gift given to some Christians by the Holy Spirit, enabling them to distinguish between those who spoke through the true inspiration of the Holy Spirit and those who pretended to convey God's word but were inspired by false or evil spirits (I Cor. 12:10; I John 4:1).

dis·ci′ple. A pupil (Matt. 10:24), esp. the follower of a public teacher, like John the Baptist (9:14). It is used most commonly in the N.T. of all who in faith received Christ's instructions (Matt. 10:42; Luke 14:26-27, 33; John 4:1; 6:66). Contrary to popular opinion, "disciple" is not a special designation for one of the Twelve (Mark 3:14-18; Matt. 10:1-4; Luke 6:13-16), though the word is often applied to one or more of them; the Twelve are more accurately called apostles.

Di'ves. The name commonly applied (although it does not appear in the Bible) to the rich man in the parable at Luke 16:19–31. The Latin word for "rich" is *dives.*

div·i·na'tion. The act or process of attempting to read the future or determine the unknown by magical or mystical means, esp. by a kind of inspiration or by the interpretation of certain signs, such as the appearance of water being poured into a container, the flight of birds, the shape and appearance of an animal's liver (Ezek. 21:21), the casting of lots, etc. The Hebrews also included in divination necromancy, foretelling the future by calling up the spirits of the dead and conversing with them (I Sam. 28:8). The Israelites were constantly warned in the O.T. that diviners, unlike prophets of God, were imposters; that no reliance could be put in them; and that consulting them was a crime.

di·vin'er. A person who practices divination; a soothsayer. See DIVINATION.

doc'tor. A learned man; a teacher (Luke 2:46); an expert in the law of Moses (Luke 5:17; Acts 5:34). A medical doctor was called a physician.

Do'eg. An enemy of David (I Sam. 21:7; 22:9–23).

dog. The dog was among the first animals domesticated by man. It was widely used by the ancients for hunting and was trained to aid the shepherd in protecting the flock against beasts of prey and thieves. The breeds of the dogs mentioned in the Bible cannot be determined. The majority of the references are to scavenger dogs, prowling about the cities and suburbs, unclean and often vicious. The term "dog" is applied in a figurative sense to those who are incapable of appreciating what is high or holy

(Matt. 7:6).

dol'phin. See LEVIATHAN; WHALE.

Dor'cas. Also called Tabitha (Acts 9:36–42).

dove. Another name for the pigeon, but usually applied to the smaller pigeon species. Four such species occurred in Palestine: the ring-dove, the stock dove, the rock dove and the ash-rumped rock dove. The last-named is the dove described in Jer. 48:28. Jesus refers to it as proverbially harmless (Matt. 10:16). It was bought and sold within the Temple courts (Matt. 21:12; Mark 11:15; John 2:14), for it was used in sacrifice (Luke 2:24). The dove is a symbol of the Holy Spirit (Luke 3:22).

DOVE

dox·ol'o·gy. A hymn or acclamation, generally short, of praise to God. There is one at the end of each of the 5 parts into which the book of Psalms is divided (Ps. 41; 72; 89; 106; 150). Sometimes they are found at the beginning of a prayer (I Chron. 29:10; Dan. 2:20; Luke 1:68).

drag'on. In the O.T. the word "dragon" is occasionally used to translate a Hebrew word that generally means "sea monster." But there are also traces of myths about battles between the Lord God and a monster or dragon (Isa. 51:9), where "dragon" is the right word, as it is throughout the book of Revelation. See also JACKAL, LEVIATHAN.

dram. A Persian gold coin, better known as a daric (I Chron. 29:7; Ezra 2:69; Neh. 7:70). It is the first coin mentioned in the Bible; previously unminted metals (principally silver and gold) had been used.

drink of'fer·ing. A drink offering was one of 3 kinds: drink; vegetable or meal; and animal offerings or sacrifices. It was not offered by itself, but always with one or both of the other kinds (Num. 29:11, 16, 18).

drom'e·dar'y. See CAMEL.

Dru·sil'la. Daughter of Herod Agrippa I and wife of Felix, governor of Judea (Acts 24:24-25).

duke. 1. A tribal chieftain (Gen. 36:40; Ex. 15:15). 2. A prince or ruler (Josh. 13:21).

dul'ci·mer. The real dulcimer (wire stretched over a metal sounding board) was unknown to the ancient East. The Hebrew word translated "dulcimer" may represent a kind of bagpipe, or it may refer to ensemble playing of the various individual instruments named (Dan. 3:5, 10, 15).

E

ea'gle. A carnivorous bird of prey (Job 9:26; 39:27-30; Hab. 1:8), large (Ezek. 17:3, 7), swift of flight (II Sam. 1:23), building its nest on lofty rocks (Jer. 49:16). Since it fed on reptiles and occasionally carrion, it was "unclean" (Lev. 11:13). The Hebrews applied the name they used for eagle to other birds that eat carrion, hence confusing eagles and vultures (Matt. 24:28). Probably 2 types of eagles were commonly seen in Palestine in Bible times, the golden eagle and the imperial eagle. See also OSSIFRAGE.

ear'nest. Part payment in advance of a wage, a sum of money, or anything else promised, this being intended as a pledge or guarantee to the recipient that the bargain, contract or promise will be carried out. The Spirit in the hearts of Christians is the earnest of their inheritance and ultimate salvation (II Cor. 1:22; 5:5; Eph. 1:13-14).

Eas'ter. The annual Christian festival celebrating the Resurrection of Christ. The word comes from Eastre, a Teutonic goddess of light and spring; the name of the festival in her honor was transferred by eighth-century Anglo-Saxons to the Christian festivals.

E'bed-me'lech. An Ethiopian who rescued Jeremiah from the dungeon (Jer. 38:7-13; 39:15-18).

Eb'en·e'zer. A stone set up by Samuel to mark a victory over the Philistines (I Sam. 7:10-12); also the name of the location at which the Israelites themselves had been defeated by the Philistines (ch. 4).

eb'on·y. A wood obtained from India or Ceylon (Ezek. 27:15), traded for in the markets of Tyre. The inner wood is black, very hard and heavy. Ebony is used for inlaying and ornamental wood-turning.

E'den, Gar'den of. "Eden" in Hebrew means "pleasantness." Efforts to determine an exact location for it have been fruitless. The story of the garden of Eden that God planted for Adam is told in Gen. 2:8-3:24. It is referred to in Isa. 51:3; Ezek. 28:13; 31:9, 16-18; 36:35; Joel 2:3.

ed'i·fi·ca'tion. Moral or spiritual instruction or improvement, especially seen in the development or confirmation of faith in God as opposed to the destruction or weakening of such faith (Rom. 15:2; I Cor. 14:3).

ed'i·fy. 1. To instruct or improve morally or spiritually (Eph. 4:29). 2. To make strong or healthy; to build up (Acts 9:31; Eph. 4:12; I Thess. 5:11).

E'dom. The name given Esau; the Edomites collectively (e.g. Num. 20:18). See EDOMITES; ESAU.

E'dom·ites. The descendants of Edom (Esau), who intermixed with the Canaanites, Ishmaelites and Horites of Seir (Gen., ch. 36). Through most of O.T. times they lived between the Dead Sea and the Red Sea, in mountainous country which abounded in copper and iron and through which lay important trade routes (I Kings 9:26-28). Although in Mosaic law they were regarded as brothers of the Israelites (Deut. 23:7-8), the old bitterness between Jacob (Israel) and Esau continued (Gen. 25:23; Num. 20:14-18; II Kings 14:7) and the Edomites joined Nebuchadnezzar in destroying Jerusalem (Obad. 10-16; cf. Ps. 137:7). During the captivity the Edomites moved up into the s. of Judah; "Idumea" (land of the Edomites) then included the cities of Beersheba and Hebron. In the 4th century B.C. the Nabateans came into the old Edom territory from the s. and e. and established their own capital, Petra; some Edomites stayed and were assimilated, others migrated n.w. to Idumea. The Herods were Idumeans. See also ESAU; HEROD; ISRAEL.

E'lah. Among other O.T. names: 1. A king of Israel (I Kings 16:6-14). See KINGS, TABLE OF. 2. The valley where David met Goliath (I Sam. 17:19).

eld'er. *n.* A person who was head of a family, of a tribal family or of the tribe itself (I Kings 8:1-3; Judg. 8:14, 16). Ordinarily only men of mature age came into these positions; hence the designation "elder." Each town, too, had its elders, who were probably the heads of the several families residing there, and these elders administered its civil and religious affairs (Deut. 19:12; 21:2; Ruth 4:2-11; I Sam. 11:3; Ezra 10:14). The office of elder in the Christian church was evidently suggested by the office of elder among the Jews, and was given similar authority. In the churches founded by the apostles, elder or presbyter and bishop were interchangeable designations (Acts 20:17; Titus 1:5, 7); the distinctions among them came only in the second century. *adj.* The older (as an elder brother).

El'e·a'zar. A number of men bear this name in

the O.T.; the most important is Aaron's
third son (Ex. 28:1), who succeeded him as
high priest and helped distribute the lands
of Canaan (Num. 3:2-4; 16:37-40; 20:25-28;
Deut. 10:6; Josh. 14:1; 24:33). See HIGH
PRIEST.

e·lec'tion. In the O.T. the term refers to God's
choice of Israel (Isa. 45:4) and of the Servant of the Lord (42:1). In the N.T. it is
used of God's choice of an individual
(Rom. 9:11) but especially of His choice of
the Christians, who are thus called "the
elect" (II Tim. 2:10; Titus 1:1). The ground
of God's choice is His love (Deut. 7:7-8).
The purpose of His choice is to redeem and
nurture a holy people (Eph. 1:4), who will
be His witnesses to the rest of mankind (Isa.
43:10; John 15:16). The fact of having been
chosen must arouse in the elect a sense not
of complacency, but of gratitude and responsibility (II Peter 1:10).

e·lect' la'dy. The addressee of the Second
Epistle of John (1:1). It may really mean an
actual lady, but many scholars believe that
John uses it as an expression for a local
church.

el'e·phant. Large herds of elephants roamed
in Syria in early biblical times. Pharaoh
Thutmose III of Egypt (c. 1450 B.C.) in an
Asiatic expedition once captured 120. They
continued to exist there until about 850 B.C.
Their tusks furnished ivory. In the wars of
the Maccabees in the period between the
Testaments, the elephant was used for attack purposes.

E'li. A Hebrew word meaning "my God"
(Matt. 27:46). See ELOI.

E'li. A high priest and judge of Israel for 40
years. At his sons' death and the loss of the
Ark in the defeat of the Israelites, Eli also
died (I Sam. 2:22-4:18). Samuel then became the religious leader of the people, and
the office of judge lost its importance for a
long time.

E·li'ah, E·li'as. See ELIJAH.

E·li'a·kim. The most prominent men of this name were: 1. The overseer of King Hezekiah's household, who laid Sennacherib's demands before Isaiah for divine counsel (II Kings 18:18-19:2). Isaiah seemed to regard him as a type of the Messiah (Isa. 22:20-22). 2. A son of Josiah, made king by Pharaoh (II Kings 23:34). See also JEHOIAKIM.

E·li'hu. A young man who reasoned with Job (chs. 32-37). There are others of the same name mentioned in the O.T.

E·li'jah. One of the greatest prophets;

> predicts drought and famine; is fed by ravens; restores widow's son (I Kings, ch. 17)

> exposes priests of Baal, proves power of God (I Kings, ch. 18)

> flees to Mt. Horeb; casts mantle upon Elisha (I Kings, ch. 19)

> denounces Ahab (I Kings 21:17-19)

> calls down fire against Ahaziah's armies (II Kings, ch. 1)

> divides waters of Jordan; taken up into heaven by whirlwind (II Kings, ch. 2)

> appears at Transfiguration (Matt. 17:3; Mark 9:4; Luke 9:30).

It was thought that he would return again (Mal. 4:5) and some believed that Jesus was Elijah (Matt. 16:14). In the O.T. he is twice referred to as Eliah, in the N.T. as Elias. See also ELOI.

El'i·phaz. One of Job's 3 friends (2:11; 4; 15; 22; 42:9).

E·lis'a·beth, E·liz'a·beth. A descendant of Aaron, cousin of the Virgin Mary, and mother of John the Baptist (Luke, ch. 1).

El'i·se'us. See ELISHA.

E·li'sha. Elijah's successor as prophet (I Kings 19:15-21);

> accompanies Elijah; divides Jordan; mocked by children (II Kings, ch. 2)

> his miracles (II Kings, chs. 3-6)

> prophesies plenty during siege; foretells kingship of Jehu and death of Jezebel

(II Kings, chs. 7-9)
his death; life restored to man who touches his bones (II Kings 13:14-21) referred to as Eliseus (Luke 4:27).

E·lo′i. An Aramaic form of a Hebrew word for God: part of an exclamation by Jesus (Mark 15:34) while on the cross, literally translated "My God." In Matt. 27:46 the Hebrew form "Eli" is used. Both words are an attempt to reflect in a Greek gospel the opening words of Psalm 22 which Jesus uttered. Some of the bystanders thought that Jesus was calling on Elijah (Matt. 27:47; Mark 15:35), whose prophetic association with the day of the Lord (Mal. 4:5) probably added to the misunderstanding. The rest of the quotation, *lama sabachthani* (lä′mä sä-bäk′tä-nē), means "why hast thou forsaken me?"

El′y·mas. A sorcerer temporarily blinded by Paul for his false teachings (Acts 13:6-12).

em′er·ods. Hemorrhoids (Deut. 28:27). They were inflicted on the Philistines (I Sam. 5:1, 6, 9-12; 6:11). But probably this was a bubonic plague, a periodic scourge of Bible lands, which often is fatal. It is transmitted by rodents.

Em·man′u·el. See IMMANUEL.

em′u·la′tion. 1. A desire to equal or surpass others; esp. a desire to imitate the good qualities of others (Rom. 11:14). 2. Ambitious rivalry and jealous quarreling (Gal. 5:20).

en·chant′er. A person who uses ritual charms and magical words either to summon the aid of spirits or to drive spirits away or out of persons they are supposedly tormenting (Deut. 18:10; Jer. 27:9, KJV; the RSV uses the word "augur").

en·chant′ment. The use of magic, etc. (II Chron. 33:6) was denounced by Mosaic law (Deut. 18:9-12).

en·due′. To endow or furnish, as with honors or property (Gen. 30:20).

en′gine. A mechanical device used for mili-

tary purposes, such as battering rams, cata-
pults and towers on wheels to provide a
high platform for archers.

en'mi·ty. A strong, settled feeling of hatred;
the attitude or feelings of an enemy (Num.
35:21-22); esp. feelings that are unrighteous
and hostile to God's will (Rom. 8:7; James
4:4).

E'noch. 1. A prophet (Jude 14) who was
translated (conveyed to heaven) without
death (Gen. 5:18-24; Heb. 11:5); called He-
noch in I Chron. 1:3. 2. A son of Cain, and
the city named for him (Gen. 4:17). Possibly the same as (1).

en'sign. 1. An ornamental emblem probably
placed on top of a long pole, as an insignia
of an army or people (Num. 2:2); used figuratively as a signal or symbol of protection
(Isa. 11:12; 30:17; 31:9). 2. A sign, standard
or other symbol that is easily seen (Zech.
9:16).

ENSIGN

Ep'a·phras. A fellow laborer in Christ with
Paul (Col. 1:7; 4:12; Philemon 23).

E·paph'ro·di'tus. See PHILIPPIANS, in "Sum-
mary of the Books of the Bible."

e'phah. A unit of dry measure, equivalent to
1.05 U.S. bushels. See MEASURES.

e'phod. 1. An upper garment, richly embroidered, worn by the high priest. It was one of
6 sacred vestments he was required to put

on when about to conduct the worship of God (Ex. 28:4), and was of gold, blue, purple, scarlet and fine twined linen. Further details are given in Ex., ch. 28. 2. A much simpler ephod of linen was worn by ordinary priests (I Sam. 22:18), by young Samuel (2:18) and by David when officiating before the Ark (II Sam. 6:14). 3. In some instances "ephod" seems to refer to an image or idol (Judg. 8:27; 17:5), or an instrument of divination (I Sam. 23:9-12; 30:7-8).

EPHOD

Eph'pha·tha. The transliteration into English of the Greek form of the imperative of the Aramaic verb "to open"; that is, "Be opened" (Mark 7:34).

E'phra·im. 1. Son of Joseph (Gen. 41:52), he was adopted by his grandfather Jacob (48:5), who blessed him as "greater" than his older brother Manasseh, signifying that he should be the ancestor of many peoples (48:8-20). 2. His people were called Ephraim, Ephraimites and Ephrathites (Josh. 16:10; Judg. 15:14; I Sam. 1:1), and the 10 tribes of which Ephraim later became the head were also known as Ephraim (e.g. Isa. 7:2). The growth of the tribe was slowed by the death of 2 of Ephraim's sons (I Chron. 7:20-22), and many were slain in battle against Jephthah (Judg. 12:1-6; see also

SHIBBOLETH). Joshua was an Ephraimite (Josh. 13:8, 16); Jeroboam, the first king of Israel after the kingdom divided, was also (I Kings 11:26-40), and built his capital, Shechem, in that territory (12:25; cf. Josh. 16:5-10).

Eph'rath·ite. See EPHRAIM.

E'phron. Sells Machpelah to Abraham (Gen. 23:10-20).

Ep'i·cu·re'ans. Followers of Epicurus (341-270 B.C.), a Greek philosopher whose moral teaching held that the goal of man should be a life of pleasure (including those derived from use of the mind and the moral faculty), regulated by morality, temperance, serenity and cultural development. The Epicureans were mostly men of soft temperament and many of them degenerated into searchers after physical, sensual pleasures only, and for this reason their philosophy was rejected by early Christians. See also STOICS.

E·pis'tles. The name given to 21 of the 27 books of the N.T. Today we would call them "Letters." They are letters that were written by the apostles, or that received apostolic approval; and they are addressed to particular churches or to individuals or to Christians generally. The titles of the letters were not part of the original composition, but were supplied afterward. They are lacking in early manuscripts and are not part of Scripture.

The letters that are not addressed to any particular church, group or individual and that are concerned with broad general problems rather than local issues, are called "General Epistles." Though the titles of II and III John do not bear the word "General," these books are included with James, I and II Peter, I John and Jude, making 7 General Epistles in all.

Three letters of Paul—I and II Timothy and Titus—are called "Pastoral Epistles" because they deal with matters of interest to pastors and church administrators.

E·sa'ias. See ISAIAH.

E'sar·had'don. Son of Sennacherib, king of Assyria, Esarhaddon became king when his brothers assassinated their father in 681 B.C. (II Kings 19:36-37; Isa. 37:37-38). After overcoming Manasseh, king of Judah, and the kings of Edom, Moab, Ammon and Gaza, among others, Esarhaddon continued s. and conquered all of Egypt. He even claimed to have conquered Ethiopia as well. He died in 661 B.C. See ASSYRIA.

E'sau. Son of Isaac and Rebekah, twin brother of Jacob (Gen. 25:24-28);

> sells birthright for pottage; is called Edom ("red") (Gen. 25:29-34)
> is cheated of blessing (Gen., ch. 27)
> comes to meet Jacob (Gen., chs. 32-33)
> generations of (Gen., ch. 36; I Chron. 1:35).

Because of the name given him when he sold his birthright, Esau's descendants were known as Edomites, and their land, originally called Seir or mount Seir, became known as Edom, later Idumea (Ezek. 35:15; Mal. 1:1-4). See EDOMITES.

Es'dra·e'lon. See JEZREEL.

Esh-ba'al. See ISH-BOSHETH.

es·pouse'. To betroth or promise in marriage (II Sam. 3:14; Matt. 1:18; Luke 1:27). Used figuratively of the union of the church with Christ (II Cor. 11:2).

Es'ther. Xerxes' queen; her story is told in the book of Esther. See also PURIM.

e·ter'nal life. The true life attained through the work of Christ and the faith of the believer; life without end in fellowship with God (John 17:3). Eternal life is pictured as both a present state and a future condition (Matt. 25:46; John 6:54; Rom. 2:7).

Eu'ty·chus. A young man of Troas who fell from a window while Paul was preaching and was restored to life by him (Acts 20:9-10).

e·van'ge·list. The Greek word means "a mes-

senger of good tidings." In the early church,
evangelists were distinct from apostles, pastors and teachers (Eph. 4:11). Their name
implied that their special function was to
announce the glad tidings of the gospel to
those before ignorant of them. As they were
not pastors of particular churches, they
were able to go from place to place preaching. At a later date the name "evangelist"
was given to the writers of the Four Gospels. See also GOSPEL.

Eve. The woman created by God to be a help-
meet for Adam; the story of her deception
and disobedience occurs in Gen. 2:20-5:4;
see also II Cor. 11:3; I Tim. 2:13.

eve'ning sac'ri·fice. The burnt offering of a
yearling lamb that took place every evening
(a similar one took place each morning) as
one of the two daily sacrifices at the Temple
directed in the Mosaic law (Ex. 29:38-39;
Ezra 9:4-5).

e'ven·tide. Evening (Gen. 24:63; Josh. 8:29,
KJV; Isa. 24:11, RSV).

e'vil. The opposite of good; physical or moral
disorder; anything which does not conform
to the will of God (John 3:19-20). Physical
evil is that which works against man's physical well-being (Job, chs. 1; 2). Moral evil is
disorder in the moral realm arising from
man's sinful inclinations (James 1:13-15).
Man in exercising his freedom of the will
may choose either what is good or what is
evil. God is not the author of sin, but He
permits it, that His justice may be known in
its punishment and His mercy in its forgiveness.

E'vil-me·ro'dach. King of Babylonia, 562-560
B.C., son of Nebuchadnezzar (II Kings
25:27-30).

e'vil spir'it. A supernatural, demonic influence, often in human form, that causes disease, pain, unhappiness or other misery (I
Sam. 16:14, 23; 18:10). In the N.T. the idea
becomes more personalized (Luke 7:21; 8:2;

Acts 19:12): the "evil spirit" becomes a "demon" or even a "devil" subject to the devil, Satan.

e'vil thing. 1. A condition that causes suffering or other misery (Luke 16:25). 2. An emotion or feeling that shows up as an evil thought or passion (Mark 7:23).

Ex'ile. The period during which the Jews were held in captivity in Babylonia in the sixth century B.C. It was begun by the first capture of Jerusalem in 597 by Nebuchadnezzar and ended with the decree of Cyrus, the Persian conqueror of Babylonia in 538 (Ezra 1:1-4).

Ex'o·dus. Literally, "a going out." The departure of the Israelites from Egypt, after they had been divinely freed from bondage in that land. The exact route is not certainly known.

ex'or·cist. A magician or sorcerer; esp. one who uses incantations or magic formulas to drive out evil spirits (Acts 19:13). Jesus cast out demons by the "Spirit of God" (Matt. 12:28) and by his own word (Matt. 8:16; Mark 1:25; 5:8; 9:25, etc.). This power was handed on to his disciples (Matt. 10:1).

ex'pi·a'tion. See PROPITIATION.

eye serv'ice. Work done only under the observation of a supervisor, or work done for flattery or favors (Eph. 6:6; Col. 3:22).

E·zek'iel. One of the great O.T. prophets, he grew up in Jerusalem in the time of Jeremiah. He was among those carried into captivity to Babylon along with King Jehoiachin, and began his prophetic mission 5 years later (II Kings 24:8-16; II Chron. 36:9-10). See also CAPTIVITY; PROPHET; TEMPLE.

Ez'ra. A priest and scribe authorized by King Artaxerxes to lead a group of Jewish exiles in Babylon back to Jerusalem, where he still lived at the time of Nehemiah (Ezra-Neh.). See SCRIBE.

F

faith. Faith has been defined as "the substance of things hoped for, the evidence of things not seen" (Heb. 11:1). As far as a difference exists between belief and faith, belief is assent to testimony and faith is assent to testimony with trust. The distinction between belief and faith is that between "believe me" and "believe on me." To the ancient Hebrews, faith was trust in the absolute truthfulness of every statement that comes from God (Gen. 15:6). In the N.T. it is reliance on God's word concerning the mission and atoning death of His Son (John 5:24) and on the testimony of Jesus regarding himself (John 3:18; Acts 3:16). Faith is a gift of God, and faith in the Redeemer is essential to salvation (John 3:15-16, 18).

fal'con. A bird of prey active in daytime only. The falcon family also includes hawks, kites and eagles. See EAGLE; KITE.

Fall, the. The Fall of man is narrated in Gen., ch. 3. God created man, male and female, after His own image. But upon being left to the freedom of their will, they yielded to temptation and transgressed the commandment of God. Through their disobedience they fell from the state of innocency and sinlessness. The result of the Fall is original sin, into which state all men are born. Paul assumes, as needing no proof, that man's sinfulness is the result of Adam's fall. Just as Adam is related to the race as the author of sin and death, so Christ is the author of righteousness and life. At one end are Adam and sinful humanity; at the other, Christ and redeemed humanity (Rom. 5:12-21; I Cor. 15:21-22, 45-49). See also SIN.

false Christ. A person who falsely claimed to be the Messiah and who would attempt to lead the Christians (Matt. 24:24; Mark 13:22).

false proph'et. A person who claims to speak

for God, but who has not been divinely inspired; his messages are usually adapted to the attitude of his audience, containing prophecies he thinks will be pleasant for them to hear (Matt. 24:11, 24; Luke 6:26; II Peter 2:1). In the book of Revelation the false prophet is an agent of Satan.

fa·mil'iar spir'it. The spirit of a dead person which professed mediums claimed to summon to consultation (Deut. 18:11), to reveal the future (Isa. 8:19). Consulting persons who supposedly had this power was forbidden (Lev. 19:31).

far'thing. An English coin equal to one-fourth of an English penny. The coin so translated (Matt. 5:26) was a Roman quadrans, worth in the first century about one quarter of a U.S. cent.

fast. *v.* To abstain from food. *n.* The period during which it takes place. One might fast to express grief over the death of a loved one (I Sam. 31:13); to punish oneself before God because of sin (Ps. 35:13); to attempt to gain the favor of God before a dangerous undertaking (Esth. 4:16); or to try to ward off evil or threatening misfortune (I Kings 21:27). *adv.* Firmly; soundly, as fast asleep.

fat. 1. The Mosaic law stated that the fat of sacrificed animals belongs to the Lord (Lev. 3:16); fat was not to be eaten by the people of Israel (Lev. 3:17; 7:23-25), though this provision was apparently abolished with respect to animals slain solely for food (Deut. 12:15-16, 21-24). 2. A wine vat (Joel 2:24; Isa. 63:2).

fa'ther, Fa'ther. 1. In Genesis esp. this word can mean the immediate progenitor of a person (Gen. 42:13), or grandfather (28:13) or more remote ancestor (17:4). He may also be the founder of an occupation or social group (4:20), or one who acts with fatherly kindness and wisdom (45:8). 2. God, either as the Creator of man (Mal. 2:10) or as the begetter and loving guardian of His spiritual children (Rom. 8:15; Gal. 4:6) or as standing in a more mysterious relation to Jesus (Matt. 11:26; Mark 14:36; Luke 22:42).

fath'om. A measure used in reckoning depth of water (Acts 27:28). The Greek word denoted the length of a man's outstretched arms: the English fathom is 6 feet.

fat'ling. A bull, steer or ox fattened before being slaughtered, esp. for sacrifice (I Sam. 15:9; Isa. 11:6).

Feast. See under UNLEAVENED BREAD; WEEKS, FEAST OF, etc.

Fe'lix. Governor of Judea. When Paul was sent before him, Felix was impressed by his speech, but, hoping in vain for bribery, left Paul in bonds for Porcius Festus, his successor, to deal with (Acts, chs. 23–24). See PROCURATOR.

fel'low·ship. The basic idea is that of sharing a common life or interest. In this fellowship Christians join in partaking of the Lord's Supper (I John 1:3-7). See also COMMUNION.

fer'ret. See LIZARD.

Fes'tus. Successor of Felix as governor of Judea under Nero. Finding Paul still imprisoned, he would have sent him to Jerusalem for trial, but Paul asked to stand before Caesar. King Agrippa and his sister Bernice visited Festus, who brought Paul forth to speak to them (Acts 24:27–26:32). See PROCURATOR.

fi'er·y ser'pent. A poisonous snake that caused many deaths among the Israelites (Num. 21:6; Deut. 8:15), probably so called because of the painful bite and resultant inflammation.

fig, fig tree. A tree bearing edible fruit (Judg. 9:10, 11) and the fruit itself. The young tree does not bear fruit unless the ground is cultivated (Luke 13:6-9), and old trees speedily deteriorate and fail when neglected (Prov. 27:18). The young fruit appears in spring before the leaves open, on branches of the last year's growth; this is the green fig

(S. of Sol. 2:13). The first ripe fruit is ready in June. The late figs grow on the new wood, keep appearing during the season, and are ripe from August onward. They are dried and pressed into cakes and form a staple article of food (I Sam. 25:18; 30:12). As

FIG TREE

with the vine, the fig tree was highly prized, and to sit under one's vine and one's fig tree was a symbol of prosperity and security (I Kings 4:25; Micah 4:4; Zech. 3:10).

fil'let. A narrow band or collar of gold or silver placed around the top of a pillar, used both as an ornament and a fixture in which hooks were set from which curtains were hung (Ex. 27:10-11). Also, to furnish with fillets (v. 17).

fin'ger. About ¾ inch. See Measures.

fire'pan. A receptacle made of bronze, gold or silver, used for carrying fire or hot coals to the altar (Ex. 27:3; II Kings 25:15).

fir'kin. A liquid measure, approximately 10 gallons (John 2:6).

fir'ma·ment. The expanse stretched across the sky to separate the upper and lower waters (Gen. 1:6-7). Also the vault of heaven as it appears to human eyes (Ps. 19:1).

first'born. The first child born of a family; if a male he was considered sacred to God and could be redeemed only by the offering of a sacrifice (Ex. 13:13, 15). The firstborn son ordinarily inherited the leadership of the family and received as his birthright a double portion of his father's property. See also BIRTHRIGHT.

first'fruits. The first crops or fruits of a harvest, to be given as an offering to the Lord, on behalf of the nation at the Feast of Unleavened Bread and the Feast of Weeks (Lev. 23:10, 17) and by individuals (Ex. 23:19; Deut. 26:1-11). The term is used figuratively in Rom. 8:23; 11:16; 16:5; I Cor. 15:20, 23; 16:15; James 1:18; Rev. 14:4. See also PASSOVER.

first'ling. The firstborn of an animal, considered to belong to the Lord (Gen. 4:4; Ex. 13:12; Deut. 12:6, 17). If of a "clean" animal, it was to be sacrificed to God; if of an "unclean" animal, it was to have its neck broken, or it could be replaced by the sacrifice of a lamb (Lev. 27:26). See UNCLEAN ANIMALS.

fish'es. The Sea of Galilee was the chief fishing ground of the Israelites. The Bible does not distinguish among the many varieties of fish. All fish with fins and scales were regarded as "clean"; those without either or both were "unclean" (Lev. 11:9-12). Fish that could not be eaten promptly were salted, dried or pickled. In such form fish was a staple item in the diet of the Hebrews. For fishing, lines, hooks and spears were used (Job 41:1, 7; Isa. 19:8; Amos 4:2; Matt. 17:27), and nets were cast from boats (Luke 5:4-7). The fish mentioned in Matt. 17:24-27 may have been a catfish, the common kind being very voracious and known to swallow many objects, including coins.

fitch. This plant, which grows about 18 inches high, was sown broadcast, and when its fruits were ripe, they were beaten out with a staff to separate the seeds. The pods yield black acrid and aromatic seeds, which in the East are sprinkled over some kinds of bread. In Isa. 28:25, 27, the RSV says "dill"; in Ezek. 4:9, "spelt." See SPELT.

flag. The word used in the KJV to represent all aquatic vegetation, esp. the crowded mass of water plants, rushes, reeds and sedges along a river's brink, esp. by the edge of the Nile (Ex. 2:3, 5; Job 8:11). See also BULRUSH.

flag'on. 1. A vessel for holding liquids (Isa. 22:24). 2. A cake of dried and pressed raisins (II Sam. 6:19; I Chron. 16:3; S. of Sol. 2:5; Hos. 3:1).

flax. A plant cultivated in Egypt and elsewhere (Ex. 9:31), the oldest known of textile fiber plants. Flax stalks were spread on flat housetops and dried in the sun (Josh. 2:6). The fine, woody fiber (Prov. 31:13) of

FLAX

the bark furnishes the flax fiber of which linen is woven, and the seeds are the linseed (linen seed) from which the valued oil is extracted.

flea. An insect, a universal pest in Palestine.

flesh'hook. A 3-pronged, hooked fork used for lifting pieces of meat at the altar in the Tabernacle and Temple.

flesh'pot. A pot for cooking meat (Ex. 16:3). "Fleshpots" today, used figuratively, stand for conspicuous consumption, licentiousness, etc.

flood. 1. The great rivers of Bible lands often flooded (Jer. 46:7; Amos 8:8; Josh. 24:2; Ps.

66:6). 2. The Deluge in the time of Noah
(Gen. 6:14–8:19) may have been universal
and have covered the globe, but it is better
to regard it as having been confined to a
locality of greater or less extent. The purpose of the Flood was to destroy the corrupt race of man (Gen. 6:7, 13, 17; 7:4). The
incident has theological and spiritual meaning: God works among men; He is inter-
ested in humanity and is merciful.

flux. See BLOODY FLUX.

fly. A 2-winged insect; usually a domestic fly
is meant. So troublesome are flies of various
kinds in hot countries (Isa. 7:18; Eccl. 10:1)
that the Ekronites worshiped a god Baal-
zebub, lord of the flies, who was supposed
to avert them (II Kings 1:2). The biting fly
of Egypt (Ex. 8:21; Ps. 105:31) was a vicious
stinger.

foot'men. Foot soldiers, infantry (Num. 11:21;
II Kings 13:7).

foot'stool. A low stool for supporting the feet
of a seated person (II Chron. 9:18). Figuratively: 1. The Ark of the Covenant as the
resting place for the symbolic presence of
God (I Chron. 28:2). 2. The earth, supporting the feet of God when heaven is spoken
of as His throne (Isa. 66:1; Matt. 5:35).

for·bear'. To bear with; to exercise patience
(Col. 3:13).

for'mer rain. See RAIN.

four'square'. Having 4 equal sides and 4 right
angles; hence, firm on every side, as an altar
(Ex. 27:1); strong, unyielding, as a city
(Rev. 21:16).

fowl. Any bird (Gen. 1:26; Lev. 11:13–19). In
Neh. 5:18 wild game birds or pigeons, or
possibly domestic fowl, were meant.

fowl'er. A person who hunts wild birds for
food or sport, using a snare; figuratively,
one who ensnares the innocent and leads
them to ruin (Ps. 91:3; 124:7; Hos. 9:8).

frank'in·cense. A fragrant gum of a tree, white
in color. In its pure form or as an ingredient
it had many uses in Hebrew ritual (Ex.

30:34; Lev. 2:1-2, 15-16; 24:7). The frankincense of antiquity was obtained in gum resin form from exotic trees found in India, on the Somali coast of Africa and on the s. coast of Arabia. Stores of it were kept in the Temple (I Chron. 9:29; Neh. 13:5, 9).

FRANKINCENSE

Freed'men. See LIBERTINES.

free'man. 1. A person not in slavery. 2. A Christian who is free from the bondage of sin, but chooses to be a slave to the will of God (I Cor. 7:22).

free'will' of'fer·ing. See PEACE OFFERING.

friend of the king. A high court official (I Kings 4:5), probably the king's confidential adviser.

fringe. An ornamental tuft of threads of equal length hanging loosely from the knot tying them together. These tufts or tassels were fastened to the 4 corners of an Israelite's garment by a blue ribbon and were for the purpose, due to their conspicuousness, of reminding the wearer of God's commandments and of his obligations to God (Num. 15:38-39; Deut. 22:12).

frog. An amphibious animal (Ex. 8:3; Rev. 16:13) that was judged by the Hebrews to be "unclean" (Lev. 11:10), though eaten by Egyptians and other Bible peoples.

front'let. A band for the forehead, worn at
prayer time, usually with an amulet affixed
to it between the eyes (Ex. 13:16). In later
years the amulet was replaced by phylacteries. See PHYLACTERIES.

full'er. One who cleanses undressed cloth of
oil and grease and renders it thick or compact by the application of pressure; or one
who thoroughly cleanses soiled garments
(Mark 9:3). The clothing was steeped in
soap and water (Mal. 3:2), spread out to dry
in a field and then tramped on.

fur'long. 630.8 English feet; see MEASURES.

G

Gab'ba·tha. A paved court outside the residence in Jerusalem of the Roman governor,
who sat here to hear cases (John 19:13). Its
location is uncertain.

Ga'bri·el. An angel; interprets visions to the
prophet Daniel (Dan. 8:16–27; 9:21–27); announces to Zacharias the birth of John the
Baptist; hails Mary as the chosen mother of
the Messiah (Luke 1:11–38).

gad. To wander about, to rove (Jer. 2:36).

Gad. 1. Seventh son of Jacob, first by Zilpah
(Gen. 30:10–11; 35:26), his 7 sons founded
tribal families (46:16; cf. Num. 26:15–18). 2.
His descendants, also called Gadites (Num.
1:25), and their territory (II Sam. 24:5).
They joined the tribes of Reuben and half
Manasseh in settling e. of the Jordan and n.
of the Dead Sea (Josh. 12:4–6). The city of
refuge Ramoth in Gilead was in Gadite territory (Josh. 20:8). 3. A prophet who advised David (I Sam. 22:5; II Sam. 24:11–14)
and wrote an account of his reign (I Chron.
29:29).

Gad'a·renes. The people who lived in Gadara,
a Greek city e. of the Jordan, about 5½
miles s.e. of the Sea of Galilee (Mark 5:1;
Luke 8:26). See GERGESENES.

Ga'ius. 3 different companions of Paul; III
John may have been addressed to one of
them.

gal'ba·num. An aromatic spice (Ex. 30:34), an ingredient in the incense burned at the golden altar in the Holy Place. It is generally supposed to have come from the gum of a perennial plant of the *Ferula* family that grows esp. in Persia.

Gal'i·lee. Originally a district in the hill country of Naphtali (II Kings 15:29; I Chron. 6:76). The name Galilee gradually extended until it included the country as far south as the Plain of Esdraelon. Many of its inhabitants were carried off into exile by the Assyrians (II Kings 15:29). It formed part of the kingdom of Herod the Great, and on his death passed under the authority of Herod Antipas, the tetrarch. It was the most northerly of the 3 provinces into which Rome divided the land of the Jews. The mixture of races in Galilee at the time of Christ tended to produce a distinct accent or even dialect (Mark 14:70; Luke 22:59). The people also were supposed to be one that never would produce a prophet (John 7:41, 52). Nevertheless, nearly all the apostles were Galileans, and Jesus made Galilee the chief scene of his ministry: Capernaum, Cana, Nazareth, Nain, Bethsaida and Chorazin are all in Galilee.

Gal'i·lee, Sea of. A fresh-water lake, fed by the river Jordan. It was called originally Sea of Chinnereth (Num. 34:11), later Lake of Gennesaret (Luke 5:1), and Sea of Galilee or Tiberias (John 6:1; 21:1). Its greatest length (n.-s.) is 12¾ miles; its width 7½ miles. It is 682 feet below sea level. Lying so low, it has a semitropical climate, but it is subject to sudden and violent storms rushing down from ice-crowned Mt. Hermon in the late afternoons. The water abounds in fish: 22 species have been identified.

gall. 1. The bitter secretion of the liver, bile (Job 16:13; 20:25); figuratively, venomous hatred against that which is good. 2. In the KJV, a poisonous, bitter herb (Deut. 29:18;

32:32; Ps. 68:21). A sore punishment was likened to a drink of gall water (Jer. 8:14; 9:15; 23:15). According to Matt. 27:34, Jesus was offered "vinegar mingled with gall" on the cross (Mark 15:23 says "wine mingled with myrrh"). "Vinegar" was a raw, sour wine that Roman soldiers drank, usually with a sweetening oil added. The Romans gave wine with frankincense to criminals before execution to soften the pains to be inflicted; in Jesus' case gall or myrrh was used. The RSV usually translates this term as "bitter fruit." 3. Anything painful or bitter to endure (Acts 8:23).

gal'ley. A low, flat-built vessel with one or more banks of oars, usually manned by slaves or convicts (Isa. 33:21).

GALLEY

Gal'li·o. Roman deputy at Achaia who refused to judge Paul and Sosthenes (Acts 18:12-17).

Ga·ma'li·el. 1. Leader of the tribe of Manasseh (Num. 1:10; 2:20; 7:54-59). See MANASSEH. 2. A teacher of Paul who advised against persecuting the apostles (Acts 5:34-39; 22:3). See PHARISEE.

gar'land. A wreath of flowers, leaves, etc. used in heathen sacrifices (Acts 14:13). The garland might be placed about the neck of the victim to be sacrificed, the neck of the priests officiating or on the idol to whom the sacrifice was being made.

gar'ner. *v.* To gather, as the harvest (Isa. 62:9, RSV). *n.* A granary or storehouse (Matt.

3:12; Ps. 144:13).

gar'ri·son. A military post; also the body of troops stationed in a fort (I Sam. 13:23; 14:1; II Cor. 11:32).

ga·zelle'. See DEER.

gaz'ing·stock. A condemned person stared at as an object of ridicule (Nahum 3:6; Heb. 10:33).

geck'o. See LIZARD.

Ged'e·on. See GIDEON.

Ge·ha'zi. Elisha's servant, whose avarice and falsehood brought leprosy upon him (II Kings 5:20-27).

Ge·hen'na. The Valley of the son of Hinnom (Josh. 15:8), near Jerusalem, where some Hebrew monarchs made human sacrifices to the god Molech (II Chron. 28:3). Later, possibly to discourage consideration of it as a sacred place, the people were persuaded to dump their garbage and other refuse there. This practice necessitated the burning of fires there to destroy the fly-infested filth. Because of its abhorrent appearance, Gehenna became a symbol for the fires of hell, where the wicked are to be punished after the last judgment. See also TOPHET.

gen'e·al'o·gy. A recorded history of the descent of a person or family from an ancestor or ancestors, kept for the purposes of determining inheritance, proving the right of succession to office, maintaining the family honor, etc. (I Chron. 5:1; Neh. 7:5). Genealogical records are traceable from the beginning of the Hebrew nation (Num. 1:2, 18; I Chron. 5:7, 17). Two genealogies of Jesus are given: by Matthew in the direct line of descent, from Abraham to Joseph (Matt. 1:1-16) and by Luke in the reverse order, from Heli (Mary's father) to Adam (Luke 3:23-38).

Gen'e·ral E·pis'tles. See EPISTLES.

gen'er·a'tion. 1. A begetting or producing, and then the person or thing produced (Gen. 2:4; 5:1). 2. Each succession of persons from a common ancestor (Gen. 50:23; Ex. 20:5;

Deut. 23:2). 3. The age or period of all persons born at about the same time or living in the same period of time (Matt. 24:34; Phil. 2:15).

Gen·nes'a·ret, Lake of. See GALILEE, SEA OF.

Gen'tiles. All nations of the world other than the Jews (Isa. 49:6; Rom. 2:14; 3:29).

ge'rah. See WEIGHTS.

Ger'a·senes. See GERGESENES.

Ger'ge·senes. The people of Gergesa (Matt. 8:28, KJV). Some scholars believe that "Gadarenes" was the original word here, as in Mark 5:1; Luke 8:26 of the KJV; the RSV, however, calls them "Gerasenes" in the latter two instances.

Geth·sem'a·ne. A garden near Jerusalem, traditionally considered to be across the river Kidron, on the slopes of the Mount of Olives. It was the site of the betrayal and arrest of Jesus (Matt. 26:36; Mark 14:32). "Gethsemane" is an Aramaic word meaning "oil press." The garden was presumably of olives, furnished with a press to squeeze oil from the fruit.

ghost. In the KJV, "ghost" is used only in the phrases "give up the ghost" (Jer. 15:9) and "yields up the ghost" (Gen. 49:33), meaning "to die." The RSV uses the word as meaning a disembodied spirit wandering the earth (Isa. 29:4; Matt. 14:26; Mark 6:49). See also HOLY SPIRIT.

gi'ant. A person of great size and strength; member of any of several tribes living in and about Palestine, who were thought to be the offspring, and descendants of the offspring, of the sons of God and the daughters of men (Gen. 6:1-4). The tribes designated as giants included the Rephaim (Gen. 14:5), of which Og, king of Bashan, was a member (Deut. 3:11), the Anakims (9:2), the Emims (2:10, 11), and the Zamzummims (2:20). There were also giants among the Philistines (II Sam. 21:16), esp. Goliath (I Sam. 17:4).

Gid'e•on. Also called Jerubbaal, "contender against Baal." Judg., chs. 6-8 tell of his life amid the early struggles in Israel between the settlers and the nomads, and between Yahweh and the followers of Baal, and of his refusal to become the Israelites' king. In the N.T. he is called Gedeon.

gier' ea'gle. See VULTURE.

gift. 1. Something given; a present. In this sense, "gift" in Scriptures is intended to convey the same meaning as the word does today (Num. 8:19; Prov. 21:14). 2. A grace or divine influence given to a person through the influence of the Holy Spirit (Rom. 12:4-8; I Cor. 12:9). All Christian virtues, manifestations of the Spirit in the hearts of believers, are graces, that is, gifts. God bestows various gifts upon men, qualifying them in various ways as He will for different forms of work in the kingdom (Rom. 12:6; I Cor. 7:7; 12:4, 9; Eph. 4:7-16).

Gil'e•ad. The mountainous country e. of the Jordan River, assigned to the Gadites, Reubenites and the half-tribe of Manasseh (Num., ch. 32; Deut. 3:12-17). Within its limits grew the celebrated balm (Jer. 8:22). See CANAAN.

gin. 1. A snare or trap, probably consisting of a noose hidden on the ground to encircle the legs of the victim: used to capture animals, birds and men (Job 18:9; Amos 3:5). 2. Figuratively, anything, such as a sin, that may entangle one (Ps. 141:9).

gird. To encircle with a belt, band or girdle (worn at the waist); to tie or strap one's robes or weapons to the body so as to allow one to move more freely (II Sam. 20:8; I Kings 20:32).

Gir'ga•shite. A tribe of Canaan (Gen. 10:15-16; 15:21; Deut. 7:1; Josh. 3:10; 24:11; Neh. 9:8).

girt. Fastened with a girdle, belt, etc.; girded (II Kings 1:8; John 21:7).

glean. To collect the portion of the crop left in

a field or vineyard by the regular reapers and vintagers. The owner of the land was required by Mosaic law to leave for the poor people and strangers those crops (such as grain and grapes) that the harvesters had failed to gather (Lev. 19:10; Jer. 49:9).

glede. The red kite is probably meant (Deut. 14:13). See KITE.

glo'ri·fy. 1. To give glory to; to make full of glory (John 13:32; 17:1; Rom. 8:30). 2. To honor; to praise highly, as to praise God.

glo'ry. 1. Applied to men, "glory" is used to describe the condition of highest achievement, splendor, wealth, etc. (Isa. 8:7; Matt. 6:29). 2. When used in speaking of God, "glory" denotes great honor and admiration; it is a recognition of His supreme excellence and divine perfections (Ps. 19:1; John 11:4). If the word in this sense is applied to man, it is an acknowledgment that he has achieved righteousness (Jer. 13:11). 3. The physical manifestation of God's glory, often in the form of a dazzling light (Ezek. 1:28; Luke 2:9). Such heavenly brightness was looked upon as a sign of the presence of God or of heavenly beings (II Cor. 3:18; Luke 9:31-32).

gnash. To grind or strike the teeth together. The gesture could be employed to express feelings of anger (Ps. 35:16) or maddening sorrow (Matt. 13:42).

gnat. Any of various small 2-winged insects or flies, esp. such as bite. "To strain *at* a gnat" in Matt. 23:24 of the KJV is a misprint in the original edition of 1611 for "strain *out*."

goad. A long pole sharpened at the point or iron-tipped, used to urge cattle forward (I Sam. 13:21). Used figuratively, a goad is anything that prods or stirs one into action.

goat. The goat was very abundant in ancient Palestine. Goats were tended with the sheep by the same shepherd (Gen. 27:9; 30:32), but in separate companies (Matt. 25:32). Their hair was woven into cloth (Ex. 25:4; 35:26), the flesh and milk were used for food (Lev. 7:23; Deut. 14:4; Prov. 27:27). They were an important item in a cattle-owner's wealth (Gen. 30:33-43; 31:1; I Sam. 25:2; II Chron. 17:11). The goat was a sacrificial animal, used for burnt offering and sin offering (Gen. 15:9; Ex. 12:5; Lev. 1:10; 4:24; Num. 7:17; 15:27; Ezra 6:17; 8:35; Heb. 9:12).

goat's hair. The hair of goats, woven into a coarse fabric which was made into garments, curtains, tent cloth, etc., or was used for filling pillows (Ex. 26:7; I Sam. 19:13).

god'head. 1. God (Acts 17:29). 2. The divine quality of God; divinity (Rom. 1:20; Col. 2:9).

god'li·ness. The quality or state of being godly; esp. loyalty and devotion to God, and the love for one's fellow man that is a result of such an attitude (I Tim. 4:7, 8; Titus 1:1).

god'ly. 1. In God's way; according to how God would have carried it out (II Cor. 7:9-11). 2. Of, from, or as if from God (Mal. 2:15; I Tim. 1:4). 3. Devoted to God, pious, devout (Titus 2:12; II Peter 2:9). 4. Having, feeling, or showing mercy; merciful (Ps. 4:3; 32:6).

God'ward. Before God (Ex. 18:19), or toward God (II Cor. 3:4).

Gog. 1. A descendant of Reuben (I Chron. 5:4). 2. A prince of the land of Magog, a symbol of evil and heathenism. Ezekiel (Chs. 38-39) prophesied that Gog would invade Israel and be defeated. 3. With Magog, symbolical names of enemies of the Kingdom of God (Rev. 20:8).

go'ings. 1. Steps, or the action of stepping (Job 34:21). 2. Courses or manners of conduct or procedure; paths (Isa. 59:8). 3. Movements (II Sam. 5:24). The phrase, "goings out" of borders, coasts, etc., means boundaries, borders (Num. 34:5, 8, 9, 12).

Gol'go·tha. See CALVARY.

Go·li'ath. The giant slain by David (I Sam., ch. 17; 21:9).

Go'mer. 1. A grandson of Noah (Gen. 10:2). 2.

Wife of Hosea the prophet (Hos. 1:3).

Go·mor'rah. A city in the Plain of the Jordan (Gen. 10:19; 13:10). Like Sodom, its neighboring city, it was destroyed by fire from heaven for its wickedness (Gen. 18:20; 19:24-28). Its site is unknown, but many scholars believe that Gomorrah may have been submerged by the waters of the Dead Sea as a result of an earthquake. A possible site, then, is on the s.e. shore of the Dead Sea.

good'ly. Of pleasing appearance; handsome (Gen. 39:6).

go'pher wood. The word "gopher" (Gen. 6:14) is simply the Hebrew word turned into the corresponding letters of our alphabet. No one knows certainly what tree the Hebrew word represents.

gos'pel. 1. The gospel is the glad tidings, esp. the good news concerning Christ, the kingdom of God and salvation. In the N.T. it never means a book, but rather the message or "good tidings" which Christ and his apostles announced. The word "gospel" comes from the Anglo-Saxon word "godspell" meaning "good news" or "good story," which was also the meaning of the original Greek word *evangelion,* from which we get the word "evangelist." 2. About A.D. 150 the word "gospel" was applied also to the writings in which the testimony of the apostles to Jesus was contained. Each one of them was called a gospel. See also EVANGELIST.

gourd. The plant that sheltered Jonah from the heat of the sun (Jonah 4:6-10, KJV) was one of two fast-growing plants of the Near East that grow to a considerable height in a few days, ultimately attaining 8-10 feet. The "wild gourds" of II Kings 4:39 were probably the cucumber-like fruits of a hardy, wild, vine-like plant that flourishes even in drought. The fruit is unfit for eating, fiery hot, a cathartic, but a valuable if dangerous medicine.

gov′er·nor. A ruler, guardian or person of authority; in James 3:4 (KJV), pilot or captain.

grace. 1. Unmerited love and favor of God toward man; the quality of God that leads Him to bestow eternal blessings on man and provide salvation from sin on the only condition that he exercise faith in Christ (Rom. 11:6; Eph. 2:5). 2. A divine influence acting in man to make him pure and morally strong, and enabling him to persevere in leading the Christian life (Acts 20:32; II Cor. 9:14). 3. An expression of gratitude or thanksgiving for a favor received (I Cor. 10:30). 4. Joy and gladness used in a greeting, such as "grace be to you and peace from God" (II Cor. 1:2; Col. 1:3). To "fall from grace" is to act wickedly, to do wrong, to sin (Gal. 5:4).

grass′hop·per. Three Hebrew words are translated "grasshopper" in the KJV. The first is the migratory locust (Judg. 6:5; 7:12; Job 39:20; Jer. 46:23); see LOCUST. The second is a small variety of locust (Num. 13:33), a voracious eater, and so numerous as to cover the ground or hide the sun (Eccl. 12:5; Isa. 40:22). The third is the grass-devouring insect of Amos 7:1 and Nahum 3:17.

grate, grat′ing. A bronze framework or lattice used on the sides of the altar of burnt offering (Ex. 27:4; 35:16; 38:4–5; 39:39). Its use, function and meaning is not known.

grav′en im′age. An image of a god, made out of wood or stone and carved with a graving tool; or made by pouring molten metal over a form and carving and finishing it after the metal hardens (Isa. 44:9, 10; Hos. 11:2). The Second Commandment expressly forbade the people of God to make them (Ex. 20:4; Deut. 5:8).

grav′ing tool. A carving tool used by a sculptor or engraver for shaping and decorating wood, stone or metal.

Great Sea. The Mediterranean Sea (Num. 34:6; Josh. 15:47). Also called the uttermost

or utmost sea (Deut. 11:24; Joel 2:20), or
the sea of the Philistines (Ex. 23:31), or just
"the sea."

greaves. Protective armor for the legs below
the knees, consisting of thin plates of metal,
with laces (I Sam. 17:6).

Gre'cian. 1. A native or inhabitant of Greece;
a Greek (Joel 3:6). 2. A Jew who spoke
Greek, esp. one absorbed in the Greek culture of the first century A.D., distinguished
from a Jew who spoke Aramaic and remained conservative culturally (Acts 6:1;
9:29).

grey'hound. Scholars do not know the meaning of the Hebrew word which is translated
"greyhound" in the KJV (Prov. 30:31); its
meaning is only "well knit in the loins."

grove. A wooden pillar or sacred tree erected
or planted (Deut. 16:21) on a high place beside the altar of a pagan Canaanite goddess
of fertility, Asherah, associated with Baal (I
Kings 18:19). It was the symbol of the goddess thought to give life. It was also, perhaps, an emblem of life itself surviving from
ancient tree worship. These pillars were
symbols of idolatry and the worship of foreign gods, and as such were to be cut down
(Ex. 34:13) or burned (Deut. 12:3); their destruction was encouraged by the prophets
(Isa. 27:9; Mic. 5:14), who considered the
elimination of the groves one step toward
abolishing such idolatrous worship. See
also ASHERAH.

guilt. Conduct that involves wrongdoing;
crime; sin (Deut. 19:13; 21:9). Also the feeling that accompanies recognition of one's
wrongdoing.

guilt of'fer-ing. An offering to God made by
one who had unintentionally done wrong
or harm, either legal or moral, sins of which
the effects came to rest primarily on another person, as in unintentional damage to
or destruction of property. Along with the
sacrifice of a ram, restitution was made

through the hands of the priest to the person injured (Lev. 5:16–17; 6:5; Num. 5:7–8). Deliberate sins for which the penalty was death could not be expiated (Num. 15:30–31). See also OFFERINGS.

guil'ty. Having done wrong or committed an offense, either legal or moral; deserving blame or punishment; the wrongdoing may have taken place knowingly or unknowingly (Lev. 4:13). It may be shared individually or collectively (Rom. 3:19) in the sense that all mankind has offended God and is therefore under condemnation.

H

Ha·bak'kuk. A prophet of Judah, probably of c. 600 B.C.

ha'ber·geon. A coat of mail to protect the breast and neck (Ex. 28:32; II Chron. 26:14; Neh. 4:16). In Job 41:26 the English word "javelin" is better. See also COAT OF MAIL; JAVELIN.

hab'i·ta'tion. 1. A place to live; a dwelling (Lev. 13:46). 2. Anything in which something or someone resides: for example, the people of God reside in Him (Ps. 91:9), and justice and judgment reside in and form an integral part of the throne of God (Ps. 89:14).

Ha'dad. A common name: 1. An ancient weather god, also known as Baal. See BAAL. 2. An Edomite prince, a lifelong adversary of David and Solomon (I Kings 11:14–22).

Had'ad·e'zer. A Syrian king defeated in battle by David (II Sam. 8:3; 10:15–19). In chs. 18–19 of I Chron. he is called Hadarezer.

Ha·das'sah. The Hebrew name for Esther (2:7). See ESTHER.

Ha'des. See HELL.

Ha'gar. Sarah's Egyptian maid, who bore Abraham's son Ishmael and was cast out with him into the desert (Gen., chs. 16; 21). She is referred to symbolically in Gal.

4:24-25 as Agar.

Hag'ga·i. A prophet contemporary with Zechariah, who encouraged rebuilding of the Temple (Ezra 5:1-2; 6:14).

hal'low. 1. To make holy or sacred; to set apart for sacred use (Ex. 28:38; Ezek. 20:20). 2. To honor as sacred (Matt. 6:9; Luke 11:2).

Ham. Youngest son of Noah (Gen. 5:32), his undutiful behavior brought a curse upon Canaan (9:22). His descendants and those whose property he annexed are listed in 10:6-14.

Ha'man. A high official in the Persian court who plotted the destruction of the Jews, but was frustrated by Esther (Esth. 3:1-8:7). See also PURIM.

Ham'mu·ra'bi. An early king of Babylonia, whose code of laws probably influenced the laws of Israel (e.g. Ex. 20:21-23:33). See AMORITES.

Ha·na'ni. A prophet; see ASA.

Han'a·ni'ah. The name of perhaps 14 different men in the O.T.

hand'breadth. The width of the human palm; see MEASURES. The word is also used figuratively for the shortness of life (Ps. 39:5).

hand'maid, hand·maid'en. A woman or girl servant, slave or attendant (Gen. 16:1; Judg. 19:19; Luke 1:48). The word is used figuratively for a humble servant of God (Ruth 3:9; I Sam. 1:11).

hand'pike, hand'stave. A weapon, a battle-ax or more probably a javelin, a long-shafted weapon with a metal spearhead at the end (Ezek. 39:9).

Han'nah. Mother of the prophet Samuel (I Sam. 2:1-10).

Ha'nuk·kah. See DEDICATION, FEAST OF.

hare. The common hare of Palestine is 2 inches shorter than the European hare, and has slightly shorter ears. It frequents wooded and cultivated places. The common hare of s. Judea and the Jordan Valley has very long ears and light tawny fur. Both are rodents, both were "unclean" (Lev. 11:6; Deut. 14:7).

har′ness. See BREASTPLATE.

hart. See DEER.

has′ty fruit. The first ripened fig of the season, considered a delicacy and hence quickly eaten. In Isa. 28:4 "hasty fruit" is a symbol for beauty's rapidly fading quality.

hav′oc, hav′ock. Great devastation (Acts 8:3).

hawk. The word "hawk" in the Bible includes more than one species of the smaller predatory birds abundant in Palestine, such as the sparrow hawk and the kestrel.

HAWK

Haz′a·el. A Syrian king who murdered King Ben-hadad and whose cruel reign was foretold by Elisha and Elijah (I Kings 19:15; II Kings 8:7-15; 10:32; 12:17-18; 13:4-7). See also ASSYRIA.

hearth. 1. The stone or brick floor of a fireplace, often extending out into the room (Isa. 30:14). 2. A container to hold burning coals, placed in a hollow in the center of a room to provide warmth and to furnish heat for cooking (Jer. 36:22-23).

heath. A shrub with minute, narrow, rigid leaves (Jer. 17:6; 48:6). The RSV translates this once as "shrub," once as "wild ass," in both cases implying something stunted for lack of nourishment.

hea'then. Any nation or people who do not worship the God of the Bible, esp. if they worship idols. The word was originally applied to people of the lands surrounding Israel, many of whose customs and attitudes were abhorred, particularly idolatry and the eating of "unclean" foods (II Kings 16:3; Ezra 6:21). By N.T. times these views were modified and Paul encouraged preaching to the heathen (Gal. 1:16; 2:9).

heav'en. 1. The sky, the expanse around the earth, in which the sun, moon and stars appear (Gen. 2:1; Isa. 13:13; Jer. 14:22). The "heaven of heavens" (Deut. 10:14; I Kings 8:27) means the heavens in their widest extent; the Hebrews were fond of dividing the heavens into different layers, the highest being regarded as God's dwelling place. 2. The place where God's immediate place is manifested (Gen. 28:17; Ps. 80:14; Isa. 66:1; Matt. 5:12); where the angels are (Mark 13:32) and where the redeemed shall ultimately be (Matt. 6:20; 18:10; Eph. 3:15; I Peter 1:4). Christ descended from heaven (John 3:13), and ascended to heaven again (Acts 1:11), whence he will come to judge the quick and the dead (Matt. 24:30; Rom. 8:34; I Thess. 4:16; Heb. 6:20; 9:24). 3. The inhabitants of heaven (Luke 15:18; Rev. 18:20). See also PARADISE.

heave of'fer·ing. This term translates a Hebrew word meaning every hallowed thing that the Israelites heaved—that is, took up, took away from a larger mass and set apart for the Lord and also the priests (Lev. 22:12; Num. 5:9; 18:8; 31:28-29). Heave offerings may have originated in the practice of tossing up, or heaving, grain offered to God, onto the threshingfloor. Later, heave offerings would include firstfruits of oil and fruit as well as grain, flesh from redeemed fatlings not required to be burnt on the altar and cakes from the first dough made from the new meal of the year (Num. 15:20-21). See also OFFERINGS.

hedge'hog. An insect-eating mammal whose hair is mixed with prickles and spines. It is common in Palestine. The porcupine is a burrowing rodent of a different order. The Hebrew words translated "hedgehog" and "porcupine" in the RSV are rendered as "bittern" in the KJV (Isa. 14:23; 34:11).

heir. See BIRTHRIGHT; INHERITANCE.

He'li. The father of Mary's husband Joseph or the father of Mary, mother of Jesus (Luke 3:25). The latter interpretation is reached by punctuating the Greek differently from the way it is rendered in the KJV. See GENEALOGY.

hell. The place of the dead; the Hebrew word is "Sheol," the Greek, "Hades." The ancient Hebrews, like other Semites, thought of Sheol as beneath the earth (Num. 16:30-33; Ezek. 31:17; Amos 9:2). Though ending earthly life, a dead person did not entirely cease to exist, however dark, chaotic and silent Sheol might be. Sheol was not a place of punishment, torture or torment. An infernal hell, a place of eternal punishment, was a development of N.T. times and thought (Matt. 5:29-30; 25:41).

help'meet. The meaning of these two words in Gen. 2:18 is: "I will make a helper *fit* (or suitable) for him." Through usage the two words have been joined (sometimes in the form "helpmate") to signify a wife.

hem'lock. Not our well-known evergeen, but a poisonous herb that grows up spontaneously even in the furrows of the field (Hos. 10:4). Similar plants are gall and wormwood. In the KJV, Amos (6:12) uses hemlock as a symbol of injustice. The juices of all these plants are unpalatable and noxious.

hen'na. See CAMPHIRE.

He'noch. See ENOCH.

her'ald. A person who announces significant news; a messenger (Dan. 3:4).

herbs, bit'ter. See BITTER HERBS.

herd'man, herds'man. A person who tends

cattle or sheep (Gen. 13:7-8; Amos 1:1).

her'e·tic, her'e·tick. A person who professes a heresy, that is, one who holds beliefs not in accord with official church doctrine (Acts 24:14; Titus 3:10).

Her'mes. See MERCURIUS.

Her'od. A dynasty of princes, Idumean, not Jewish by blood, the founder of which, Antipater, was forced to adopt Judaism when conquered by John Hyrcanus. 1. Herod the Great, friend of the Romans, who made him king of Judea, had 10 wives, and his personal life, as well as his political career, was in his later years one of suspicion and violence. After he had murdered many of his rivals, including 3 of his sons, he learned that a child had been born who was to be King of the Jews, and ordered all children 2 years old and under to be slain (Matt., ch. 2). He died c. 4 B.C. See also TEMPLE. 2. Herod Antipas the tetrarch, a son of Herod the Great. He competed with his brother Archelaus for their father's kingdom, but received from the Herods' Roman overlords only Perea and Galilee (Luke 3:1). He married the notorious Herodias, previously wife of Herod Philip, his half-brother. Jesus referred to him as "that fox" and was sent before him by Pilate (Luke, chs. 13; 23; Acts 4:27). This Herod died in exile, after seeking elevation to kingship in Rome. See ARCHELAUS; HERODIAS; PHILIP (3); TETRARCH. 3. Herod (the King) Agrippa I, a grandson of Herod the Great, educated in Rome, where he became the friend of future Roman emperors Caligula and Claudius, who assigned him the territories of Philip the tetrarch and later added Herod Antipas' district, Galilee, making Agrippa a king. He slew James, the brother of John, imprisoned Peter and, according to Acts 12:1-23, receiving adulation as if he were a god, he was smitten by an angel, eaten by worms, and died. 4. Agrippa, commonly known as Herod Agrippa II, was son of Herod Agrippa I and brother of Bernice and Drusilla. He was king under the Roman emperors Claudius and Nero, first of Chalcis, then of much larger Roman provinces. He and Bernice visited Festus and were present at the interview with Paul recounted in Acts 25:13-26:32. After the fall of Jerusalem, he and Bernice went to Rome, where he died A.D. 100. See also CAESAR.

He·ro'di·as. Granddaughter of Herod the Great; reproved for her wicked ways by John the Baptist, she plotted his death (Matt. 14:1-12), aided by her daughter Salome, who danced before the king. See HEROD.

her'on. A bird generally of large size, with a long bill, long bare legs adapted for wading and large wings, though its flight is comparatively slow. It feeds mainly on fish and reptiles. Lev. 11:19 and Deut. 14:18 forbade the eating of "the heron after her kind," probably meaning "herons of any kind."

Heth. See HITTITES.

Hez'e·ki'ah. King of Judah, son of Ahaz;
     eliminates idolatry (II Kings 18:1-8)
     attacked by Assyrians; Isaiah's prophecy (II Kings, ch. 19)
     his life extended (II Kings, ch. 20; Isa., chs. 38; 39)
     his piety (II Chron., ch. 29)
     keeps Passover (II Chron., ch. 30)
     Sennacherib defeated; Hezekiah's death (II Chron., ch. 32).
See KINGS, TABLE OF; SENNACHERIB.

high place. A place of worship, as a shrine or altar or temple, originally located on lofty heights (Num. 22:41; I Kings 11:7; 14:23), in or near towns (II Kings 17:9; 23:5), and later even in valleys (Jer. 7:31). The Canaanites possessed them, and the Israelites were strictly told to destroy them when they entered Canaan (Num. 33:52; Deut. 33:29). Sacred prostitution, a feature of Canaanite religion, was often connected with

the worship on high places (Hos. 4:11-14).
On a leveled piece of ground stood an altar
(I Kings 12:32); near the altar was a
wooden image or symbol of Asherah, Canaanite goddess of fertility, usually with a
pillar or pillars of stone nearby. Benches
afforded a place for the worshipers to sit
and partake of the sacrificial feast (I Sam.
9:12-13, 22). Priests were assigned to the
high place (I Kings 12:32; II Kings 17:32).
At times the worship of the Hebrew Lord
God was conducted by the Israelites on
high places; but this was forbidden by law,
which eventually insisted upon one altar,
Jerusalem, for all Israel. Throughout Hebrew history the high places provided a
constant temptation and were attacked by
prophets and reforming kings. See also A-
SHERAH.

high priest. The chief priest of the Hebrew
priesthood; spiritual leader of ancient Israel, he was regarded as the representative
of the nation before God. The legal head of
the house of Aaron held the office, and the
succession was probably through the first
son, unless legal disabilities interfered (Lev.
21:16-23). Political considerations, also, not
infrequently played a part in his selection (I
Kings 2:26-27, 35). His special duties were
the oversight of the sanctuary, its service
and its treasure (II Kings 12:7-8; 22:4); the
performance of the service on the Day of
Atonement, when he was obliged to enter
the Holy of Holies; and the consultation of
God by Urim and Thummim. Later he pre-
sided also over the Sanhedrin, the Jewish
governing body under Roman rule (Matt.
26:57; Acts 5:21). At first the high priesthood was for life, but Herod the Great and
afterward the Romans made and unmade
the high priests as they wished. The unique
official garments of the high priests included a bejeweled breastpiece, within
which were kept the Urim and Thummim;
the ephod, an enriched, embroidered vest-

ment; the robe of the ephod, worn underneath it, entirely blue with an ornamental fringe; and a miter, a cap or turban of linen, surmounted in later years by a triple crown of gold. See also LEVITES; PRIEST; SADDUCEES; URIM AND THUMMIM.

Hil·ki'ah. Among others of this name in the O.T., a high priest in the time of King Josiah, who found the book of the law (II Kings 22:3-23:4; II Chron. 34:9-22).

hill coun'try. A rugged, uneven region of low mountains, running n. and s. from Judea west of the Jordan Valley to the mountains of Lebanon (Josh. 13:6; 21:11; Luke 1:39, 65).

hin. A unit of liquid measure. See MEASURES.

hind. See DEER.

hind'er sea. This term, used in Zech. 14:8, is elsewhere translated the "utmost" or "uttermost" sea (Deut. 11:24; Joel 2:20) or the "sea of the Philistines" (Ex. 23:31). In all cases the Mediterranean is meant. It was "hinder" because all Hebrew directions started from facing east—not north, as we do today—so the Mediterranean was behind them, s. to the right, n. to the left.

hind'most. Farthest back, last (Num. 2:31; Josh. 10:19). Also "hindermost" (Gen. 33:2; Jer. 50:12).

Hin'nom, Valley of. A valley that passed around the w. and s. sides of Jerusalem, its Hebrew name became corrupted into "Gehenna." See GEHENNA.

hip'po·pot'a·mus. See BEHEMOTH.

Hi'ram. 1. A king of Tyre who was a friend of both David and Solomon and helped rebuild the Temple (II Sam. 5:11; I Kings 5:1-12; II Chron. 2:3-16; 8:1-2; 9:21). 2. A metalworker employed by King Hiram in rebuilding the Temple (I Kings 7:13-46; II Chron. 2:13; 4:16). Both men are also called Huram. See also PHOENICIANS.

hire'ling. A person who works for the wages he is paid; a servant who is not a slave (Job 7:1-2; Isa. 16:14). It was common for men

to be hired for certain stated periods (Lev.
25:50-55).

hiss. 1. To show hatred or disapproval by
making a sound by forcing breath between
tongue and teeth, the equivalent of a boo
today. 2. To summon, signal or lure by
whistling (Isa. 5:26; 7:18).

Hit'tites. The people of an empire which
flourished in Asia Minor between c. 1900
and c. 1200 B.C. Their racial affinities are
not clearly understood. They were not Semites. It seems that the modern Armenians
are the lineal descendants of one group of
this nation. The Hittites were short and
stocky, and had thick lips. According to the
monuments, they wore heavy clothing, long
coats, high woolen headdress and shoes
turned up at the toes—all suggestive that

they came from snowy mountains. The
Anatolian Hittite culture seems to have
centered in Cappadocia, today the central
part of Turkey. Scholars now generally
agree that Hittite belongs to the Indo-European languages, not Semitic. The word Hittite occurs 47 times in the O.T., while Heth,
which means the same thing, is found 14
times. The Hittites are often mentioned in
the list of nations inhabiting Canaan before
the Conquest (Gen. 15:20; Ex. 3:8; Deut.
7:1; 20:17; Josh. 3:10; 11:3; 24:11). Abraham purchased the cave of Machpelah from
Ephron the Hittite (Gen. 23:10-18). Esau
took Hittite wives (Gen. 26:34), and later
Israelites intermarried with Hittites (Judg.
3:5-6). David had Hittite associates (I Sam.
26:6), and he married Bath-sheba, the wife
of Uriah the Hittite. Apparently the Hebrews did not regard the Hittites as a home-
less, nondescript people; they recognized a
land of the Hittites (Josh. 1:4). The kings of
the Hittites are mentioned in the same sentence with those of Syria (I Kings 10:29; II
Chron. 1:17). As a sign of their greatness
they are placed in the same category as the

Egyptians (II Kings 7:6). One king (c. 1620 B.C.) plundered Babylon and ended the Amorite dynasty of Hammurabi there. Later the Hittites fought and lost a major battle with the Egyptians at Megiddo. By 1350 B.C. the Hittite Empire was the most powerful state in w. Asia. About 1200 B.C., during the period of the Israelite judges, the Hittite Empire in Cappadocia fell to an invading Aegean (Greek) people. The Hittites not in Asia Minor were now grouped around Carchemish on the upper Euphrates as their capital. Finally (717 B.C.) Carchemish fell into the hands of Sargon II of Assyria. Thus the n. Syria and e. Asia Minor portions of the former Hittite Empire were gradually absorbed by Assyria.

Hi′vites. One of the races of Canaan before the conquest by the Hebrews (Gen. 10:17; Ex. 3:17; Josh. 9:1). A body of them dwelt at Shechem in the time of Jacob (Gen. 33:18; 34:2, 14-24). Another Hivite group dwelt in the area of Gibeon; they obtained a treaty of peace from Joshua by stratagem, but on the discovery of their deceit, they were made hewers of wood and drawers of water (Josh., ch. 9). Their native land was probably in the Lebanon Mountains. It is not known whether the Hivites as a people ever had a real or separate existence. Confusion between Hivite and Horite is found in Gen. 36:2, where Zibeon is a Hivite, and vv. 20 and 29, where he is a Horite. Perhaps the Hivites were a subdivision of the Horites, or a local name for Hurrians. See HORITES.

hoar. White, gray or grayish-white, as hairs (Isa. 46:4). "Hoar frost" is white, frozen dew on the ground, leaves, plants, etc. (Ex. 16:14; Ps. 147:16). "Hoary" means as if covered with hoar frost (Job 41:32).

Ho′bab. See JETHRO.

hock, hough. To disable by cutting the tendons of the hind leg; to hamstring (Josh. 11:6).

ho′ly. 1. Set apart, sacred; said of God (Lev. 19:2; 21:8). His uniqueness and moral perfection separate Him from all created things. 2. Devoted to religious use; made or declared sacred; consecrated; hence, removed or separated from immorality or defilement; said of utensils (I Chron. 22:19), church officers (Titus 1:7-8), certain days (Ex. 20:8), etc. 3. Spiritually pure; untainted by sin (Eph. 1:4).

Ho′ly Com·mu′nion. The sacrament or formal ceremonial observance commemorating the Lord's Supper: bread and wine are consecrated and received as symbols of the body and blood of Jesus Christ, in a manner similar to the custom begun by Jesus at the original Lord's Supper. The partaking of these "elements" is usually accompanied by a reading of Paul's record of the words of Christ spoken at the time (I Cor. 11:24-25). The idea of calling this rite "communion" has probably developed out of I Cor. 10:16.

ho′ly day. A feast day; religious festival (Ps. 42:4; Isa. 58:13; Col. 2:16).

Ho′ly Ghost. See HOLY SPIRIT.

Ho′ly of Ho′lies. The innermost room of the Tabernacle. See MOST HOLY PLACE.

ho′ly place. The larger, outer chamber of the Tabernacle and the Temple; the chamber adjacent to the Most Holy Place, separated from it by a veil of fine twined linen, decorated with figures of cherubim. The holy place contained the altar of incense, table of showbread and golden lampstand (the holy place in Solomon's Temple had 10 such lampstands). See Ex. 28:29, 35, 43; II Chron. 29:7. See also SHEWBREAD; TABERNACLE.

Ho′ly Spir′it. The spirit of God, the third person of the Trinity. In modern speech the word "spirit" now more correctly expresses the concept than does "ghost," which now commonly means a disembodied spirit wandering on earth. The underlying meaning of both the Hebrew and Greek words

for "spirit" is "breath" or "wind." In the
O.T. the Spirit is the divine agency performing the will of God (Ps. 51:11; Isa.
63:10-11). The Spirit acts in works of creation (Gen. 1:2), and as leader of God's
people (Judg. 3:10). In the N.T. the term
has a deeper connotation: with the descent
of the Holy Spirit on the Day of Pentecost,
the Spirit becomes active in the life of the
church (Acts, ch. 2; 9:31; Phil. 2:1-2; I Cor.,
ch. 12). Jesus indicates in John's gospel that
he would continue to be with the apostles
in the person of the Holy Spirit as companion (John 14:3), as helper (v. 16) and as
leader (v. 26). The recognition of the Holy
Spirit as distinguishable from the Father
and the Son, and yet inseparable from them
in the total life of the Godhead, becomes
evident as one reads the N.T. The Holy
Spirit is spoken of as "he" rather than "it,"
whose special office it was to bring to fulfillment in human experience the redemptive
work of Christ.

home'born. 1. Of domestic origin; native (Ex.
12:49). 2. Designating a servant or slave
born to parents who were also in servitude
(Jer. 2:14).

ho'mer. A unit of liquid and dry measure. See
MEASURES.

hoo'poe. See LAPWING.

Hoph'ni. A son of Eli, who disgraced his
priestly office (I Sam. 2:22-4:11).

Ho'rites. 1. Called Horims in Deut. 2:12, 22,
"Horites" was the specialized name given
to the inhabitants of Mt. Seir (Gen. 36:20),
a region later occupied by Edomites. They
were governed by chieftains (Gen.
36:29-30). 2. Where the O.T. deals with a
people called "Horites" inhabiting central
Palestine (e.g. Josh. 9:7), and not those in
Edom to the far south, such "Horites" are a
branch of the Hurrians, a race not mentioned in the Bible, but widely spread
through the ancient Near East, whose original home was probably in the mountains of

Armenia. Hurrians were the most important ethnic element in the Mitanni Empire, whose great period was c. 2500 B.C., with its center in the Middle Euphrates Valley in the vicinity of Biblical Haran. Hurrians were found in central Palestine.

horn. In early times the Israelites converted the horns of animals into trumpets (Josh. 6:13), or into flasks for such substances as oil (I Sam. 16:1; I Kings 1:39). When God exalts the horn of an individual, the meaning is that He confers great power and prosperity (I Sam. 2:10); but when a person exalts or lifts up the horn, it means that he becomes arrogant and insolent (Ps. 75:4-5). The horn is the emblem of strength and political power, the image being drawn from bulls that attack with their horns (Ps. 132:17; Jer. 48:25). In the language of prophets, horns signify a kingdom or kings (Dan. 7:8; Zech. 1:18-19; Rev. 17:12). Horns of the altar were projections slightly resembling horns placed at the corners of the altar of burnt offering (Ex. 27:2). Apparently the horns provided a sanctuary for criminals; since the horns were sacred the offender could avoid capture by clinging to them. To break or cut off the horn of someone was to crush or weaken him (Jer. 48:25; Lam. 2:3).

hor'net. The hornet is of the same genus as the

HORNET

wasp, but larger and more formidable. The common hornet and a closely allied species are well known in Palestine (Ex. 23:28).

horse. The horse was domesticated in early antiquity somewhere e. of the Caspian Sea by Indo-European nomads. Horses were used for military purposes c. 1900 B.C. and horse-drawn chariots c. 1800 B.C. in Asia Minor and Syria. Mountainous Palestine was not well adapted for the use of the horse, and in early times its use was restricted to the maritime plain and the Valley of Jezreel. The horse was found in Egypt (Gen. 47:17; Ex. 9:3), introduced there by the Hyksos. Pharaoh's pursuing army was equipped with chariots and horses (Ex. 14:9; 15:19), as was Sisera's army (Judg. 4:15; 5:22). Solomon imported them in great numbers, and later exported them to the kings of the Hittites and the Syrians (I Kings 10:28-29; II Chron. 1:16-17; 9:28). Horses were used in war, hunting and transportation but little in agriculture or pulling burdens, which was done by oxen. Royal stables at Megiddo have been excavated, showing stalls and feeding troughs for 450 horses at this chariot city.

horse'leach. A large leech, common in Palestine. It is noted for its insatiable appetite for blood, and frequently lodges in the throats of animals that drink from pools. See Prov. 30:15.

Ho·san'na. This is a Greek transliteration of a Hebrew word meaning "Save now!" It was the acclamation of the multitude on the occasion of Jesus' triumphal entry into Jerusalem. The word originally was used in connection with prayer (Ps. 118:25), but as the context in the Gospels shows (Matt. 21:9; Mark 11:9-10), it had become an ejaculation of joy.

Ho·se'a. A prophet in the Northern Kingdom in the time of Jeroboam II (c. 786-746 B.C.), the few known facts about his life are to be found in the book of Hosea.

Ho·she′a. Among others in the O.T.: 1. The
early name of Joshua (Num. 13:16). 2. The
last king of Israel (II Kings 15:30). The
story of his conspiracy with and the later
invasion of Israel by Shalmaneser V of Assyria is told in II Kings 17:1-4. Hoshea was
taken captive, and Samaria, after being besieged for 3 years, fell to Sargon, Shalmaneser's successor. See KINGS, TABLE OF.

hos·pi·tal′i·ty. The friendly and generous acceptance of guests into the home esp.
strangers and travelers. This was important
in O.T. times because of the lack of public
lodging places. Hospitality was recognized
as one of the important expressions of
Christian virtue and good will (Rom. 12:13;
I Tim. 3:2; Titus 1:8).

host. A multitude, esp. when organized (Gen.
21:22; Judg. 4:2).

host of heav′en. The stars, in their beautiful
order and wonderful array (Deut. 4:19; I
Kings 22:19; Isa. 40:26).

hosts, Lord of. This phrase means more than
that the Lord is the God of the armies of
Israel (I Sam. 17:45; Isa. 31:4). The Lord
did fight for His people, but the "Lord of
hosts" was more than the war god of Israel.
The word "hosts" here means the armies of
the universe; it pictures the universe in its
various aspects as forming a vast army, in
numerous divisions, of various kinds of
troops, all in orderly array under the command of God. One division was of angels,
another of the stars, another all the forces of
nature, who stand ready to serve the bid-
ding of the Lord (Neh. 9:6; Jer. 29:17).

hough. See HOCK.

hour. 1. The twelfth part of a day (John 11:9),
a day being from sunrise to sunset (Acts
2:15), and later the twelfth part of a night as
well. Since the rising and setting of the sun
varied with the seasons, the hours based on
this division were not uniform in length. 2.
A point or period of time for a particular
activity or occasion (John 13:1; Rev. 14:7).

hu·mil'i·ty. 1. The absence of pride, vanity or self-assertion; being conscious of one's defects or shortcomings; modesty; recognition of the equality of one's fellow man (I Peter 5:5).

hun'ger·bit'ten. Famished (Job 18:12).

Hu'ram. See HIRAM.

Hur'ri·ans. See HIVITES; HORITES.

hus'band·man. 1. A farmer; one who cultivates land (Gen. 9:20; II Tim. 2:6). 2. A tenant vinedresser; a farmer who rents land for use as a vineyard (Matt. 21:33-35, 38).

hus'band·ry. 1. Farming or domestic management (II Chron. 26:10). 2. Land under cultivation (I Cor. 3:9).

Hu'shai. A faithful counselor of David (II Sam. 15:32-37; 17:5-16).

husk. A kind of food eaten by cattle and swine (Luke 15:16). It is the pod of the carob tree, and is also called locust bean and St. John's bread. In times of famine the legumes, often a foot long, were eaten by humans. In the RSV it is called "pods."

HYENA

hy·e'na. The "wild beasts of the islands" of the KJV (Isa. 13:22, 34:14; Jer. 50:39) are called in the RSV the hyena, which in modern times has been the commonest beast of prey in Palestine after the jackal. The hyena is essentially an eater of carrion, lives in caves

and tombs, comes forth after dark to seek
his prey, and has a piercing, unearthly
howl. He is not mentioned by this name in
the KJV.

Hy'me·nae'us. One excommunicated by Paul
for blasphemy (I Tim. 1:20; II Tim.
2:17-18).

hys'sop. A plant of Egypt and Palestine (Ex.
12:22) well adapted for sprinkling and purification rites. Its thick, hairy leaves and

HYSSOP

branches can be made into a bunch that
will hold liquids. The leaves have a pun-
gent, aromatic flavor. Like peppermint, at
first it tastes hot, followed by a cooling, refreshing feeling. In John 19:29 a reed or a
pike may have been used to administer the
vinegar and hyssop to Jesus.

I

i'bex. See PYGARG.

i'bis. A wading bird, related to the heron.

Ich'a·bod. Grandson of Eli, born when his father and grandfather died and the Ark was
captured (I Sam. 4:19-22).

Id'do. The O.T. mentions several men of this
name, the most prominent being a seer who
wrote accounts of the reigns of Solomon,

Rehoboam, Jeroboam and Abijam (II Chron. 9:29; 12:15; 13:22).

I'du·me'a. The name used by Greeks and Romans, in slightly different spelling, for the country of Edom or of the Edomites (Mark 3:8; Isa. 34:5-6; Ezek. 35:15; 36:5). See EDOMITES; ESAU.

Im·man'u·el. The name, meaning "God (is) with us," given to a son who will be born to "a young woman" as a sign to King Ahaz in a time of national crisis in Judah (Isa. 7:14). Some unknown mother, Isaiah tells the king, will call her son "Immanuel" as an expression of faith that God is with His people and will save them; confidence lies not in political alliances but only in faith in God. "Immanuel" (God with us) was not a sign to compel faith, but one that called for faith on the part of Ahaz and the people. Isa. 7:14 has been interpreted by many Christians throughout history as referring to the coming Messiah, as did Matthew (1:23).

in'cense. A substance producing a pleasant odor as it is burned during certain rituals of worship (Ex. 25:6; 37:29). The ingredients were stacte, onycha, galbanum and frankincense in equal proportions, tempered with salt. An altar of incense, made of acacia wood overlaid with gold, was set in the holy place, just outside the veil which concealed the Holy of Holies; here each morning the high priest burned incense (Ex. 30:1-9; Luke 1:8-10).

in·gath'er·ing. Harvest; the "Feast of Ingathering" is a harvest festival (Ex. 23:16; 34:22), the same as the "Feast of Booths" or "Feast of Tabernacles." See TABERNACLES, FEAST OF.

in·her'it·ance. 1. Something inherited or to be inherited; property received or to be received by one person as the heir to another. The laws of inheritance were concerned primarily with land, which in Hebrew society was considered to belong to the family, and upon the death of the father was passed along to the sons of a legal wife, with the firstborn son possessing the birthright, a double portion (Deut. 21:15-17; I Chron. 28:8; Ezra 9:12). When there were no sons, the property went to the daughters. 2. Any possession coming as a gift, as the land (Canaan) given to Abraham and his descendants by God (Gen. 15:7; I Kings 8:36). 3. God and His Kingdom, as He gave or will give both to His people (Josh. 13:33; Matt. 25:34), Israel and mankind collectively, and also to each man individually (Ps. 16:5), provided he lives in righteousness and maintains the faith (Gal. 5:21). In a figurative sense, believers are heirs of God and joint heirs with Christ (Rom. 8:17). See also FIRSTBORN.

in·i′qui·ty. 1. Lack of righteousness or justice; wickedness; evil; sin (Eccles. 3:16; Matt. 7:23; Acts 3:26). 2. Failure to abide by the law; lawlessness (II Thess. 2:7; Heb. 1:9). 3. Punishment because of sin (Gen. 19:15).

ink′horn. A small case or container made of horn, used to hold ink and reed pens, that could be carried tucked into one's girdle (Ezek. 9:2-3). The ink was made of soot or charcoal mixed with gum arabic and diluted with water.

inn. In the ancient Near East, a public inn was a mere place of shelter for man and beast. Like modern khans in this region, it was probably a large, quadrangular court, with a well in the center and unfurnished rooms around the sides for travelers, chambers for goods and stalls for cattle. The traveler provided food for himself and fodder for his cattle. Rarely was there a host from whom food could be purchased (Luke 10:34-35).

in′ner (or in′ward) man. The spiritual nature of man, contrasted with man's mortal, or perishable, being (II Cor. 4:16). The spirit of God resides in the inner man of a Christian, to help him control outer man's physical desires (Rom. 3:16; 7:22).

in'spi·ra'tion. An act of God whereby certain men were empowered through the Holy Spirit to speak on matters of life and of doctrine. This influence of the Holy Spirit resulted in the writing of the Scriptures; see II Tim. 3:16, where inspiration is thought of as the infusion of the breath of God into these writings. The authority of the Scriptures rests upon the concept that the Spirit of God inspired the writers and guided them in recording the truth. See also ORACLE.

in'ward part. An inner chamber where motives and feelings are stored, and where the secrets of the soul are deposited: often thought to be the heart (Ps. 5:9; 51:6; Isa. 16:11).

I'saac. Abraham's second son, born to Abraham and Sarah in their old age. His story and that of his twin sons, Esau and Jacob, can be found in Gen., chs. 17–35.

I·sa'iah. The son of Amoz, born c. 770 B.C. and active as a prophet for about 40 years, during the reigns of Uzziah, Jotham, Ahaz and Hezekiah (see KINGS, TABLE OF). He is called Esaias in the N.T., where he is referred to many times.

Is·car'i·ot. See JUDAS.

Ish–bosh'eth. Fourth son of Saul, his name was changed from Esh-baal (I Chron. 8:33) because "Baal" came to imply idolatry. The story of his short reign as king of Israel and his traitorous murder is told in II Sam. 2:8–4:12.

Ish'i. 1. See BAALI. 2. The name of 4 men in the O.T.

Ish'ma·el. Oldest son of Abraham, by Hagar, Sarah's maid (Gen., ch. 16); mocks Isaac, is sent away with Hagar into the desert, where an angel saves them (21:9–21; cf. Gal. 4:22–31).

isle, is'land. 1. A relatively small land mass surrounded by water (Acts 27:16; 28:1). 2. Any region having land along the sea, whether an island or part of the mainland; coastland (Gen. 10:5; Isa. 24:15). 3. Any distant land or far-off region (Isa. 49:1; Zeph. 2:11). 4. In Isa. 40:15 simply dry land is meant.

Is'ra•el. 1. The name given to Jacob at the brook Jabbok (Gen. 32:22-32). 2. The whole body of the descendants of Jacob at any one time (Gen. 34:7; Ex. 32:4; Deut. 4:1). 3. The tribes that acted independently of Judah; the 10 northern tribes or Northern Kingdom. As compared with Judah, Israel had twice the population and nearly 3 times the territory. Its capital was first Shechem, then Tirzah, then Samaria built by Omri (I Kings 12:25; 14:17; 15:21; 16:23-24). The Assyrian army captured Samaria in 722-721 B.C., and a large number of inhabitants were carried off to Assyria. 4. For Israel as God's suffering servant, see Isa. 49:3. 5. For the Christian Church as the true Israel, see Rom. 9:6-8, 30-32; 10:12-13; Gal. 3:6-9, 14, 23-29; 6:16).

Is'sa•char. Jacob's ninth son, fifth by Leah (Gen. 30:17-18; 35:23; see also I Chron. 7:1). His tribe received territory in the fertile valley of Jezreel (Josh. 19:17-23), between Mt. Tabor and Mt. Gilboa, lands which were the scene of many battles (e.g. Judg., chs. 4; 5; I Sam., chs. 28-31).

is'sue. *v.* 1. To go, pass, come or flow (out); to emerge; to discharge. 2. To be born, to be descended (II Kings 20:18). *n.* 1. A place or means of going out, an outlet, exit; an escape (Ps. 68:20). 2. A child or children; offspring (Matt. 22:25). 3. A discharge of blood, pus, etc., from the body (Lev. 15:25; Luke 8:43-44); a man's disease, called "running issue," probably blennorrhea (Lev. 15:2-15); an issue of blood is a female menstrual disorder (Matt. 9:20).

I•tal'ian band, co'hort. A cohort (a military unit consisting of 600 foot soldiers) called the Italian was stationed in Syria (Acts 10:1). Presumably the men were recruited in Italy.

Ith'a·mar. Aaron's youngest son, he followed him in the priesthood and founded a priestly family (Ex. 28:1; I Chron. 24:1-6).

It'ta·i. A loyal follower of David (II Sam. 15:18-22).

i'vo·ry. A substance derived from the tusk of the elephant, it was a token of luxury and wealth. Ancient ivory objects, some elaborately carved, have been found in Palestine, Syria and Babylonia. It was brought from abroad by Solomon's ships (I Kings 10:22; II Chron. 9:21); it seems also to have come from India and Africa, and thrones, beds and even houses were made or overlaid with it (I Kings 10:18; Amos 6:4; Ps. 45:8).

J

Ja'chin and Bo'az. Jachin was the right-hand, Boaz the left-hand of 2 pillars set up in the vestibule of Solomon's Temple (I Kings 7:15-22). It is not known whether the pillars supported the roof or were freestanding and strictly ornamental or symbolic. The meanings of the names are obscure: perhaps they both are abbreviations of inscriptions on them in praise of God; or Jachin may be a symbol of Firmness, Boaz of Strength.

ja'cinth. A precious stone, probably the sapphire (Rev. 21:20).

jack'al. This member of the dog genus is not mentioned in KJV. However, in some places where KJV reads "monster" or "dragon" a mammal is meant (Lam. 4:3) that dwells in the wilderness (Isa. 35:7; 43:20) and in deserted places (Isa. 34:13-14; Jer. 49:33; 51:37). The jackal is most likely. It differs from the dog in its long, pointed muzzle. Its length is 30 inches, its height 17. It frequents ruins, hunts in packs and feeds chiefly on carrion. In Palestine its terrible wailing howl is a common sound in the night.

Ja'cob. Son of Isaac and Rebekah, twin brother of Esau (Gen. 25:24-28);

> purchases Esau's birthright (Gen. 25:29-34)
>
> receives blessing meant for Esau (Gen., ch. 27)
>
> serves Laban; marries Leah and Rachel (Gen., chs. 29-31)
>
> wrestles with angel, who names him Israel (Gen., ch. 32)
>
> 12 sons (Gen., ch. 35)
>
> grieves for Joseph (Gen., ch. 37)
>
> sends sons to Egypt (Gen., chs. 42-45)
>
> goes to Egypt, meets Pharaoh (Gen., chs. 46-47)
>
> blesses Joseph's sons, dies (Gen., chs. 48-50).

The Hebrew nation, as descended from Jacob, is often called the people, or children, of Israel (Ex. 14:16, etc.). The prophets often use Jacob and Israel in their poetic couplets (Deut. 33:10, etc.).

Ja'el. The story of Jael's murder of the sleeping Sisera is told in Judg., chs. 4; 5.

Jah. A shortened form of the Hebrew name for God, occurring in poetry (Ps. 68:4).

Ja'i·rus. Ruler of the synagogue, whose young daughter was healed by Jesus (Matt. 9:18-26; Mark 5:21-43; Luke 8:40-56). See MINSTREL.

James. 1. Son of Zebedee, brother of John and one of the 12 apostles (Matt. 4:21; 10:2, etc.); he and John received from Jesus the name Boanerges, "sons of thunder" (Mark 3:17), and both were present at the Transfiguration and at Gethesmane (Mark 9:2; 14:33, etc.) and in the upper room (Acts 1:13). Herod put James to death (Acts 12:2). 2. Son of Alphaeus, also one of the 12, sometimes referred to as James the Less (Matt. 10:3; Mark 3:18; 15:40; Acts 1:13). Nothing further is certainly known of him. 3. The Lord's brother, mentioned only twice in the Gospels (Matt. 13:55; Mark 6:3); though not one of the 12, he became the leader of the Jerusalem church (Acts 12:17; Gal. 1:19, etc.). See BRETHREN OF THE LORD. After Acts 21:18 the N.T. tells us nothing of this James; history says that he was martyred in an uprising of the Jews after the death of the procurator Festus, before the arrival of his successor. See FESTUS. 4. The father or brother of Judas (Luke 6:16; Acts 1:13).

Jan'nes and Jam'bres. The two Egyptian magicians who attempted to thwart the work of Moses (II Tim. 3:8). In Ex. 7:11; 8:7; 9:11 they are unnamed.

Ja'pheth. The third son of Noah, who received his blessing (Gen. 9:18-10:2).

Jash'ar, Jash'er, book of. A book known only from the three citations from it in Scriptures (Josh. 10:12-13; II Sam. 1:18; and I Kings 8:53 in the Greek Version). Judging from these citations, the book was evidently a collection of religious poems or national songs which described great events in the history of Israel.

Ja'son. A kinsman of Paul (Acts 17:4-9; Rom. 16:21).

jas'per. A precious stone, probably an opaque green variety of quartz (Ex. 28:20; Ezek. 28:13; Rev. 21:18).

jave'lin. A small kind of spear, intended to be thrown (Num. 25:7; I Sam. 18:10-11; Job 41:29).

jeal'ous. 1. Resentfully suspicious of a rival or a rival's influence (Num. 5:14). 2. Demanding exclusive loyalty; unwilling to tolerate the worship of other gods: said of God in His desire to maintain a unique and pure relationship between Himself and His people (Ex. 20:5; Josh. 24:19). 3. Watchful or solicitous in guarding or keeping (I Kings 19:10, 14; Joel 2:18).

jeal'ous·y of'fer·ing. The so-called offering of jealousy (Num. 5:15) calling for a cereal offering before a priest, was more truly a trial by ordeal of a woman suspected of unfaithfulness to her husband (Num. 5:14-31). See also BITTER WATER.

Jeb'u·sites. The name of a tribe of Canaan before the conquest by the Hebrews (Gen. 10:16; 15:21; Ex. 3:8). They are known only as dwelling at Jebus, a clan name—a city that later became Jerusalem. Jebusites still held the stronghold of Zion as an enclave at the beginning of David's reign (II Sam. 5:6-7). Jebusites very possibly were of Hurrian background.

Jec'o·ni'ah. See JEHOIACHIN.

Jed'i·di'ah. A name given to Solomon by Nathan the prophet (II Sam. 12:25).

Je·ho'a·haz. 1. King of Israel, son and successor of Jehu; destroyed by the Syrians (II Kings 13:1-9, 22). 2. King of Judah; a younger son of Josiah, placed by the people on the throne upon Josiah's death. He was deposed after only 3 months and taken in chains to Egypt (II Kings 23:30-34; II Chron. 36:1-4). Jehoahaz was also called Shallum (Jer. 22:11). 3. See AHAZIAH. See also KINGS, TABLE OF.

Je·ho'ash. See JOASH.

Je·hoi'a·chin. King of Judah, son of Jehoiakim, at age 18 he ruled just 3 months, then surrendered the city to Nebuchadnezzar (II Kings 24:8; 25:27-30; cf. II Chron. 36:9) and was carried, with all his royal family and officials, into exile in Babylon (Jer. 52:28; II Kings 24:14). Jeremiah (22:24) sometimes refers to him as Coniah. Another spelling is Jeconiah (I Chron. 3:16, etc., RSV). See KINGS, TABLE OF.

Je·hoi'a·da. A high priest who defied Queen Athaliah, placed Joash (Jehoash) on the throne of Judah and repaired the Temple (II Kings 11:4-12:16; II Chron. 22:10-24:15). Others of the same name appear in the O.T.

Je·hoi'a·kim. King of Judah; a son of Josiah, he was originally called Eliakim. Pharaohnechoh made him king of Judah after deposing his brother, Jehoahaz, and forced him to collect tribute (II Kings 24:34-37).

As Babylon arose as the dominant power,
Jeremiah (ch. 36) sent him a warning which
he ignored. Jehoiakim's disastrous relations
with Nebuchadnezzar are told in II Kings
24:1-5 and II Chron. 36:5-8. See KINGS,
TABLE OF.

Je·ho'ram. 1. (Also Joram). Son of Ahab, king
of Israel, he overcame the Moabites with
the help of the Edomite ruler and Jehoshaphat of Judah (II Kings 3:1-27). He was
killed by Jehu, who succeeded him as king
of Israel (II Kings 8:28-29; 9:15-26). 2. A
king of Judah, son of Jehoshaphat (I Kings
22:50; II Kings 8:16-23), he killed all his
brothers on gaining the throne (II Chron.
21:1-4). His wife was Athaliah, later queen
(21:6). Elijah foretold his sickness and
death (21:12-20). See KINGS, TABLE OF.

Je·hosh'a·phat. In the O.T. 5 Jehoshaphats
can be identified. Most important is the
king of Judah, son of Asa, whose reign was
mostly a worthy one except for his war alliance with Ahab of Israel against the Syrians. His story is found in I Kings, ch. 22, II
Kings, ch. 3 and II Chron., chs. 17-20. See
JUDGE; KINGS, TABLE OF; MOAB.

Je·hosh'a·phat, Valley of. A symbolic name
for a valley where all nations shall be gathered by God for judgment (Joel 3:2, 12). So
far as evidence goes, no valley actually bore
this name. Joel doubtless chose it because
Jehoshaphat means "the Lord has judged,"
which symbolizes the event it predicted.

Je·hosh'e·ba. Sister of Ahaziah, she rescued
his infant son Joash (Jehoash) from slaughter and kept him hidden until Queen Athaliah's death (II Kings, ch. 11; in II Chron.,
ch. 22 she is called Jehoshabeath).

Je·hosh'u·a. See JOSHUA.

Je·ho'vah. A name given to God in the O.T. It
is a medieval and modern translation of
what was an attempt to vocalize the ancient
Hebrew sacred name for God. The name
was written with 4 consonants YHWH or
JHWH, by themselves unpronounceable,

because the Lord's name was considered too sacred to utter. *Adonai* was often written beneath YHWH or JHWH, and after a time the vowels of *Adonai* were inserted between the consonants (the first *a* becoming an *e*) of the sacred name. This produced ultimately the modern word "Jehovah" (see Ex. 6:3; Ps. 83:18).

Je'hu. Among others in the O.T.: 1. A prophet in the time of King Jehoshaphat (I Kings 16:1; II Chron. 19:2; 20:34). 2. A commander in the army of King Ahab of Israel who was anointed by Elisha and commissioned by him to destroy the house of Ahab, represented by Jehoram, Ahab's son, and the queen mother, Jezebel. How he carried out their deaths and those of Baal's priests in a blood bath is told in II Kings, chs. 9 and 10. But Jehu himself took no heed to walk in the law of God and did not depart from the calf worship (II Kings 10:29, 31) which separated the Northern Tribes from the Southern Kingdom with its Temple worship in Jerusalem. Jehu's reign ended in disaster. See KINGS, TABLE OF.

jeop'ard. To risk loss, damage or failure of; to jeopardize (Judg. 5:18).

jeop'ard·y. Danger, risk (Luke 8:23).

Jeph'thah. Judg. 10:6–12:7 tells of the illegitimate son cast out of Gilead by his half-brothers but later urged to return and lead the Gileadites against the Ammonites, and of his rash oath. See AMMONITES.

Jer'e·mi'ah. The most important of those named in the O.T. is the great prophet, who carried on his lonely work through the reign of 5 kings of Judah, beginning under Josiah and continuing even after the fall of Jerusalem. In the N.T. he is called Jeremy and Jeremias (Matt. 3:17; 16:14). See KINGS, TABLE OF.

Jer'o·bo'am. 1. Jeroboam I, founder of the Northern Kingdom;
Solomon's overseer (I Kings 11:27-28)

Ahijah's prophecy, Solomon's threat (I
Kings 11:29-40)
speaks for Israel to Rehoboam (I Kings
12:3-12; II Chron. 10:3-4)
chosen king of the 10 tribes (I Kings
12:20; cf. II Chron. 13:6)
his idolatry (I Kings, chs. 12-14; II
Chron. 13:8)
his defeat and death (II Chron. 13:14-20;
I Kings 14:20).
See KINGS, TABLE OF; REHOBOAM; also AL-
TAR.

2. Jeroboam II, son of Jehoash (Joash), a
much later king of the 10 tribes (II Kings
14:16, 27-29), whose 41-year reign was mili-
tarily successful and prosperous, but irreligious and immoral (Amos, chs. 1-8). See
KINGS, TABLE OF.

Jer'ub-ba'al. See GIDEON.

Jesh'u•a. Several O.T. men. The best known
is the high priest who encouraged Zerubbabel in rebuilding the Temple (Ezra 2:2;
3:2-8; Neh. 7:7); in Zech., chs. 3; 6 he is
called Joshua. This priest was assisted by a
Levite also named Jeshua (Ezra 2:40; 3:9;
Neh. 7:43, etc.).

Je'sus. In addition to our Lord, this name,
which was common during N.T. times, referred to the Joshua who succeeded Moses
as leader of the people (Acts 7:45; Heb.
4:8); an associate of Paul (Col. 4:11); and
Barabbas. See also CHRIST.

Jeth'ro. A shepherd and priest. Moses married his daughter Zipporah (Ex. 3:1;
4:18-20; ch. 18). He was also called Hobab
(Num. 10:29) and Reuel (Ex. 2:18).

jew'el. A costly ornament (Ex. 3:22).

Jez'e•bel. Wife of King Ahab; her evil life and
the horrible end foretold by both Elijah and
Elisha are recounted in I Kings
16:31-21:29; II Kings 9:10, 30-37). The
name, which has come to mean wickedness,
is also applied to an evil woman in Rev.
2:20. See also AHAB.

Jez're•el, Valley of. The great plain intersecting Palestine e. to w. immediately n. of Carmel, also known as the Plain of Esdraelon. Jezreel was the fortified town at the w. entrance to it. Throughout all bygone time this valley has been a battlefield of nations (I Sam. 31:1-5, 11; Judg. 6:33). See ARMAGEDDON.

Jo'ab. David's nephew and loyal commander of his army (II Sam. 8:16), he was unsparing to his enemies (3:27; 14:1-15:15; 18:5-19:7; 20:4-13). His support of Adonijah as successor to the throne cost him his life (I Kings, chs. 1; 2).

Jo·an'na. The wife of Herod's steward; ministers to Jesus and visits his tomb (Luke 8:3; 24:10).

Jo'ash, Je·ho'ash. Most notable of 6 O.T. men of this name are: 1. Grandson of Queen Athaliah, from whom he was hidden for 6 years; becomes king of Judah at her death (II Kings, chs. 11-12; II Chron., chs. 22-24). 2. King of Israel, whose victories over the Syrians are prophesied by Elisha; he defeats King Amaziah of Judah (II Kings 13:9-14:16). See KINGS, TABLE OF.

Job. In Gen. 46:13 "Job" is probably an error for "Jashub." Nothing is known of the author of the book of Job.

Jo'el. The name appears frequently in the O.T. Of the author of the book of Joel, nothing is known except that he was the son of Pethuel.

John. 1. Son of Zebedee, brother of James and one of the 12 apostles (Matt. 4:21-22, etc.). Jesus gave him and James the name Boanerges, "sons of thunder" (Mark 3:17); see BOANERGES. Sometimes referred to as the "beloved disciple," he was especially close to Jesus (Matt. 17:1; Mark 9:2; John 13:23), and some mistakenly thought that he was not to die (21:20-23). When Paul returned to Jerusalem after his first missionary journey, John was still there, a pillar of the church (Acts 1:12-4:32; Gal. 2:9). The

Fourth Gospel, I, II and III John are commonly held to be of his composition; uncertain tradition also assigns Revelation to this John, probably incorrectly. 2. Mark the evangelist. See MARK. 3. A Jew who may have been related to the high priest Annas (Acts 4:6).

John the Bap'tist. The forerunner of Jesus;

> born to Zacharias and Elisabeth as foretold by angel Gabriel (Luke 1:5-25; 40-45; 57-80)

> baptizes the people; teaches them to repent and pray (Matt. 3:1-12; Mark 1:1-8; Luke 3:1-18; John 1:6-34; 3:23-36; Acts 13:24)

> baptizes Jesus (Matt. 3:13-15; Mark 1:9; Luke 3:21; John 1:32; 3:26)

> imprisoned (Matt. 4:12; Mark 1:14; Luke 3:19-20)

> sends disciples to question Messiahship; Jesus' answer (Matt. 11:2-19; Luke 7:19-29)

> his death brought about by Herodias (Matt. 14:1-12; Mark 6:14-29)

> disciples who knew only his teachings (Acts 18:24-19:4).

join'ing. A clamp, as for holding together two pieces of wood or metal (I Chron. 22:3).

Jon'a-dab. See RECHABITES.

Jo'nah. There is no historical evidence that Jonah, the son of Amittai (II Kings 14:25; Jonah 1:1) was actually the author of the book of that name.

Jon'a-than. Most important of those bearing this popular name was the oldest son of King Saul, who led an army against the Philistines, routing them; he is saved from death by the people (I Sam., chs. 13-14); he is a close friend of David (chs. 18-20), who mourns his death (31:2; II Sam. 1:17-27).

Jo'ram. See JEHORAM.

Jo'seph. A common name in the Bible. Chief among them: 1. Jacob's eleventh and favorite son (Gen. 35:24; 37:3). Gen., chs. 37,

39-50 tell how his brothers sold him into slavery in Egypt, where he was imprisoned but later made ruler; how his sons, Ephraim and Manasseh, were blessed and adopted by Jacob; and of Joseph's death. His bones were taken to the Promised Land in the Exodus (Ex. 13:19; Josh. 24:32). 2. Espoused (engaged) to Mary, Joseph, a carpenter of Nazareth, learned in a dream of the coming birth of Jesus. As a descendant of David, he had to go to Bethlehem to be taxed, and took Mary, now his wife, with him. See esp. Matt. 1:18-25; 2:13-23; Luke 2:1-5, 41-51; also BRETHREN OF THE LORD. 3. Joseph of Arimathaea, a member of the Sanhedrin, who had voted against the conviction of Jesus. He begged the body of Jesus from Pilate and laid it in his own new tomb (Matt. 27:57-66; Mark 15:43-46; etc.).

Josh'u·a. Although the name appears elsewhere in the O.T., the best known is the son of Nun, called also Oshea and Jehoshua (Num. 13:8, 16). Sent with Caleb to report on Canaan (Num. 14:6-10), he returns and is designated Moses' successor as leader of the Israelites (Num. 27:18-23; Deut. 31:14, 23). After Moses' death he leads his people across the Jordan. See also JESHUA; TABERNACLE.

Jo·si'ah. The story of Josiah, son of Amon, who became king of Judah at the age of 8, is found in II Kings, chs. 22-23 and II Chron., chs. 34-35. Influenced by the high priest Hilkiah, at age 20 he destroyed idols and wicked places; at age 26 (621 B.C.) he repaired the Temple; in the process the book of the law (Deuteronomy) was found. Josiah then initiated a full-scale reform and celebrated a solemn Passover. In 609 he was mortally wounded in a battle against Pharaoh-nechoh, and was greatly lamented. See KINGS, TABLE OF.

jot. Jesus' words in Matt. 5:18 ("jot and tittle") undoubtedly were spoken in Aramaic. "Jot" therefore refers to the Hebrew letter *yōd*, which was the smallest letter in the current Aramaic-Hebrew writing. Hence, figuratively, "jot" signifies a matter that seems to be of small importance.

Jo'tham. 1. Youngest son of Gideon, he escapes slaughter by Abimelech; utters parable of trees anointing a king (Judg. 9:5-21). 2. A king of Judah who rules first as regent when Uzziah is smitten with leprosy (II Kings 15:5, 30-38). See KINGS, TABLE OF.

joy. The feeling of pleasure and happiness that one experiences when there is a healthy relationship between God and a person; also the spiritual happiness that a righteous man finds through his belief in God: this joy is the greater because of the anticipation of fuller joy in the kingdom of heaven (Rom. 14:17). Aside from this ultimate joy, the word is used to relate other less exalted emotions, as the happiness found in nature (Ps. 96:11), the thrill derived from victory in battle (I Sam. 18:6), the ecstasies of feasting (I Chron. 12:40), all of which come from doing God's work, or seeing it carried out, and from furthering the kingdom of God. God is also spoken of as experiencing this feeling as He watches His people living righteously and walking in the ways of truth (Neh. 8:10; Luke 15:7). Jesus and Paul taught the joy found in suffering itself (Matt. 5:12).

ju'bi·le, ju'bi·lee. A year-long celebration held after 7 times 7 years had been counted from the last jubilee (Lev. 25:8-10). It derived its name from the custom of proclaiming it by a blast on the trumpet. This proclaimed liberty to all Israelites who were in bondage to a countryman and the return of ancestral belongings to any who had been compelled by poverty to sell them. Mortgaged lands, except lots or houses inside walled cities, were restored to the original owners, and the land was left fallow to regain its fertility (Lev. 25:8-17). Historical evidence is lacking that the year of jubilee was ever observed in actual practice. But even if this remained ideal legislation, its social values lay in teaching personal liberty, restitution of property and the simple life. The sabbatical year (every seventh year) was observed, in which most of the provisions of the jubilee year were carried out.

Ju·dae′a, Ju·de′a. See JUDAH.

Ju′dah. 1. Though the fourth son of Jacob and Leah, he received the birthright (Gen. 29:35; chs. 37–38; 43–44; 46; 49). See BIRTHRIGHT. He was an ancestor of David and of our Lord (Matt. 1:3–16). 2. The descendants of Judah (Num. 1:26) and their territory (cf. Luke 1:39, "Juda"). David was king of Judah alone before reuniting Saul's kingdom and building a new capital, Jerusalem, on the border between Judah and the northern tribes. When the 10 tribes revolted against Rehoboam, Judah and the Simeonites and a large part of Benjamin remained loyal, forming the kingdom of Judah, or Southern Kingdom. When Jerusalem fell to Nebuchadnezzar, great numbers of the people of Judah were deported to Babylon. After the Exile, the region was known as Judea (Ezra 5:8).

Ju′das. A common late O.T. and N.T. name, the Greek form of Judah. 1. One of the 12 apostles, carefully distinguished from Judas Iscariot (John 14:22), also called Lebbaeus or Thaddaeus (Matt. 10:3; Luke 6:16; Acts 1:13; etc.). 2. A brother of Jesus (Matt. 13:55; cf. Mark 6:3). See BRETHREN OF THE LORD. 3. Judas of Galilee, who perished in a revolt against taxation (Acts 5:37). 4. A man in Damascus with whom Paul lodged (Acts 9:11). 5. Judas, surnamed Barsabas, associated with Barnabas and Paul (Acts 15:22, 27, 32).

Ju′das Is·car′i·ot. The disciple who betrayed Jesus (Matt. 10:4; 26:25; Mark 3:19, etc.). "Iscariot" seems to be a Greek word meaning "a native of Kerioth," a town in Judah.

Thus he would be the only apostle from Judea; the rest were Galileans.

    rebuked by Jesus (John 12:4-8)

    covenants with priests and gives sign (Matt. 26:14-16, 47-49; Mark 14:10-11, 43-45; Luke 22:3-6, 47; cf. John 14:26; 18:2)

    confesses and kills himself (Matt. 27:3-5; cf. Acts 1:16-18).

See also ACELDAMA.

Jude. An English form of the name Judas, given to the writer of the Epistle of Jude. Nothing is known of his life.

judge. 1. A civil magistrate (Ex. 21:22; Deut. 16:18). Moses first organized the judiciary of Israel (Ex. 18:13-26). Later the king became the supreme judge in civil matters (II Sam. 15:2; I Kings 3:9, 28; 7:7). Jehoshaphat organized the judiciary in Judah still further (II Chron. 19:5-8). 2. A man whom God raised up to lead a revolt against foreign oppressors and who, having freed the nation and shown thereby his call to God, was looked to by the people to maintain their rights. The period of the judges was between Joshua and Samuel.

judg'ment. 1. An order or sentence given by a judge or law court; a legal decision (II Kings 25:6). 2. The power of comparing and deciding; the ability to tell right from wrong; good sense (Prov. 13:23; Matt. 7:2). 3. Sound reason; rightfulness; justice (Ex. 23:2, 6; Matt. 23:23). 4. The just and righteous commandments and the acts of God as the divine Judge (Isa. 10:1-4; Jer., ch. 5).

judg'ment, day of. In the O.T., this phrase first conveyed the idea of a day when the Lord would manifest Himself in triumph over His foes and deliver His people from them. The "day of the Lord," as it is most often called in the O.T., was therefore a day to be desired. While there would be a national dissolution, it would only be in order to usher in a glorious reconstruction. But the prophet Amos gave the term a new signif-

icance when he spoke of the day of the
Lord as God's judgment upon Israel (Amos
5:18-20; also chs. 2-4). Later prophets used
the phrase to portray impending doom resulting from the nation's persistent sinfulness. While the day of the Lord is a judgment primarily on Israel, it also includes
the Gentiles (Ezek. 30:1; Obad. 15-17). The
day of the Lord, then, is the final and universal judgment. Although that day will
cause men terror and anguish, it is also a
cause of universal rejoicing, for then begins
the reign of God. In the N.T. the same basic
idea is expressed in new words: the day of
Christ, the day of his coming in the glory of
the Father. It is a day of wrath (Rom. 2:5),
a day of judgment (Matt. 10:15; Rom. 2:16),
a great day (Jude 6). Sometimes it is called
"that day" (Matt. 7:22; I Thess. 5:4) or simply "the day" (I Cor. 3:13). God through
Christ (Rom. 2:5, 16) will bring all men under judgment; He will pass condemnation
on the wicked and will establish the perfect
kingdom of righteousness in which all true
believers will ever be with the Lord (Matt.
25:46; II Cor. 5:10; Rev. 20:11-15).

judg'ment seat. The seat in which a governor,
king or other official sat when hearing and
deciding legal cases (Matt. 27:19; John
19:13; Acts 18:12; 25:17). Figuratively, the
bench of Jesus Christ before which all men
must appear to be judged (Rom. 14:10; II
Cor. 5:10).

ju'ni·per. Although several species of juniper
do occur in Lebanon, Galilee and Bashan,
the evergreen, cone-bearing juniper we are
familiar with is not the one referred to (I
Kings 19:4-5; Job 30:4; Ps. 120:4, KJV), but
rather the broom tree, a much-branched
bush-like tree which grows in the Jordan
Valley, Arabia and the Sinai Peninsula.

Ju'pi·ter. The supreme god of the Romans.
He corresponded to Zeus of the Greeks
(Acts 14:12-13). See BARNABAS; TEMPLE.

jus'ti·fi·ca'tion. The gracious, divine act by

which sinful man is forgiven, declared righteous, and freed through faith from the penalty of his sin. Although this man is unworthy because of his transgression of God's law, he is accepted by God as worthy of being saved because he has shown himself to be a believer, and because Christ, as his substitute, has borne his guilt on the cross. Thus the process of his salvation has begun (Rom. 4:25; 5:16, 18).

K

kab. A unit of dry measure. See MEASURES.

Ke·tu'rah. Abraham's second wife or concubine (Gen. 25:1-4; I Chron. 1:32). Her children were not treated as Isaac was, but were sent away (Gen. 25:6).

key. An Oriental key (Judg. 3:25) consists of a piece of wood with pegs fastened on it, corresponding to small holes in a wooden bar

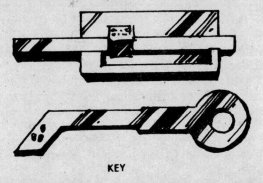

KEY

or bolt within. The action of such a key was to lift and push the bar inside the door; it was not turned like a modern key. The key is the symbol of authority (Isa. 22:22; Matt. 16:19; Rev. 1:18; 3:7; 9:1; 20:1).

kid'ney. Either of a pair of organs in the upper abdominal cavity of animals, the surrounding fat of which was considered a choice item for burning as an offering to God (Ex. 29:13; Lev. 3:4, 10, 15); hence the finest part of anything (Isa. 34:6; Deut. 32:14, where "the fat of kidneys of wheat" means the choicest wheat).

kin'dred. 1. Relatives or family; kinsfolk (Gen. 24:4). 2. A group of people associated due to a common reputation, experience, etc. (Ezek. 11:15). 3. A group of people having the same ancestry; a tribe, clan, race (Acts 7:19; Rev. 14:6).

kine. See COW.

king'dom of God, of heav'en. The spiritual realm of God throughout which His will is in complete control. The phrase does not appear in the O.T. The kingdom begins to become a reality as the will of God is revealed in Jesus Christ (Luke 17:21). Evidences of its workings are seen in the deeds, miracles and healings performed by Jesus; but he suggests in a parable (Matt. 13:31) that it is still in the germination stage, and elsewhere (Luke 9:27) he speaks of the fulfillment and culmination of the kingdom as still being in the future. Seeking the kingdom must be the first goal of the Christian (Matt. 6:33)—that is, conforming to the will of God and recognizing His sovereignty over all of life. Once this is achieved, all of the already established marks of the kingdom, such as salvation, eternal life, etc., will become realities for each person. The kingdom may be thought of as a world-wide family of God's children who, under the Lordship of Christ, will attain everlasting bliss.

Kings of Judah and Israel. The chronology of the divided kingdom based on that prepared by Dr. W. F. Albright is widely accepted. The ruled crosslines mark changes in dynasties.

JUDAH

	B.C.
Rehoboam	c. 922–915
Abijah (Abijam)	c. 915–913
Asa	c. 913–873
Jehoshaphat	c. 873–849

Jehoram (Joram)	c. 849-842
Ahaziah	c. 842
Athaliah	c. 842-837
Joash (Jehoash)	c. 837-800
Amaziah	c. 800-783
Uzziah (or Azariah)	c. 783-742
Jotham (regent and king)	c. 750-735
Ahaz	c. 735-715
Hezekiah	c. 715-687
Manasseh	c. 687-642
Amon	c. 642-640
Josiah	c. 640-609
Jehoahaz (or Shallum)	c. 609
	B.C.
Jehoiakim	c. 609-598
Jehoiachin	c. 598-597
Zedekiah	c. 597-587
Fall of Jerusalem	587

ISRAEL

Jeroboam I	c. 922-901
Nadab	c. 901-900
Baasha	c. 900-877
Elah	c. 877-876
Zimri	c. 876
Omri	c. 876-869
Ahab	c. 869-850
Ahaziah	c. 850-849
Jehoram (Joram)	c. 849-842
Jehu	c. 842-815
Jehoahaz	c. 815-801
Joash (Jehoash)	c. 801-786
Jeroboam II	c. 786-746
Zechariah	c. 746-745
Shallum	c. 745
Menahem	c. 745-738
Pekahiah	c. 738-737
Pekah	c. 737-732
Hoshea	c. 732-724
Fall of Samaria	722-721

kite. A bird of prey of the falcon family. It was "unclean" (Lev. 11:14; Deut. 14:13). Kites are of various kinds: the black, the yellow-billed and the red kite are known in Palestine.

KITE

knave. A deceitful, unscrupulous person.

knead'ing trough. A shallow, open vessel, usually of wood and portable, in which dough is worked (kneaded) into a well-mixed mass, before baking (Ex. 12:34).

knowl'edge, tree of. See TREE OF KNOWLEDGE.

Ko'rah. Best known of this name is a Levite who, together with Dathan, Abiram and On, rebelled against Moses and Aaron (Num., ch. 16); the rebels and their households perished in an earthquake, but the sons of Korah were spared (26:10-11).

L

La'ban. Brother of Rebekah, he gave his daughters, Leah and Rachel, to Jacob in marriage in return for 14 years' service (Gen. 24:29-31; ch. 29; 30:25-31:55).

lace. A band or lacing (Ex. 28:28).

la'ma. See ELOI..

Lamb of God. Jesus, who like the lamb at Passover, is sacrificed for the guilt and sin of others (John 1:29, 36). The lamb was frequently chosen for sacrifice (Ex. 12:3, 21) because of its purity, gentleness and uncomplaining submission to suffering, and in these qualities also it resembled Jesus. The word "Lamb" alone is used elsewhere as a symbolic reference to Jesus (Rev. 5:12; 13:8). See PASSOVER.

lam'en·ta'tion. An outward expression of grief or sorrow (Gen. 50:10; Ps. 78:64; Amos 8:10). Lamentations often took the form of speeches (II Sam. 1:17-27) or poems that lamented a great man who had died. The book of Lamentations contains poems of mourning over the destruction of Jerusalem and the sufferings of the people.

lamp. A vessel designed to contain oil to be burned by means of a wick to give light. The earliest household lamps were made of clay in a saucer shape, with a spout formed for the wick to lie in; they were very small—perhaps 3 inches across—and were carried in the palm of the hand. Nothing like the gold lamps of the Tabernacle and the Temple (Ex. 37:35; I Kings 7:49) has survived. See CANDLESTICK; SNUFFERS.

lamp'stand. See CANDLESTICK.

lan'cet. A kind of small spear (I Kings 18:28).

lap'wing. While Palestine is visited by a member of the lapwing family in winter, it is probable that the word in Lev. 11:19 and Deut. 14:18 of the KJV should be "hoopoe," a grayish-brown bird about a foot long with a crest of feathers upon its head.

last days. The time during which all things will be summed up and in which final judgment will be pronounced before the end of life on earth. At this time the final glory of God will be disclosed and the destiny of man will be revealed (Isa. 2:2; Dan. 10:14; Heb. 1:2).

last judgment. See JUDGMENT, DAY OF.

Last Sup'per. See LORD'S SUPPER.

lat'ter rain. See RAIN.

la'ver. A basin or trough for water in which to wash. In the O.T. the word refers to a bronze basin used in rites of purification in the Tabernacle services (Lev. 8:11). It stood upon a base of bronze in the court between the altar and the door of the Tabernacle, and was used by the priests for washing their hands and feet before ministering at the altar or entering the sanctuary (Ex. 30:17-21). In Solomon's Temple the one laver was replaced by a "molten sea" and 10 lavers (I Kings 7:23-26, 38-40, 43)

law. Of the several meanings of the word "law," two are used in Scripture: 1. A uniformly acting force which determines the regular sequence of events, as for example a law of nature. 2. More importantly, a rule of conduct enjoined by a competent authority and, if need be, enforced by penalties. Law may have its source in custom, or a king's decree, or in revelation, as in the case of Moses, who in a supernatural manner at Sinai received the law from God. The term "the law," without any other qualifying word, occasionally refers to the whole O.T. in general (John 12:34; I Cor. 14:21); but it is employed much more frequently as the title of the Pentateuch (the first 5 books of the O.T.), called *Torah* ("The Law") by Jews. Ultimately the body of statutes that comprised the law controlled the general form of worship, protected human rights, regulated personal conduct and prescribed sacred seasons and sacrifice. See BOOK OF THE LAW; TEN COMMANDMENTS.

law·giv'er. 1. One who draws up, introduces or enacts a code of laws for a nation or a people, esp. God (Isa. 33:22; James 4:12). Moses was the lawgiver of Israel (John 1:17; 7:19). 2. The scepter or staff held by a ruler on ceremonial occasions as a symbol of his authority (Gen. 49:10; Num. 21:18) and law-creating power.

law'yer. The N.T. meaning is that of a person with a thorough knowledge of the oral and written law of the Hebrews; one who decided questions of law and taught others on matters of law. In some instances of its appearance (Matt. 22:35; Mark 12:28), "lawyer" is equivalent to "scribe."

lay'ing on of hands. The symbolic act of placing one's hands on another (normally on the head) as an act of blessing in the presence of God or for the purpose of identifying oneself with that person or animal, specifically: 1. The laying of hands on the head of an animal that one is offering as a sacrifice at the altar (Lev. 1:4), thereby identifying it as one's own representative to God; 2. The laying of hands on one's children (Gen. 48:14), indicating parental blessing, or on the sick (Mark 8:23), conveying the blessings of God, etc.; 3. The act of an apostle, missionary, etc., laying his hands on a person, thus signifying that that person is devoted to the service of God (I Tim. 4:14).

Laz'a·rus. 1. The beggar carried to heaven (Luke 16:20-25). 2. Brother of Martha and Mary of Bethany, raised from the dead (John 11:1-46).

league. An agreement made by nations, groups or individuals for the purpose of doing a specific thing, or preventing something; a covenant (II Sam. 5:3; I Kings 5:12).

Le'ah. Daughter of Laban, she was given to Jacob in marriage first, in place of Rachel (Gen. 29:15-17, 23-25, 31-35; 30:14-21; 49:31).

Leb·bae'us. See JUDAS (1).

leech. See HORSELEACH.

leek. A delectable vegetable, a favorite food in Palestine and Egypt from earliest times (Num. 11:5). It looks like an elongated onion, with dark green leaves at the top.

lees. Dregs or sediment that settled at the bottom of a wineskin. The wine was allowed to remain on the lees so that its color and flavor would improve (Isa. 25:6). To "settle on one's lees" was to become complacent, to feel self-satisfied (Jer. 48:11; Zech. 1:12). In Ps. 75:8, to drink the lees or dregs of the cup (of wrath) means to taste the full bitterness of the punishment.

le'gion. 1. The chief subdivision of the Roman

army. It originally contained 3,000 foot soldiers with a contingent of 300 cavalrymen. During the time of the N.T. its size had grown to 6,000 infantrymen; a legion consisted of 10 cohorts, each cohort of 3 maniples, each maniple of 2 centuries. 2. Any large number, as in the name "Legion" given by the unclean spirit in the demoniac (Mark 5:9, 15; Luke 8:30) to indicate that many demons had entered the man.

len'til, len'tile. A plant (II Sam. 23:11) of the pea family, bearing small, broad legumes, full of starch. It was boiled as a pottage or thick soup (Gen. 25:29, 34) and in times of scarcity was made into bread (Ezek. 4:9). The plant grows wild in Moab and is cultivated in all parts of Palestine. Pottage made from it is red.

leop'ard. A large and ferocious spotted cat of Africa and s. Asia. It was very swift (Hab. 1:8). Its usual food was the kid (Isa. 11:6), but it sometimes attacked man (Hos. 13:7-8), lurking for the purpose in the vicinity of towns or villages (Jer. 5:6). It was found in Palestine until 1911, but now seems to be extinct there.

lep'ro·sy. 1. A chronic skin disease of more than one variety (Lev., ch. 13), probably the most common type was what we today call psoriasis and not the dreaded Hansen's Disease. Psoriasis is characterized by scaly, reddish patches. However, whether it was psoriasis, ringworm, boils, eczema or some other curable disease, it was believed to be infectious and, for that reason, isolation of the victim was prescribed. True leprosy (Hansen's Disease) may also have been known but this has been curable or controllable only in this century, and many Biblical references (esp. Lev. 14:1-32) indicate only temporary sufferings from "leprosy." 2. Mildew, mold, dry rot, or a fungus growth that affected clothing and houses (Lev. 14:33-57). Since these all have the characteristics of decay and deformity, they were identified with the skin disease, and repair or destruction was required.

Le'vi. 1. Third son of Jacob and Leah (Gen. 29:34; 35:23), his story appears in Gen. 34:25-31; 49:5-7. He died in Egypt at an advanced age (Ex. 6:16). See LEVITES. 2. Another name for the apostle Matthew (see MATTHEW). 3. Two ancestors of Christ (Luke 3:24, 29-30).

le·vi'a·than. An aquatic monster found in the Canaanite literature of the city of Ugarit (15th and 14th century B.C.). In the O.T. it is mentioned only in poetic passages. In Job 41 it appears to be the crocodile. In Ps. 74:14, leviathan is a primeval dragon subdued by God at the time of Creation. In Isa. 27:1 it is viewed as symbolizing the fierce and terrible powers of the world that have afflicted the people of God, but whom God will ultimately destroy. In Ps. 104:25-26 "leviathan" seems to mean the dolphin or whale.

Le'vites. 1. The descendants of Levi, a son of Jacob. Levi had 3 sons: Gershon or Gershom, Kohath and Merari, each of whom founded a tribal family (Gen. 46:11; Ex. 6:16; Num. 3:17; I Chron. 6:16-48). Moses and Aaron were Levites of the house of Amram and family of Kohath (Ex. 6:16-26). 2. The men of the tribe of Levi charged with the care of the sanctuary. Aaron and his sons were set apart for the priesthood, and the office made hereditary, including the high priesthood, which was transferred from Aaron to his son Eleazar (Num. 20:25-28). But the care and transportation of the costly sanctuary and the preparation of materials, the cleaning, etc., for the elaborate services entailed labors to which no one man, no one family, was equal. The firstborn sons belonged to God; but instead of the firstborn of all the tribes, the Levites were chosen for service in connection with the sanctuary (Ex. 32:26-29; Num. 3:9, 11-13, 40-41, 45; 8:16-18). It was the duty of the Levites to transport the Tabernacle and its furniture when the camp moved, and when the camp rested, to erect the tent, have the care of it and assist the priests in their varied work (Num. 1:50-53; 3:6-9, 25-37; 4:1-33; I Sam. 6:15; II Sam. 15:24). In David's time a Levite began his apprenticeship at age 20; became eligible for higher offices, such as gatekeeper or musician or administrator, at age 30; and retired at age 50; some might become judges (I Chron., ch. 23). David also divided them into classes, and also into "courses," to serve in rotating shifts (I Chron., chs. 24-26). They were not required to devote their entire time to the sanctuary, or to dwell continuously near it.

Because of their special role in Israel, the sons of Levi did not participate in the distribution of Canaanite territory, but were assigned rights in 35 towns (not counting special rights granted to Levites who were also full-fledged priests), these towns being in Judah, Simeon and Benjamin. See also HIGH PRIEST; NETHINIMS; TABERNACLE; TITHE.

Le·vit′i·cal. The adjective form from Levite: of the Levites or their duties (Heb. 7:11).

lewd. 1. Wicked; lawless; worthless (Acts 17:5). 2. Lustful; unchaste (Ezek. 16:27).

Lib′er·tines. Persons who formed a section of the Jewish community in Jerusalem and who were among the foes of the first martyr, Stephen (Acts 6:9). The word so translated means "Freedmen"—probably Jews who had once been taken prisoners by Pompey or another Roman general, had been bondsmen in Rome and then freed and returned to Palestine.

Lib′y·ans. See LUBIM.

lice. Small insects, hurtful to man, are meant (Ex. 8:16-18; Ps. 105:31), either lice or gnats.

lig′ure. See JACINTH. It is impossible to identify the *ligurius* of the ancients with any known gem.

like′mind′ed. Having the same ideas, plans, tastes, etc.

lil′y of the field. Neither the Hebrew (O.T.) nor Greek (N.T.) word for "lily" was used in the modern scientific sense, but included with the true lily various plants that resembled it. Most authorities regard the red anemone or windflower, 6 inches tall, growing from a bulb, as the famous lily of the field referred to by Jesus. It is one of the most conspicuous and brilliantly colored field flowers. But it is doubtful whether our Lord had any particular lilies in mind. More likely he referred to all the splendid colors and beautiful shapes of the numerous wild flowers included under the general designation of lily.

lil′y work. The carved work in the form of lilies on the tops of the columns on the porch of Solomon's Temple (I Kings 7:19, 22). The large water lily or lotus of the Nile served as a model.

lin′tel. The horizontal crosspiece over a doorway, carrying the weight of the structure above it (Amos 9:1). The blood of the sacrificial lamb was sprinkled on the lintels of the homes of Israelites in Egypt to notify the angel of death to spare the residents. See PASSOVER.

li′on. The lion once roamed over most of Africa and much of s. and w. Asia. In Biblical times it was common in Palestine, but it disappeared there after A.D. 1300. In the O.T. allusion is made to its strength (II Sam. 1:23; Prov. 30:30); its courage (II Sam. 17:10; Prov. 28:1); to its teeth (Joel 1:6); to its crouch-and-spring (Gen. 49:9); its preying on other animals (I Sam. 17:34; Isa. 11:6-7) or upon man (I Kings 13:24; Jer. 2:30); and to its roaring (Job 4:10; Prov. 20:2; I Peter 5:8). A special haunt of lions seems to have been among the trees and bushes fringing the Jordan (Jer. 49:19).

liz'ard. Any of a suborder of reptiles known as Lacertilia. Lizards abound in the Arabian desert, the Sinai Peninsula, the Judean wilderness. They prefer parched, barren regions. One of the common Palestinian lizards is the gecko, that frequents houses, running over walls and ceilings, feeding at night on spiders and insects. This is probably the "ferret" of Lev. 11:30 (KJV). Larger lizards (up to 5 feet long) eat snails, mice, birds' eggs and small birds, small reptiles, etc. Lizards were forbidden as food.

lo'cust. The insect called the migratory locust is 2 inches or more in length. It has 4 wings and 6 legs. On the front 4 legs it walks, while the hindmost pair, much longer than the others, it uses for springing. The mouth has cutting jaws, which nip off leaves and blades of grass. Locusts were clean insects (Lev. 11:21-22). John the Baptist ate them, as do Orientals today. They are slightly roasted, dried in the sun, and salted. Head, wings, legs and intestines are usually re-

LOCUST

moved, and only the fleshy portion eaten. This locust or "grasshopper" is very destructive to vegetation (II Chron. 7:13). The locust is distinguished from the grasshopper by the shortness of its antennae. See also CATERPILLAR; GRASSHOPPER.

lodge. *v.* To dwell in a place temporarily, as for the night (Gen. 24:23). *n.* A shelter or hut (Isa. 1:8).

loft. An upper room or story (Acts 20:9).

log. A unit of liquid and dry measure. See MEASURES.

long'suf'fer·ing. When this word, as a noun or adjective, is applied to God, the idea being conveyed is "slow to anger": God is delaying the infliction of a deserved punishment in the hope that the sinner may come to repent; God is patient. When applied to men, longsuffering is one of the virtues, a fruit of the Spirit (Gal. 5:22), a quality that helps bind the community together (Eph. 4:2).

look'ing glass. A polished surface intended to reflect objects, esp. the face (Ex. 38:8; Job 37:18; II Cor. 3:18; James 1:23); a mirror. Glass had not been invented. Mirrors were made of various alloys of copper, of silver and even of gold, and were round, oval and square and often with handles.

Lord, LORD. In your Bible, when Lord is printed in small letters with only the initial a capital, it is a translation of a Hebrew word meaning "master" (Ex. 23:17; Ps. 114:7) or much more frequently another Hebrew word meaning "my master" or "my lord" (Ex. 4:10; Isa. 40:10). When printed in capital letters, LORD represents the Hebrew 4-consonant word JHWH or YHWH, the most sacred and incommunicable name of God. See JEHOVAH.

Lord of Hosts. See HOSTS, LORD OF.

Lord's day. The day especially associated with the Lord Jesus Christ. The expression is found but once in the N.T., at Rev. 1:10. Various interpretations have been suggested: 1. that John was speaking of the Sabbath, the seventh day of the Jewish week; 2. that "the Lord's day" is the same as "the day of the Lord" mentioned at II Peter 3:10, where it undoubtedly means the day of the Second Advent; 3. that it refers to the first day of the week (Sunday), the day on which the early Christians assembled to worship (I Cor. 16:2). This day was observed to commemorate the Resurrection of Jesus Christ from the dead (John 20:1-19). See also JUDGMENT, DAY OF; SABBATH.

Lord's Pray'er. The prayer which Jesus taught his disciples (Matt. 6:9-13; a shorter version appears in Luke 11:2-4).

Lord's Sup'per. The name given by Paul (I Cor. 11:20) to the meal Jesus shared with his disciples before he was crucified. At this Passover feast, held in an upper room in Jerusalem, Jesus (speaking the words of institution, Matt. 26:26-28) blessed bread and wine and instructed the disciples to eat and drink them in his memory and the memory of his sacrifice (Matt., ch. 26; Mark, ch. 14; Luke, ch. 22). See also LOVE FEAST.

lot. The use of the lot to determine doubtful questions was much in vogue among ancient peoples (Esth. 3:7; Jonah 1:7; Matt. 27:35). Stones or inscribed tablets or the like were put into a vessel and, having been shaken, were drawn forth or cast out. The act was commonly preceded by prayer, and was an appeal to God to decide the matter (Acts 1:23-26). The land of Canaan was divided among the 12 tribes by lot (Josh. 14:2; 18:6); Saul and Jonathan cast lots against each other (I Sam. 14:40-45), etc. See URIM AND THUMMIM.

Lot. Abraham's nephew (Gen. 12:5); his story appears in Gen. 13:5-12; chs. 14; 19 (cf. Luke 17:28-32). See also AMMONITES; MOABITES.

love feast. A social meal (also called *agape* and *feast of charity*), held by members of the original Christian community in connection with the celebration of the Lord's Supper. All distinctions of rank, wealth and culture were ignored at these gatherings as the people shared this feast to promote Christian fellowship and brotherly love. A collection was often taken for the poor and

the needy, esp. the widows. It seems that
originally the sacrament of the Lord's Supper, or Eucharist, took place at the end of
the love feast. But clearly by the middle of
the second century A.D. the two phases, love
feast (social) and Lord's Supper (sacramen-
tal) were sharply distinguished from each
other, if not wholly separated.

lov'ing·kind'ness. Kindness, mercy and loyalty
are all included in this word. Man needs the
lovingkindness and mercy of God; because
God is faithful to the covenant, He is merciful and exercises lovingkindness toward the
sinner. The word is always said of God's
attitude toward man and never used of a
feeling or emotion expressed by man (Ps.
36:10; Isa. 63:7; Jer. 9:24).

low coun'try, low plains. The region of low
hills between the Plain of Philistia along
the Mediterranean and the high central
range of Palestine, from which it is separated by a series of valleys that run n. and s.
from Aijalon to Beer-sheba. It is itself cut
by several wide, fertile valleys that lead
from the Judean ridge to the sea. On the
slopes of the hills in the "low country" the
olive flourishes.

Lu'bim. The Libyans, from whom Pharaoh
Shishak drew part of his army (II Chron.
12:3; 16:8; Nahum 3:9).

Lu'cas. See LUKE.

Lu'ci·fer. Latin name for the planet Venus
when it is the morning star, "Lucifer"
meaning "light-bearer." The application of
the name Lucifer to Satan, the rebel angel
hurled from heaven, first appeared in the
third century A.D. It was based on the incorrect supposition that Luke 10:18 is an ex-
planation of Isa. 14:12. See also Rev. 9:1;
12:7-10.

lu'cre. Money, riches, wealth (I Sam. 8:3).
"Filthy lucre" (I Tim. 3:3, 8; Titus 1:7, 11; I
Peter 5:2) is money or wealth obtained by
dishonest or unworthy methods.

Lud, plural **Lu'dim.** A people classed among the Semites (Gen. 10:22), but believed instead to be the Lydians of Asia Minor, near the Ionian coast. They are mentioned as bowmen in the armies of Egypt and Tyre (Isa. 66:19; Jer. 46:9; Ezek. 27:10; 30:5).

Luke. "Beloved physician" and companion of Paul (Col. 4:14; II Tim. 4:11; Philemon 24). Little is known of his life, and the time and manner of his death are unknown.

lu'na·tic. The word attempts to describe a person afflicted with an intermittent disease affected by the light or the periodic changes of the moon (*luna* = moon). Lunacy is distinguished from possession by demons (Matt. 4:24), yet possession by a demon might give rise to lunacy (compare Matt. 17:15 with Mark 9:17-18; Luke 9:39). A study of these passages has led to the modern medical opinion that epilepsy is what is meant.

lust. *v.* To have an eager, esp. a sinful, desire (Jas. 4:2). *n.* A sensuous desire; a violent or degrading passion (I John 2:16, 17).

lust'y. Full of life and vigor (Judg. 3:29).

lye. In ancient times the cleansing power of lye was well known. It was obtained by burning certain plants and dissolving out the lye from the ashes.

M

Mach·pe'lah. A place e. of Mamre, bought by Abraham from Ephron, a Hittite (Gen. 23:9, 17, 19), for a burial place for Sarah and his family (Gen. 25:9-10; 49:29-33).

mag'ic. See DIVINATION.

Mag·nif'i·cat. A lyric hymn of praise sung by the Virgin Mary, before the birth of Jesus (Luke 1:46-55). It begins, "My soul doth magnify the Lord," which in the Latin text is *Magnificat anima mea Dominum;* hence the name, which does not appear in the

English version. The song appears to be modeled on the Song of Hannah (I Sam. 2:1-10), and to contain echoes of several Psalms.

mag'ni·fy. To praise highly; increase the importance of (Josh. 3:7).

Ma'gog. See GOG.

maid'serv'ant. A handmaid, or occasionally a female slave (Ex. 20:10, 17; Jer. 34:9-10).

mail. See COAT OF MAIL.

Mal'a·chi. A prophet, the writer of the last book of the O.T.

Mal'cham. 1. A Benjaminite (I Chron. 8:9). 2. Same as Milcom (Zeph. 1:5). See MOLECH.

Mal'chus. The high priest's servant whose ear Peter cut off (John 18:10).

mal'e·fac'tor. An evildoer, criminal (Luke 23:32-33; John 18:30).

mal'low. Generally thought to be a perennial shrub common in salt marshes of the Holy Land (Job 30:4).

mam'mon. The Semitic word transliterated into English means "wealth," "money," "property," "riches." Mammon is the personification of wealth as an object of worship and greedy pursuit (Matt. 6:24; Luke 16:9, 11, 13).

Ma·nas'seh. Among others of the name in the O.T.: 1. Son of Joseph (Gen. 41:51), adopted by his grandfather Jacob (48:5); although the firstborn, he was blessed after Ephraim (48:8-20). 2. The tribe that descended from Manasseh. After the Israelites took the lands of kings Sihon and Og, half the tribe of Manasseh joined with the tribes of Reuben and Gad in settling e. of the Jordan, in rich grain country. The other half took their inheritance w. of the river (Josh. 12:4-6; 17:5-10). Ephraim had cities in the lands of Manasseh (16:9) and there were towns of Manasseh in Issachar and Asher (17:11). The borders were not fixed as in modern countries, except between the Southern and Northern Kingdoms. 3. A king of Judah, son and successor of "good king Hezekiah," he ascended the throne when he was only 12 years old. He undid the religious reforms of his father, and as a penalty God left him to his enemies. His story is told in II Kings, ch. 21 and II Chron., ch. 33. See KINGS, TABLE OF.

man'drake. Mandrake plants were supposed to act as a love philter or charm (Gen. 30:14-16). The fruit is small and yellow, and ripens about the time of the wheat harvest.

man'eh. See WEIGHTS.

man'na. The chief food of the Israelites during their 40 years' sojourn in the wilderness. The account of their experience of manna appears in Ex., ch. 16 and Num., ch. 11. No substance is known that answers all the requirements of the O.T. references. Various plants exude a manna-like substance, either spontaneously or when punctured by an insect. A species of the tamarisk tree (*Tamarix gallica mannifera*) which grows in the Sinai Peninsula, produces an exudation that is dirty yellow but that turns white when it falls on stones. It melts in the heat of the sun. It is produced during a period of from 6 to 10 weeks, the height of the season being June. Arabs today use plant manna of different kinds as butter and honey. But taken in large quantities it is purgative.

man of God. A man dedicated to the service of God, said of Moses (Deut. 33:1), of the prophets (I Sam. 9:6; II Kings 4:7), and of messengers of God (Judg. 13:6, 8).

man of sin. The agent of Satan whom Paul expected to appear at the end of the age (II Thess. 2:3-10), before the Second Coming of Christ.

man'sions. Separate lodgings, apartments or rooms (John 14:2).

man'slay'er. A person who has killed another by accident, without premeditation (Num. 35:6, 12).

Mar'a·nath'a. See ANATHEMA MARANATHA.

Mar'cus. See MARK.

Mar'duk. See BEL.

Mark. The surname of John Mark, also called John, companion of Paul and Barnabas (Acts 12:12, 25; 13:5, 13; 15:37); he separates from Paul (15:38-39) but later joins him in Rome (Col. 4:10; Philemon 24) and is commended by him (II Tim. 4:11).

Mars Hill. See AREOPAGUS.

Mar'tha. Sister of Mary and Lazarus; rebuked by Jesus (John 11:1-5, 21; Luke 10:38-42).

Ma'ry. In the N.T., 6 women bear this name:
1. The Virgin Mary, mother of our Lord (Matt. 1:16);
> betrothed to Joseph (Matt. 1:18)
> visited by angel Gabriel (Luke 1:27-38)
> her song of praise (Luke 1:46-55)
> Christ is born (Luke, ch. 2)
> she witnesses miracle at wedding (John 2:1-12)
> desires to speak with Christ (Matt. 12:46; Mark 3:31; Luke 8:19)
> at Crucifixion (Matt. 27:56; John 19:25-27)
> with the apostles in upper room (Acts 1:14).

Many legends exist about Mary's later life, but nothing certain is known. As presented in Scripture, she is simply a beautiful example of a devoted and pious mother. See also BRETHREN OF THE LORD.

2. Mary Magdalene (Matt. 27:56; Mark 15:40; Luke 8:2); sees risen Lord at the tomb (John 20:1, 15, etc.). 3. Mary of Bethany, sister of Martha and Lazarus (Luke 10:39; John 11:1); anoints Jesus (Matt. 26:7-13; John 12:1-8). 4. Mother of John Mark (Acts 12:12). 5. Wife of Cleophas (John 19:25). 6. A Christian of Rome (Rom. 16:6).

Mas'chil, Mas'kil. A Hebrew word appearing in the title of 13 Psalms. Although the meaning is obscure, it may signify a didactic psalm: the "I will instruct" of Ps. 32:8 is another form of the same root word.

ma'trix. The womb (Ex. 13:12, 15; 34:19; Num. 18:15). In each passage the reference is to the firstborn.

Mat'ta·ni'ah. For the most prominent of several O.T. men of this name, see ZEDEKIAH.

Mat'thew. A publican or taxgatherer, called to be one of the 12 apostles; also called Levi (Matt. 9:9; 10:3; Mark 2:14; 3:18; Luke 5:27; 6:16; Acts 1:13); gives feast to Jesus and his followers (Mark 2:15; Luke 5:29).

Mat·thi'as. A disciple chosen by lot to fill Judas Iscariot's place as apostle (Acts 1:15-26).

meal of'fer·ing. See MEAT OFFERING.

Meas'ures.

1. Measures of length:

The unit was the cubit, about 18 inches.

4 fingers = 1 handbreadth
3 handbreadths = 1 span
2 spans = 1 cubit

1 finger therefore equaled about ¾ inch.

In the Greco-Roman period distance was measured by miles (Rome) and stades (Greece). 5,000 Roman feet = 1 Roman mile = about 4,860 English feet. The Roman mile was about .92 of an English mile. The stadium (plural stadia), or the "furlong" in the King James Bible, in the race course at Olympia equaled 630.8 English feet.

2. Measures of capacity:

Our knowledge of ancient measures is not exact, and there were variations in the standards at different periods. The equivalents in U.S. values are to be understood as representing merely approximate values.

For dry substances, the unit was the *ephah*.

For liquids, the unit was the *bath*.

The *ephah* and *bath* were of equal capacity (Ezek. 45:11).

The *ephah* contained 1.05 bushels, U.S.

dry measure.

The *bath* contained 9.8 gallons, U.S. wine measure.

Continuing with liquid measures:

12 logs = 1 hin
6 hins = 1 bath
10 baths = 1 homer, or cor

The log, accordingly, contained .54 quart, and the hin 1.62 gallons, U.S. measure.

Returning to dry measures:

4 logs = 1 cab (or kab)
6 cabs = 1 seah
3 seahs or measures or 10 omers or tenth parts = 1 ephah
10 ephahs = 1 homer

The cab (or kab) was equivalent to 1.86 quarts, U.S. measure.

The seah equaled 1.4 U.S. pecks.

The homer equaled 10.48 U.S. bushels.

meat. Food, esp. solid food, as distinguishable from drink (Ezra 3:7; Matt. 25:35; I Cor. 8:8).

meat of·fer·ing. An offering consisting of meal, cereal or flour, unleavened bread, cakes or wafers, or ears of grain, always with salt and olive oil. It was usually made as a supplemental offering to a burnt offering or a peace offering (I Chron. 21:23), except in the case of offerings by the poverty-stricken (Ezra 7:17; Neh. 13:5). In its earliest forms it also could be an offering of flesh, but it appears soon to have become distinctively limited to nonflesh offerings. It is now usually called a "cereal offering." See also OFFERINGS.

Medes. The country of the Medes lay s. of the Caspian Sea and n.e. of Babylonia. It was high tableland, with excellent pasturage, and noted for its horses. At the height of the power of Assyria, Media was a province or a tribute-paying, vassal kingdom. Under Cyaxares the Medes allied themselves with Nabopolassar and the Babylonians (c. 625

B.C.). They besieged and destroyed Nineveh, terminating the Assyrian empire in 612. The marriage of Nebuchadnezzar, son of Nabopolassar, and a daughter of Cyaxares cemented the alliance and strengthened both countries. However, in 550 the Persians, whose country lay s. and s.e. of Media, successfully rebelled, and Cyrus became king of Media and Persia. The conquerors and conquered, both of an Aryan race, became a dual nation, Medo-Persia. In 330 B.C. Media became a part of Alexander's empire. In Scriptures the Medes appear in Isa. 13:17; 21:2, 9; Jer. 51:11, 28; Dan. 5:31. See ASSYRIA; NEBUCHADNEZZAR.

Mel·chiz′e·dek. Priest-king of Salem (perhaps Jerusalem) who blessed Abraham (Gen. 14:18; Heb. 7:1-4), he was the symbol of the ideal king-priest (Heb. 5:10; cf. Ps. 110:4).

mel′on. Melons of all sorts were cultivated in Egypt (Num. 11:5), including the watermelon.

Mel′zar. The title, not the proper name, of the steward set over Daniel and his companions (Dan. 1:11, 16).

Men′a·hem. A king of Israel who slew another regicide, Shallum, after the latter's reign of 1 month. Later he exacted heavy taxes in order to pay tribute to Assyria (II Kings 15:14-22). See KINGS, TABLE OF.

me′ne, me′ne, tek′el, u·phar′sin. The Aramaic inscription written by a hand on the wall during Belshazzar's feast (Dan. 5:25). The words mean "numbered, numbered, weighed and divided." How this was to be applied Daniel explained in Dan. 5:26-28; he changed the form of the last word to provide a double meaning involving the rival Persian empire. The RSV renders this "mene, mene, tekel and parsin."

Me·phib′o·sheth. 1. Lame son of Jonathan, befriended by David (II Sam. 4:4; ch. 9; 16:1-4; 19:24-30; 21:7). In I Chron. 8:34; 9:40 he is called Merib-baal. 2. Son of Saul, executed by David (II Sam. 21:8, 9).

Mer·cu'ri·us. Mercury; the Greek Hermes, messenger of the gods and god of science and invention. When Paul healed the cripple at Lystra, the people there looked upon him as a god (Acts 14:8-18) and called him Mercurius.

mer'cy. To show mercy is to act in kindness, love, forbearance, pity and compassion—and to be constantly faithful, in God's case, in these attributes. "Steadfast love" is a modern equivalent; "lovingkindness" is another equivalent used often in the King James Bible. In the N.T., God's mercy refers esp. to the fulfillment of His promised kindness (Luke 1:54, 72) through the saving work of Christ (Titus 3:5-6; I Peter 1:3).

mer'cy seat. The covering of the Ark of the Covenant; a slab of specially refined gold, at each end of which stood a cherub fashioned out of the same material and wrought as one piece with it. The cherubim faced each other, but bent downward toward the mercy seat, with outstretched wings, so that a wing of each extended over the mercy seat and met that of the other cherub (Ex. 25:11-22). Beneath these cherubim God's glory was manifested, and there God communed with His people (Ex. 25:17-22; 30:6; Num. 7:89). Once a year, on the great Day of Atonement, the high priest entered the Most Holy Place (Holy of Holies), burned incense and sprinkled the blood of the previously sacrificed young bull on and before the mercy seat. He thereby made atonement for the sins of himself and the nation in the presence of the covenant law, written on tables of stone, kept in the Ark, and of the Lord, who appeared in the cloud of incense upon the mercy seat (Lev. 16:2, 13-17).

Mer'ib-ba'al. See MEPHIBOSHETH.

Me·ro'dach. See BEL.

Me·ro'dach-bal'a·dan. A king of Babylon during the reigns of Sargon and Sennacherib of Assyria (II Chron. 32:31; Isa. 39:1-8). In II

Kings 20:12-19 his name appears as Berodach-baladan.

Me'shach. See ABEDNEGO.

Mes·si'ah. The Hebrew word meant originally any person anointed with the holy oil, as the high priest (Lev. 4:3; 5:16; I Sam. 12:3, 5) or the king (II Sam. 1:14, 16). When God promised David that the throne and scepter should remain in the family forever (II Sam. 7:13), the title acquired a special reference and denoted the representative of the royal line of David (Ps. 2:2; 18:50; 84:9, etc.; Lam. 4:20; Hab. 3:13). David was a king of such heroic aspect that he became the type of Messiah. In Isa. 9:6-7 the child or son will occupy the throne of David; in Isa. 11:1 the Messiah is referred to as a "shoot from the stump of Jesse," David's father. The Messianic idea is further developed in Isa. 9:6-7; Micah 5:2-5; and Jer. 23:5-6. By the beginning of the Christian Era, "Messiah" had become a technical term for the deliverer whose advent was awaited, and it ultimately became a customary designation of Jesus, usually in the form of "Christ."

Me·thu'se·lah. A descendant of Seth noted for his very long life (Gen. 5:21-27).

Mi'cah. Several men in the O.T. bore this name, including: 1. An Ephraimite who made and worshiped idols (Judg., chs. 17; 18); 2. A prophet in the time of Kings Jotham, Ahaz and Hezekiah (Micah 1:1; Jer. 26:18).

Mi'cha·el. A very common name, esp. in the O.T., the best known being the archangel (Jude 9) who appeared to Daniel (ch. 10) and contended with the devil (Rev. 12:7).

Mich'tam, Mik'tam. A word of obscure meaning, appearing in the titles of Psalms 16 and 56-60. It may mean a song, the object of which is to cover or atone for sin; a psalm of expiation or atonement.

Mid'i·an. A son of Abraham by Keturah (Gen. 25:1-2).

Mid'i·an·ites. A desert people, 5 families of whom sprang from Midian (Gen. 25:4). Joseph was bought and carried to Egypt by Midianites (Gen. 37:25, 28, 36), and the father-in-law of Moses was a Midianite (Ex. 3:1). The Midianites joined with the Moabites against Israel, which nearly destroyed them (Num., chs. 22; 25; 31). In the period of the Judges, the Midianites and the Amalekites entered Canaan, with their cattle, their camels and their tents, impoverishing the land; after 7 years they were subdued by Gideon in a battle fought in the Valley of Jezreel, and their leaders put to death (Judg., chs. 6–8).

might'y men. Bold and strong heroes (Gen. 6:4; Josh. 10:2). It is also a term specially applied to foreign mercenaries and warriors of King David for outstanding exploits (II Sam. 10:7; 15:18; 17:8, 10; 23:8–39; I Kings 1:10, 38).

might'y works. The wondrous deeds performed by Jesus (Matt. 11:20, 21, 23; Mark 6:2; Luke 10:13; 19:37).

milch. Milk-giving (Gen. 32:15).

Mil'com. See MOLECH.

mile. The Roman mile was about .92 of an English mile. See MEASURES.

mil·len'ni·um. Any period of 1,000 years. The concept of "the millennium" or reign of 1,000 years is based upon a literal interpretation of Rev., ch. 20. There are various interpretations of the millennium. Premillennialism is the doctrine that the Second Coming precedes and ushers in the millennium. According to postmillennialism, the Second Coming will be after the millennium, which will come as the result of the Christianization of the world, presumably without miraculous intervention. Another interpretation, called amillennialism, denies that an earthly millennium of universal righteousness will either precede or follow the Second Advent of Christ.

mil'let. A cereal, the grain of which is nutritious and palatable food for man (Ezek. 4:9). It is also fed to poultry, and its stalks make excellent fodder for cattle.

mi′na. See WEIGHTS.

minc′ing. Using short steps, or walking with affected daintiness (Isa. 3:16).

min′is•ter. 1. A servant or attendant, esp. a personal servant in a position of honor and trust, as Joshua, a minister of Moses (Ex. 24:13; Josh. 1:1), and John Mark, a minister of Paul and Barnabas (Acts 13:5). 2. A public official, acting as a servant of the people and, therefore, of God (I Kings 10:5; Rom. 13:6). 3. An angel who is a servant and a messenger of God (Ps. 103:21; 104:4). 4. A priest or a Levite who served in the sanctuary and who was thus the agent of God (Ezra 8:17; Jer. 33:21). It is this usage, generally speaking, that has come down to us in the modern conception of the "minister"—one who conducts worship, administers the sacraments, preaches and performs the duties of God's servant. 5. Christ, as the chief minister of God (Mark 10:45), and as an equivalent to the high priest in heaven, at the right hand of God (Heb. 8:2).

min′is•tra′tion. The act of serving as a minister; the performance of God's duties as discovered in the traditional Jewish ritual service (Luke 1:23). The act of ministering, giving out, providing or serving (Acts 6:1; II Cor. 3:7-9; 9:13).

min′is•try. 1. The act of ministering, or serving as a minister of God (Acts 6:4; 12:25). 2. The office, position or function of a minister as a servant of the church, figuratively "the body of Christ" (II Cor. 4:1; Eph. 4:12).

min′strel. A musician, esp. one who played the harp or lyre (I Sam. 16:14-23; II Kings 3:15), and sang as he played. The minstrels hired by Jairus played the flute, the instrument of grief (Mark 5:21-24, 35-43; Luke 8:40-42, 49-56; Matt. 9:18-19, 23-26). Minstrels played at a wide variety of court affairs, banquets and special family occasions.

mint. An herb with a pleasant odor. Its juices are used in medicine and food-seasoning. See Matt. 23:23; Luke 11:42.

mir'a·cle. An extraordinary event effected directly by God and not by the normal operation of the known laws of nature. The term "miracle" is the English form of the Latin word *miraculum*, which meant a wonder or a marvelous thing. In the N.T., miracles are described as signs, wonders, mighty works and powers. In the Biblical sense miracles are events in the external world intended as signs or attestations of the power and love of God, and are directed toward a religious purpose. The miracles of the Bible are almost entirely confined to 4 periods: 1. the Exodus (Ex. 7:9-10; Num. 20:7-11; Josh. 6:8-20); 2. the age of Elijah and Elisha (II Kings 4:2-7; 6:5-7); 3. the Exile (Dan. 3:9-27); 4. the ministry of Jesus, when miracles attested his divine power as the Son of God (Matt. 15:33-39; Mark, chs. 22-24; John 2:1-9). The workings of miracles by the apostles were signs of their apostleship.

Mir'i·am. Sister of Moses and Aaron, a prophetess (Ex. 15:20; cf. 2:4-8; Num. 26:59); for speaking against Moses, she is stricken with leprosy but healed (Num., ch. 12); dies at Kadesh (20:1).

mir'ror. See LOOKING GLASS.

mir'y. Having the nature of a mire, or wet, soggy ground; swampy (Ps. 40:2; Ezek. 47:11).

mite. A small coin, worth about ⅛ cent (Mark 12:42). It was the coin of lowest value in circulation at the time.

mi'tre, mi'ter. The ornamental headdress or turban worn by the high priest (Ex. 28:4; 29:6; 39:28, 31; Lev. 8:9; 16:4). Made of fine linen, it was seamed at the folds; its precise form is not known. Its distinguishing characteristic was a gold plate inscribed with the words "Holy to the Lord," and affixed in front by a blue-colored lace (Ex. 28:36-39).

Mo'ab. The first son of Lot (Gen. 19:37).

Mo'ab·ites. Descendants of Moab, Lot's son, closely related to the Ammonites (Gen. 19:37-38). Originally nomads, by about 1300 B.C. they had settled along the e. coast of the Dead Sea between the land of Edom and the Plain of Heshbon. The Amorites drove them out of the country n. of the Arnon, making that river the boundary between them (Num. 21:13-15, 26-30). Although they refused to let the Israelites pass through their land (Judg. 11:17), Moses was forbidden to attack them (Deut. 2:9, 19); but when the Israelites camped nearby, King Balak of Moab sent for Balaam to curse them (Num., chs. 22-24; Josh. 14:9), thus turning Israel against them forever (Deut. 23:3-6; Num. 13:1). Early in the time of the Judges, Eglon, king of Moab, invaded Canaan, established his capital at Jericho and oppressed the Israelites until his death (Judg. 3:12-30). When David became king of Israel, he exacted tribute from the Moabites, putting many to death (II Sam. 8:2, 12; I Chron. 18:2, 11). Years later the Moabites joined with the Ammonites and Edomites to rebel against Judah and King Jehoshaphat, but the allies fought among themselves and Judah did not need to strike a blow (II Chron. 20:1-30). The prophets denounced the Moabites as types of the enemies of God (Isa., chs. 15; 16; 25:10; Jer. 9:26; 25:21; 27:3; ch. 48; Ezek. 25:8-11; Amos 2:1-2; Zeph. 2:8-11). Nebuchadnezzar overcame the Moabites, and they disappeared as a nation, though still existing as a race (Ezra 9:1). Their chief god was Chemosh (Num. 21:29, etc.). Fragments of the Moabite Stone, discovered in 1868 near the ancient town of Dibon, have been pieced together, and tell of the exploits of a Moabite king of about the 9th century B.C. Ruth was a Moabitess (Ruth 1:22).

mole. This word appears in Lev. 11:30 and Isa. 2:20. The Hebrew word so translated means "burrowing animal." There is no common mole in Palestine, its place being taken by the mole rat. The latter is very common, living underground in small groups. It is not of the same order as the mole, and is a rodent feeding on vegetables, whereas the mole eats insects. The mole rat is also larger, being 8 inches or more long. It has almost sightless eyes but very strong teeth and claws.

Mo'lech. A deity worshiped by the children of Ammon (I Kings 11:7). He was also associated with, or an aspect of, Baal (Jer. 32:35). A detestable feature of Molech's worship was the sacrifice to him of children by burning in a fire. The practice was in vogue early, and the Mosaic law decreed that any Israelite who made or permitted his children to "pass through the fire to Molech" was to be put to death (Lev. 18:21; 20:1-5). Nevertheless, Solomon in his old age erected an altar to Milcom (another name for Molech), being led into this idolatry by his Ammonite wives; and in the following centuries children were occasionally burned to Molech in the Valley of Hinnom (II Chron. 28:3; II Kings 21:6; Isa. 30:33; Jer. 7:31; 19:4-5). Northern Israelites were also sometimes guilty of this hideous rite (II Kings 17:17; Ezek. 23:27). For Josiah's reform in this regard see II Kings 23:10, 13. Molech, Moloch, Milcom and Malcham are one and the same. See also BAAL; GEHENNA; TOPHET.

Mo'loch. See MOLECH.

mol'ten sea. See BRASEN SEA.

mon'ey-chang'ers. Persons whose business was to exchange money, usually of different countries, for a fee. Several currencies, esp. Roman, were in circulation in Palestine in N.T. times, but it was customary for Jews visiting Jerusalem from foreign lands to make freewill offerings (Mark 12:41) in na-

tive Palestinian money; furthermore the
Temple tax had to be paid in specified coinage. The money-changer, therefore, moved
his place of business from the streets into
the Court of the Gentiles, outside the Temple proper, on feast days and days of worship, so as to change money for the worshipers. The fees and profits from these
transactions were limited by law and subject to the scrutiny of public officials. The
position and function of the money-changer
was necessary in the eyes of Temple authorities for the proper maintenance of the
Temple, and for the convenience and protection of all who made pilgrimages to the
Temple. This system and procedure from
time to time was open to abuse, esp. dishon-
esty and avarice incompatible with the
sanctity of the place and the noise of commerce that destroyed the quiet necessary for
worship (John 2:14-16; Matt. 21:12-13).

Mor'de·cai. Cousin of the Persian queen, Esther, his adopted daughter, his story is told
in the book of Esther.

morn'ing sac'ri·fice. See EVENING SACRIFICE.

mor'row. The next following day; tomorrow

mor'tar, mor'ter. 1. A vessel in which grain
and spices are pounded with a pestle (Num.
11:8; Prov. 27:22). 2. A substance used to
bind bricks or stones together in a wall.
Various materials were used: mud or clay
without lime (Isa. 41:25; Nahum 3:14); a
mixture of sand, lime and water, not unlike
modern mortar (Isa. 33:12); and bitumen in
regions where lime or mud is scarce (translated "slime" in Gen. 11:3).

Mo·sa'ic law. The law received by Moses
from God at Sinai and recorded in places
throughout the first 5 books of the Bible.

Mo'ses. The great Hebrew leader;
  born, hidden, found by Pharaoh's daugh-
    ter (Ex. 2:1-10)
  slays Egyptian, flees (Ex. 2:11-25)
  burning bush; 2 signs from God (Ex., chs.
    3; 4)

returns to Egypt; 10 plagues (Ex. 4:18-20;
chs. 5-12:30)

the first Passover (Ex. 12:21-28)

pillars of cloud and fire (Ex., chs. 13; 14;
40:38; Num. 14:14)

divides the sea (Ex. 14:21-31)

quails and manna sent (Ex., ch. 16)

Ten Commandments, other laws (Ex.,
chs. 20-24)

instructions for Tabernacle and priests
(Ex., chs. 25-31)

destroys golden calf and tables of the law
(Ex., ch. 32)

meets God on Mt. Sinai (Ex. 24:12-18;
34:4-35)

numbers people (Ex., chs. 1; 26)

sends spies to Canaan (Num., ch. 13)

intercedes for people (Num., ch. 14)

punishment of Korah (Num., ch. 16)

smites the rock (Num., ch. 20)

makes brasen serpent (Num. 21:9; John
3:14)

appoints Joshua (Num. 27:18-23; Deut.
3:28; 34:9)

defeats Midianites (Num., ch. 21)

shown Promised Land and dies (Num.
27:12-14; Deut. 34:1-12)

appears at Transfiguration (Matt.
17:1-4).

Moses probably lived c. 1300 B.C.

most High. God: a name applied probably to
indicate His supremacy (Ps. 9:2; 21:7; Acts
7:48). Also written "most high God," (Gen.
14:18), "Lord most high" (Ps. 7:17) and
"God most high" (Luke 8:28).

Most Ho'ly Place. With a few exceptions
(Num. 18:10; Ezek. 48:12; Dan. 9:24), these
words mean the innermost room of the
Tabernacle and later of the Temple, in
which were kept the Ark and its tablets, the
cherubim and the mercy seat. In this room
the high priest made yearly atonement for
the people. See also ARK; ATONEMENT;
CHERUB; TABERNACLE.

mote. A small particle of straw, chaff, etc.; a

speck (Matt. 7:3). Used by Jesus in contrast with a log or beam of wood.

moth. An insect proverbial for its destruction of clothing (Job 13:28; Matt. 6:19; James 5:2). Its larva feeds upon wool (Isa. 51:8), and out of the same substance builds itself a house or case, in which it lives (Job 27:18).

mul'ber-ry tree. The black (or red) mulberry, common in Palestine. A cooling drink is made from its berries, the juice being sweetened with honey and flavored with spices. The white mulberry, on whose leaves the silkworm feeds, was not introduced into Palestine until post-biblical times. The tree mentioned in II Sam. 5:23 of the KJV is called "balsam" in the RSV. See also SYCAMINE TREE.

mule. The mule is a hybrid produced by breeding a male donkey with a female horse. Mules eat grass (I Kings 18:5). They are often mentioned with horses (Ps. 32:9) and were much used for riding and for carrying burdens (II Sam. 13:29; II Kings 5:17; I Chron. 12:40). They are not mentioned before the time of David, but were in common use thereafter.

mus'tard. A garden herb (Luke 13:19), which in comparison with other herbs becomes a "great tree" from the tiniest of seeds (Matt. 13:32; Mark 4:32). It also grows wild, attaining the height of a horse and rider. The mustard seed was referred to in proverbs by Jews, as it was by Jesus (Matt. 17:20; Luke 17:6).

Muth-lab'ben. No one knows what this means (Ps. 9). It may be the opening words ("death of the son") to a well-known song to the tune of which this psalm was to be sung.

myrrh. A fragrant substance, obtained in a gummy form from the bark of a tree grown in Arabia. It was an ingredient in the oil of anointing (Ex. 30:23), and beds and garments were perfumed with it (Ps. 45:8; Prov. 7:17; S. of Sol. 3:6). The Magi

brought it from the East to the infant Jesus
(Matt. 2:11). At the Crucifixion it was offered to him in wine, probably to deaden
pain (Mark 15:23). It was an ingredient in
the spices compounded for anointing his
body (John 19:39).

myr'tle. A large evergreen shrub, with beautiful white flowers, often thought of as a tree,

MYRTLE

up to 20 feet high. It grew in the mountains
near Jerusalem. See Neh. 8:15; Isa. 41:19;
55:13; Zech. 1:8-11.

N

Na'a·man. Commander of Ben-hadad's army,
he goes to Elisha and is healed of leprosy;
though renouncing idolatry, he is permitted
to continue serving his master (II Kings, ch.
5; cf. Luke 4:27).

Nab'o·po·las'sar. Founder of the Chaldean
dynasty and king of Babylon (626-605 B.C.);
father of Nebuchadnezzar. Allied with Cyaxares, king of the Medes, Nabopolassar ut-
terly destroyed Nineveh, capital of Assyria
(612 B.C.). See ASSYRIA.

Na'both. Owner of the vineyard coveted by
Ahab, he is falsely accused by Jezebel and

slain (I Kings, ch. 21); avenged by Jehu (II Kings 9:21-26).

Na'dab. 1. Aaron's oldest son, who offered "strange fire" and died (Ex. 6:23; Lev. 10:1, 2; Num. 26:61). 2. King of Israel, son of Jeroboam I; he reigned for less than 2 years, when he was murdered by Baasha, thus fulfilling the Lord's threats against Jeroboam and his house (I Kings 14:20). See KINGS, TABLE OF.

Na'hum. A poet and prophet of Elkosh who foretold the destruction of Nineveh.

Na'o·mi. Mother-in-law of Ruth (Ruth, chs. 1-4).

Naph'ta·li. 1. Sixth son of Jacob, second by Bilhah (Gen. 30:8; 35:25). 2. The tribe descended from him, divided into the families of his 4 sons (46:24). The Naphtalites often answered the call to arms (e.g. Judg. 4:6; 6:35; I Chron. 12:34), but their land, a narrow mountainous strip on the w. coast of the Sea of Galilee (Josh. 19:32-39), was ravaged by Ben-hadad and later by Tiglath-pileser (I Kings 15:20; II Kings 15:29; cf. Isa. 9:1-7). In Matt. 4:13, 15, the land is called Nephthalim; in Rev. 7:6, Nepthalim.

Na'than. Among others mentioned in the Bible: 1. A prophet and historian in the time of David and Solomon (II Sam., ch. 7; I Chron. 29:29; II Chron. 9:29); rebukes David for his sin (12:1-15; see also PARABLE); questions the reign of Adonijah and anoints Solomon king (I Kings 1:8-46). 2. A son of David (II Sam. 5:14; Zech. 12:12; Luke 3:31).

Na·than'a·el. Not mentioned in the first 3 gospels, he is probably the same person as Bartholomew, one of the 12; he acknowledges Jesus as the Son of God (John 1:45-51) and sees him after the Resurrection (21:1-14). See also BARTHOLOMEW.

nat'u·ral force. Physical vigor (Deut. 34:7).

naught. In the KJV, this is used to mean wicked, bad (Prov. 20:14) or unfit for consumption (II Kings 2:19). In the RSV (Ezek. 12:22; Hab. 2:13), it implies "nothing." See also NOUGHT.

Naz'a•rene. 1. One born or resident in Nazareth (Matt. 2:23). 2. An adherent of the religion founded by Jesus; a Christian. It is used contemptuously in Acts 24:5.

Naz'a•rite. An Israelite, male or female, who individually and voluntarily, or as the result of the promise of a parent (Judg. 13:3-5), assumed certain religious vows, specifically abstaining from wine and any strong drink, not cutting the hair, and avoiding contact with dead bodies, even of near relatives. The period of consecration was either for a lifetime or for a limited period decided upon by the Nazarite initiate (Num. 6:2-21). There is no evidence that the Nazarites were ever organized into a monastic order of any sort. Samson (Judg. 13:4-5), Samuel (I Sam. 1:11, 28) and John the Baptist (Luke 1:15) were Nazarites; the prophetess Anna may have been one (Luke 2:36-37).

Ne'bo. The Babylonian god of writing and speech, the arts and sciences. He was regarded as the son of Marduk. His name appears as an element in the names of 3 Babylonian kings, Nabopolassar, Nebuchadnezzar and Nabonidus.

Neb'u•chad•nez'zar, Neb'u•chad•rez'zar. A king of Babylon who plundered and destroyed Jerusalem in 597 and 586 B.C., carrying away thousands of captives and beginning the Exile ended by Cyrus in 538. Jeremiah and Ezekiel prophesied during his reign, and he made Daniel ruler of Babylon. See II Kings, chs. 24-25; Jer., chs. 20-34; 37-39; Dan., chs. 1-4; BABYLONIANS; CAPTIVITY; MEDES.

Neb'u•zar•a'dan. A captain of Nebuchadnezzar; burns and plunders Jerusalem and carries away captives (II Kings 25:8-21; Jer. 52:12-30) but shows kindness to Jeremiah (39:9-40:6).

nec'ro•man'cer. A person who claims to foretell the future or explain mysteries of the
present through alleged communication
with the spirit of the dead (Deut. 18:11). See
SORCERER.

Ne'he•mi'ah. A Jew of the captivity who was
cupbearer to the Persian King Artaxerxes,
he returned to Jerusalem to rebuild the
walls and became governor of Judah.

Ne•hush'tan. The name of the serpent made of
bronze that Hezekiah destroyed. See BRA-
SEN SERPENT.

neigh. To make loud, harsh sounds, like a
horse; used figuratively by Jeremiah (5:8;
8:16; 13:27) for strong, reckless and immoral urges of people.

Neph'tha•lim, Nep'tha•lim. See NAPHTALI.

Ner'gal. The Babylonian god of the sun in its
burning, destructive aspect, also of war and
disasters (II Kings 17:30).

neth'er. Lower; said of 2 millstones between
which grain was ground (Deut. 24:6; Job
41:24), and of the lower parts of the earth,
i.e., "hell" (Ezek. 31:14, 18).

neth'er•most. Lowest, farthest down (I Kings
6:6).

Neth'i•nims. The word means "the given
ones"—i.e., to service in the Temple. These
were the Temple servants or slaves who
performed the most menial duties of the
sanctuary, such as chopping wood, drawing
water, sharpening knives, cleaning sacrificial blood from the altar, etc. Originally
they were probably prisoners of war given
as slaves into the service of the Levites, who
directed their labors.

net'tle. The Roman or pill nettle is found everywhere in Palestine (Isa. 34:13; Hos. 9:6).
It is an annual wild plant, noted for its un-
pleasant sting when touched. It springs up
wherever land is neglected (Prov. 24:31;
Zeph. 2:9).

net'work. 1. A bronze grating for the altar of
burnt offering (Ex. 27:4; 38:4). 2. Bronze
latticed work on the pillars of Solomon's

Temple (I Kings 7:18, 41-42).

new birth. The complete change in spiritual condition that takes place when a person by faith in Christ responds to divine grace and enters into fellowship with God through Christ. This transformation is the work of the Holy Spirit, who imparts to the sinner the gift of faith and the power of a new spiritual life (John 3:3). Through faith in Christ man dies to sin and rises to a new life (Rom. 6:1-11; II Cor. 5:17; Gal. 2:20).

new crea'ture. A person who has experienced a new birth (II Cor. 5:17).

new wine. Probably freshly made wine, or must, that is fermenting in wineskins (Matt. 9:17; Mark 2:22); the suggestion is that the action of fermentation will split an old wineskin.

Nib'haz. An idol, one of two worshiped by the Arvites, a tribe brought with others from Assyria to colonize Samaria after the captivity of the Northern Kingdom (II Kings 17:31).

Nic'o·de'mus. A Pharisee convinced by Jesus (John 3:1-21); takes his part against the Sanhedrin (7:50-51); helps at Jesus' burial (19:39).

Nic'o·la'i·tans. A party or sect of the churches of Ephesus and Pergamum whose practice and doctrine are severely censured. They were associated with some who held the teaching of Balaam, that Christians were free to eat things offered to idols and to commit the excesses of heathenism (Rev. 2:6, 14-15), contrary to the command issued by the apostolic council held at Jerusalem in A.D. 50 (Acts 15:29). That the Nicolaus of Acts 6:5 was the person who started the sect of Nicolaitans is a theory without proof.

nigh. Near, close.

night. The period of darkness (Gen. 1:5). See also NIGHT WATCHES.

night hag. See OWL.

night watch'es. The periods into which the

night was divided. Each period represented the segment of time that a guard or sentinel was on duty. The Hebrews divided the night into 3 such watches—sunset to 10; 10 to 2; 2 to sunrise. The Romans, to improve the alertness of the soldier-watchmen, increased the periods to 4: sunset to 9 (called "evening"); 9 to midnight ("midnight"); midnight to 3 ("cockcrowing") and 3 to sunrise ("morning"). This latter division was in use in N.T. times (Mark 6:48; Luke 12:38).

Nim'rod. A ruler and "mighty hunter" (Gen. 10:8-10; Micah 5:6).

Nis'roch. A god worshiped by Sennacherib of Assyria. It was in the temple of Nisroch that he was assassinated (II Kings 19:37; Isa. 37:38). The name has not been identified; possibly it may be the same as Nusku, the fire god.

ni'tre. Potassium carbonate or sodium carbonate, but deposits of the latter are not known in Palestine. It is an alkali (Prov. 25:20) and in solution was used in washing clothes (Jer. 2:22). To put vinegar on nitre would destroy its usefulness as a cleanser.

No'ah. Son of Lamech (Gen. 5:28-29), also called Noe (Matt. 25:37-38);
3 sons of (Gen. 5:32; 6:10)
commanded to build ark (Gen. 6:14-22)
enters ark, rain begins (Gen., ch. 7)
waters abate, all go forth (Gen., ch. 8)
covenant of the rainbow (Gen. 9:8-17)
his drunkenness mocked by Ham, he curses him, blesses Shem and Japheth (Gen. 9:22-27)
dies (Gen. 9:28-29).
As Adam had been blessed, so was Noah blessed at the beginning of a new world (Gen. 9:1; cf. 1:28); his faith was commended in Heb. 11:7, and there are other references to him in the N.T.

no'ble. A person of high birth, rank, title or exalted position because of illustrious deeds, skills or moral quality (Judg. 5:13;

Ezra 4:10; Esth. 6:9; Prov. 17:26; Isa. 32:5;
Acts 17:11; I Cor. 1:26).

noon'day, noon'tide. Noon, midday.

North'ern King'dom. See ISRAEL (3); SOLO-
MON.

nought. Worthless, or worthlessness; nothing.
See also NAUGHT.

nur'ture. An environment of education and
training (Eph. 6:4).

O

oak. A tree of considerable size and great
strength in Palestine as in the U.S. Several
Hebrew words in the O.T. are translated
"oak," except where two such words appear in one sentence, where "teil tree" or
"elm" is substituted for one. "Terebinth" (a
small European tree) may be the correct
translation of one of these Hebrew words
(Isa. 6:13; Hos. 4:13). Several oak varieties
are common in Palestine and thrive in Bashan, Galilee, Gilead and Carmel.

oath. An appeal to God to witness one's statement of intention to speak the truth, keep a
promise, remain faithful, carry out an
agreement, etc. An oath made a promise
doubly binding. Oaths were made in prom-
ising to do or not to do something specific
(Gen. 14:22); in pledging allegiance to
someone of superior rank, as a king (I
Kings 18:10); in threatening or avowing
that something will take place (I Sam.
14:24); as a public testimonial in cases concerning the damage of another's property
(Ex. 22:11) or the suspected theft of another's possessions; the alleged unfaithfulness
of a wife (Num. 5:19), etc. Certain phrases
usually accompanied the making of an
oath, such as "Behold, the Lord be between
thee and me forever" (I Sam. 20:23) or "As
the Lord liveth" (I Sam. 14:39), and it was
common to perform a gesture such as lifting
the hand to God (Gen. 14:22). On more se-
rious occasions one might place the hand

under the thigh of the person to whom the promise was made (Gen. 24:2; 47:29), or cut a sacrificial animal in half and walk between the halves (Jer. 34:18). Any man swearing an oath or making a vow to God was required to carry out his promise: for the dire consequences of rash oaths, see Jephthah (Judg. 11:30-40) and Herod the tetrarch (Matt. 14:3-12). Anyone who swore falsely by the name of God profaned the divine name (Lev. 6:3; 19:12). Jesus condemned the use of oaths, urging a simple direct "yes" or "no" statement (Matt. 5:33-37). See also vow.

O'ba·di'ah. This is a common name in the O.T. Most prominent are: 1. A prophet of Judah. 2. The governor of Ahab's palace, who hid 100 prophets of the Lord from Jezebel (I Kings 18:3-16).

O'bed-e'dom. Among others of this name, a man who sheltered the Ark for David (II Sam. 6:10-12; I Chron. 13:13-14; 15:25). See ARK OF THE COVENANT.

o·bei'sance. A gesture in token of respect or submission; a bow or curtsey (Gen. 37:7).

ob·la'tion. An offering; a sacrifice.

ob·serv'er of times. A soothsayer; a person who attempts to foretell the future by observations and interpretations of natural events, as the rustling of leaves, the buzz of insects, changing cloud formations, etc. (Deut. 18:10, 14). See also DIVINATION.

of'fer·ings. In the biblical sense of the term, sacrifice may be regarded as an external expression of man's response to the grace of God, and it may be considered as a visible form of prayer offered to God. An offering was a gift offered to God as an attempt by the giver to bring himself into a personal relationship with God by cleansing himself of sin. The gifts, or offerings, have been named in accordance with the type of thing given (drink, meat or meal offering), the manner in which they were given (burnt offering, incense offering), the state of mind of the worshiper (jealousy offering, peace offering) and the time of day at which the offering was presented (morning offering, evening offering). Offerings were made by man as an acknowledgment of his sinfulness and basic frailty, and the recognition that he could not enter into a covenant with God without obedience and faith. The laws governing sacrificial offerings are discussed in Leviticus. The practice of offering sacrifices seems to have fallen into a subordinate position, if not quite into disuse, in N.T. times. Offerings found no part in the ministry of Jesus, and his disciples placed no emphasis on them in their teachings. The sacrificial offering of Jesus was that of himself, an offering greater than all others (Heb. 7:27; chs. 9; 10). See also GUILT OFFERING; SIN OFFERING.

off-scour'ing. Something scoured off; rubbish; refuse; filth (Lam. 3:45; I Cor. 4:13).

Og. A king of the Amorites of Bashan, of huge stature (Deut. 3:1-11), he was defeated by the Israelites and his territory given to the half-tribe of Manasseh (3:13).

oil. The oil used by ancient Hebrews was chiefly olive oil. Oil was so important that "oil and wine" are frequently linked with grain as among the chief harvest products (Num. 18:12; Deut. 7:13; Neh. 10:39).

oil, ol'ive. Olive oil, obtained from olives; a household mainstay, used in cooking, lamps, ointments, etc.

oil tree. Some believe that the reference in Isa. 41:19 (KJV) is to the oleaster, a shrub abundant in Palestine, yielding an oil much inferior to olive oil. The same Hebrew words are translated "pine branches" in Neh. 8:15 and "olive tree" in I Kings 6:23. The RSV translators believed that the olive tree or olive wood was meant in all cases.

oint'ment. See PERFUME.

old wives' fa'ble. A silly story or superstitious belief such as might be passed around by gossipy old women (I Tim. 4:7).

ol'ive. A tree widely cultivated in Palestine in orchards (Ex. 23:11; Judg. 15:5; I Sam. 8:14). The olive was the most valuable tree of ancient Palestine, providing edible fruit, oil for cooking, medicinal purposes and lamps, and timber for cabinet-making, doors and other interior trim. See OIL TREE. The olive tree of Palestine is the common European variety, with leathery evergreen leaves of a dusty color. Constant cultivation, esp. pruning and grafting onto the wild olive stock is required, else the tree deteriorates. The olive was a symbol of prosperity and divine blessing, of beauty and strength (Ps. 52:8; Jer. 11:16; Hos. 14:6). An olive branch is now an emblem of peace.

o·me'ga. See ALPHA AND OMEGA.

o'mer. A unit of dry measure. See MEASURES.

Om'ri. Among others of this name, commander of the army of King Elah of Israel. Omri, upon the murder of the king by Zimri, was proclaimed king by the army. He forced Zimri's suicide in one week, but 5 more years were required to eliminate another competitor for the throne, Tibni. Omri built a new capital, Samaria, and made an impression on the Moabites and Assyrians, who recorded his name in their historical records. However, he followed the idolatries of Jeroboam. His son and successor was Ahab. A strong king, he is but briefly mentioned in the Bible (I Kings 16:23-28). See KINGS, TABLE OF.

On. See KORAH.

O·nes'i·mus. A bearer of letters to the Colossians and Philemon (Col. 4:9; Philemon).

On'e·siph'o·rus. An Ephesian who was kind to the imprisoned Paul (II Tim. 1:16-18; 4:19).

on'y·cha. One of the ingredients in a perfume made for the service of the Tabernacle (Ex. 30:34). It is believed to have been the operculum (lid) of a shell mollusk which when burned gave out a perfume.

on'yx. A precious stone, probably the same variety of agate still known by this name, with alternate layers of color, often black and white (Ex. 28:20; 39:13; Ezek. 28:13).

or'a·cle. Divine announcement; prophetic declaration; oracular saying. In the English Bible the word is used in several different ways: 1. The inner sanctuary or Holy of Holies in the Temple (I Kings 6:16, 19–21, 23, 31; Ps. 28:2). 2. The word of God (II Sam. 16:23). 3. All the recorded utterances of God in the O.T. 4. In the N.T., oracle denotes a revealed word or command of God given at Sinai or recorded in Scripture (Acts 7:38; Rom. 3:2). Oracles are spoken under the clear consciousness of divine inspiration (I Peter 4:11). See also INSPIRATION.

or'gan. A wind instrument of ancient origin (Gen. 4:21) which was used in merrymaking (Job 21:12; 30:31) and was deemed worthy of employment in the praise of God (Ps. 150:4). It apparently was a kind of shrill pipe or flute.

O·ri'on. A constellation (Job 9:9; 38:31; Amos 5:8). Orion in classical mythology is represented as a man of great strength, a worker in iron, and a hunter. He was placed in the heavens by the Roman goddess Diana.

Or'nan. See ARAUNAH.

Os·nap'par. See ASHURBANIPAL.

os'pray, os'prey. A dark brown eagle, fre-

OSPREY

quenting seacoasts and living on fish. In Palestine it occurs along the Mediterranean, esp. near the mouth of the Kishon River. It was an "unclean" bird (Lev. 11:13; Deut. 14:12).

os'si·frage. The Hebrew word so translated means "breaker"; the English name means "bone-breaker." The lammergeier (bearded eagle) of the Dead Sea and Sinai Peninsula regions is 3½ feet high and has a 9-foot wingspread; it feeds on bones, snakes and tortoises, which it breaks by taking them up to a great height and dropping them on rocks. It was an "unclean" bird (Lev. 11:13; Deut. 14:12).

os'trich. A large bird, 6-8 feet tall, unable to fly. To compensate, it is a powerful, fleet runner, able to outrun a horse. It is described poetically in Job 39:13-18. The bird prepares its nest by rolling in the sand and scooping out a hole 6 feet in diameter. An egg is laid every other day until there are 10 or 12 in the nest. Each egg weighs about 3 pounds. The male sits on the eggs for about 20 hours a day, the hen 4 hours. The male takes charge of the young brood.

out'most. Farthest outward; uttermost (Ex. 26:10).

o'ver·se'er. One who watches over and directs the work of others; a steward over the household (Gen. 39:4); a foreman (II Chron. 2:18); a choirmaster (Neh. 12:42); a leader of others (Prov. 6:7); a bishop (Acts 20:28).

owl. 1. Probably the little owl is intended in most occurrences of "owl," for it is found throughout Palestine, in olive groves as well as in rocky areas and thickets and among ruins. It often perches on highway milestones in full daylight. It is regarded by Arabs as a bird of good luck. The Hebrews considered it "unclean" (Lev. 11:17; Deut. 14:16). 2. The screech or barn owl (Isa. 34:14; RSV, "night hag") that frequents ruins. See also OWL, GREAT.

owl, great. Probably the Egyptian eagle owl that lives in caves and among ruins (Isa. 34:11) and is common about Petra and Beer-sheba. It was ceremonially "unclean" (Lev. 11:17; Deut. 14:16).

ox. The male of the species *Bos taurus,* though "ox" frequently means any animal of the kind, male or female (Ex. 20:17). The plural form, "oxen," is often a synonym for "cattle." The ox was used for plowing (I Kings 19:19), for dragging carts or wagons (Num. 7:3; II Sam. 6:6), and for treading out grain (Deut. 25:4). Oxen were eaten (I Kings 1:25; Matt. 22:4), and were much used in sacrifice, esp. in connection with burnt offerings (Num. 7:87–88; II Sam. 24:22; II Chron. 5:6; 7:5). A yoke of oxen was a pair fastened together to pull a plow, a cart, etc.

ox, wild. In Deut. 14:5 of the KJV appears a Hebrew word translated "wild ox," but which is more likely the antelope. See also UNICORN.

P

pad'dle. A tool to be used for digging a hole to bury one's excrement (Deut. 23:13).

paint. Painting the eyebrow, the eyelash and around the eye, prolonging the outer corner, was common in Egypt and Mesopotamia, but frowned upon among the Hebrews, to whom it suggested harlotry (Jer. 4:30). Antimony, burned to blackness and pulverized, was one mineral used, lead was another. In Egypt kohl, a powder obtained from almond shells, was used. In each case the powder was kept in small jars, moistened into a paste with oil, and applied with a blunt-ended stick. Oriental women also painted their finger- and toenails a reddish orange color obtained from the henna plant.

pal'let. A small bed, apparently often used to carry the sick (Mark 6:55, RSV).

palm. The palm tree in Scripture almost always means the date palm, which grows 60-80 feet high, having a single upright trunk of uniform thickness through its entire length and terminating in a circle of great feathery leaves, 4-6 feet long, perennially green. The leaves are used for covering roofs and sides of houses and for mats and baskets. The fruit, produced annually in numerous clusters (S. of Sol. 7:7-8), constitutes its chief value. Its great leaves were used as tokens of victory and peace (John 12:13).

palm'er·worm. When the King James Bible was translated, "palmerworm" meant a sort of hairy caterpillar that has no fixed abode but wanders like a "palmer" or pilgrim from place to place. The Hebrew word probably meant instead a kind of locust, or a locust in a certain stage of growth. Anyway, it devoured vines, fig trees, olive trees and gardens generally (Joel 1:4; 2:25; Amos 4:9).

pal'sy. A partial or total loss of feeling and voluntary mobility, or both, in one or more parts of the body (Mark 2:3, 9-12; Acts 9:33-35). It is produced by damage to the brain or injury to the spinal cord or particular nerves. Palsy was once a popular designation for various sorts of paralysis that can be more specifically diagnosed today.

pan'nag. A product of Palestine purchased by merchants of Tyre (Ezek. 27:17). It is not a place name. It may mean "early figs," or perhaps it is a confection.

pa'per reed. The papyrus plant (Isa. 19:7). See BULRUSH.

pa·py'rus. See BULRUSH.

par'a·ble. 1. A short, simple story which forcefully illustrates a single idea. In a parable, a moral lesson or religious truth is illustrated by an analogy derived from common experience in life. The comparison may be expressed, as by the word "like," or it may be only implied. One advantage of the use of a parable is that it is easily remembered, much more so than a plain, didactic statement of the same truth. Also a person who may be the intended target of the parable will become engaged by the story and continue to listen until he discovers who is being condemned. This was done on one O.T. occasion with great skill by the prophet Nathan (II Sam. 12:1-14), as well as many times by Jesus in the N.T. Some other O.T. parables are found in Judg. 9:8-20; II Sam. 14:4-20; I Kings 20:35-42; Isa. 5:1-7. An important part of our Lord's teaching was by means of parables; and when Scripture parables are referred to, generally those of Jesus are meant. He used the parabolic form of teaching at every period of his public ministry (Mark 3:23; Luke 6:39; 7:40-50). 2. An obscure or perplexing saying (Ps. 49:4; 78:2). 3. An intricate lecture with much poetic and ornamental speech (Job 27:1).

par′a·dise. A word of Persian origin, meaning "enclosure" or "wooded park." The garden into which Adam and Eve were placed has been called paradise, by which is meant a place of great beauty, perfection and spiritual bliss. Nowhere in the O.T. does paradise refer to a place of future reward. The word occurs only 3 times in the N.T. (Luke 23:43; II Cor. 12:4; Rev. 2:7), and in each case it means or denotes heaven. Paul attempts to identify paradise with the third heaven into which he had been caught up in a vision (II Cor. 12:4). Traditionally, paradise has been thought of as the heavenly abode of the righteous.

Par′bar. The Hebrew form of a Persian word which in other inscriptions means anteroom or vestibule. Parbar was a part of the courtyard on the w. side of the Temple.

parched corn. Better, parched grain; grains of wheat roasted in a pan (Ruth 2:14; I Sam. 25:18).

parch'ment. The skin of sheep or goats prepared for use as a writing material or other
purposes. The skin is first soaked in lime, to
remove the hair, then shaved, washed,
dried, stretched and smoothed. Papyrus was
the common writing material in O.T. times,
but sacred and more important books were
written on parchment after about 200 B.C.,
and potsherds were always in use for short
personal messages, for they were not expensive like papyrus and parchment. Paul refers to parchments of his in II Tim. 4:13.

par'lour, par'lor. 1. An upper room in a
house, a roof chamber (Judg. 3:20, 23). 2. A
chamber in the Temple, near the sanctuary
(I Sam. 9:22; I Chron. 28:11).

par'tridge. A wild bird which was hunted in
the mountains of Palestine (I Sam. 26:20).
There are 2 species in Palestine: the desert
or Hey's sand partridge, restricted to the
lower Jordan Valley; and the larger chukar
partridge, abundant in all the hilly regions.

pas'chal lamb. See PASSOVER.

Pass'o·ver. The festival commemorating the
deliverance of the Hebrews from slavery in
Egypt and the establishment of Israel as a
nation of people redeemed and adopted by
God. The Passover draws its name from the
memory that God passed over the Hebrew
houses in Egypt to spare them when He
smote the firstborn of the Egyptians on the
eve of the Exodus: the lintels of the houses
of the Hebrews had been marked with the
blood of the paschal lamb (Ex., ch. 12).
Passover is considered the most important
Hebrew festival, and it is the first of 3 annual festivals at which all men were required to appear at the sanctuary (Ex.
12:43; Deut. 16:1). It is also known as the
Feast of Unleavened Bread: the Hebrew
people had no leaven in their houses the
night of the Passover in Egypt, and consequently the dough they seized in their hurried flight was unleavened (Ex. 12:8, 34, 39).
Henceforth unleavened bread was a re-

minder of their flight, their hardships in the desert and of God's providence. The festival began on the 14th day of Abib, at evening, that is, at the start of the 15th day, with a sacrificial meal, consisting of a lamb or kid slain toward sunset, the "paschal lamb." Every step of the meal is full of symbolism for Jews. The festival period lasts until the 21st of the month. To Christians, Christ is our paschal lamb (I Cor. 5:7), without blemish (cf. Ex. 12:5 with I Peter 1:18-19). See also TABERNACLES, FEAST OF; WEEKS, FEAST OF.

pas'tor. 1. A shepherd, used figuratively, esp. by Jeremiah (2:8; 3:15; 17:16), for a minister whose duty it is to look after his flock. 2. A Christian minister (Eph. 4:11).

Pas·tor'al E·pis'tles. See EPISTLES.

pate. The crown of the head (Ps. 7:16).

pa'tri·arch. The father or head of a family, tribe or race; esp. Abraham, Isaac, Jacob and Jacob's 12 sons. The name was first given in Acts 7:8-9. In the patriarchal system the government of a clan is regarded as the paternal right, starting from the progenitor of the tribe and descending from him to the firstborn son, and so on. The head of each separate family into which the increasing tribe expands, exercises a similar government within his own limited sphere.

Paul. The great apostle to the Gentiles, born in Tarsus, the chief city of Cilicia (Acts 9:11; 21:39; 22:3). His Jewish name was Saul, and he is so called in Acts, up to ch. 13:9. Possibly Saul took his second name from the converted proconsul, Sergius Paulus, or perhaps he had been given both names by his parents, who were strict Jews and sent their young son to Jerusalem to be educated (Acts 22:3). Like other Jewish boys he was taught a trade, in his case the manufacture of tents such as were used by travelers (Acts 18:3). In Jerusalem he was instructed "according to the strict manners of the law of our fathers." He had for his teachers one of the most distinguished rabbis of the day, Gamaliel (Acts 5:34-39). The future apostle grew into manhood an ardent Pharisee with a hatred for the Christian sect. He first appears in Christian history as the man at whose feet the witnesses who stoned Stephen laid their garments (Acts 7:58). Most of what we know about the rest of Paul's history is recorded in the Acts:

as a persecutor (Acts 7:58; 8:1; 9:1)

his conversion (Acts 9:3)

first missionary journey undertaken (Acts 13:1-3)

second journey undertaken (Acts 15:36-41)

third journey undertaken (Acts 18:23)

last journey to Jerusalem (Acts 20:4)

falsely charged (Acts 21:27-29)

Paul before the Sanhedrin (Acts 23:1-10)

a prisoner in Caesarea (Acts 23:10, 35)

the hearing before Felix (Acts, ch. 24)

the hearing before Festus (Acts, ch. 25)

his defense before Agrippa (Acts, ch. 26)

the journey to Rome (Acts, ch. 27; 28:1-16)

imprisonment in Rome (Acts 28:17-21). Paul's letters written from Rome in the approximate period A.D. 61-63 (Colossians, Philemon, Ephesians, Philippians) show that he had many friends in Rome who had access to him and worked with him there and as messengers to churches throughout the Roman Empire. Paul was an "ambassador in chains" (Eph. 6:20). Although the Acts leaves Paul a prisoner at Rome, there is reason to believe that he was released after 2 years (Acts 28:30) and resumed his missionary journeys. Nero's persecution of the Christians had not yet begun; in the view of Roman law the Christians were as yet only a sect of the Jews, whose liberty to maintain their religion was fully recognized. Paul probably therefore was acquitted. His subsequent movements can only be inferred, however, from allusions in the

Letters to Timothy and Titus, and from tradition: there are suggestions that he jour-
neyed to Asia, Macedonia and Spain. In
A.D. 64 Nero began his persecution of the
Christians. Perhaps, in A.D. 67 or 68, Paul
was arrested at some point in his journeys
as a leader of the now-outlawed sect and
sent to Rome for trial. Tradition relates that
the apostle was beheaded, as became a Roman citizen, on the Ostian Way. Much of
this reconstruction, however, is uncertain.

pa·vil'ion. 1. A large booth or tentlike structure with a protective covering (I Kings
20:12). 2. A place where God will shelter
from evil those who fear Him (Ps. 27:5;
31:20). 3. In Ps. 18:11 it is the clouds that
are the pavilion of God.

peace of'fer·ing. Three kinds may be distinguished: the thank offering, in recognition
of unmerited and unexpected blessings; the
votive offering, in payment of a vow; and
the freewill offering, a spontaneous expression of irrepressible love for God (Lev., ch.
3). Any unblemished animal authorized for
sacrifice might be used, but no bird of either
sex. See also OFFERINGS.

pea'cock. Peacocks, along with ivory and
apes, were imported by Solomon (I Kings
10:22; II Chron. 9:21). It has been assumed
that the decorative peacock from India is
meant.

pearl oyster. A pearl was a precious article of
commerce (Job 28:18; Matt. 13:45-46; Rev.
21:21), used as an ornament by women (I
Tim. 2:9; Rev. 17:4). Pearls of large size and
fine quality are found in the pearl oyster
which abounds in the Indian seas, esp. in
the Persian Gulf and near Ceylon. Pearls
are also found inside the shells of several
species of *Mollusca.*

Pe'kah. A commander under Pekahiah, king
of Israel, Pekah slew him and reigned in his
stead. He made an alliance with Rezin, king
of Syria, against Jotham, king of Judah, and
warred against Jotham's successor, Ahaz (II

Kings 15:25-31). See KINGS, TABLE OF.
Since he apparently did not rule all Israel
for 20 years, the reference in 15:27 seems to
be an error, but he may have "ruled" a
province in the Galilee region under Menahem before becoming king.

Pek'a·hi'ah. A king of Israel, son of Menahem, assassinated after 2 years by Pekah (II
Kings 15:22-26). See KINGS, TABLE OF.

pel'i·can. A large, web-footed fishing bird,
with a huge, furrowed bill that has under it
a dilatable pouch in which the bird carries
fish to feed its young. Its height is 5-6 feet,
its wingspread 12 or 13 feet. Pelicans are
often seen during winter months on the Sea
of Galilee. See also CORMORANT.

PELICAN

pence. Plural form of the English penny
(Matt. 18:28; Mark 14:5). The coin referred
to was the Roman denarius (plural, *denarii*).

pen'ny. The Greek word at Matt. 20:2 and
22:19 is *denarion,* the silver coin the Romans called a "denarius." It was probably
worth about 20 cents in the time of Christ.
It was the ordinary pay of a farm laborer for
a day. We do not know why the King
James translators chose "penny" here; in
some cases a "coin" is what is meant. The
RSV uses "penny" at Matt. 5:26 to indicate

a coin of little worth. See FARTHING.

Pen'ta·teuch. See LAW.

Pen'te·cost. For the Hebrew festival some-times called Pentecost, see WEEKS, FEAST OF. For Christians, the most notable Pente-cost was their first after the Resurrection and Ascension of Christ (Acts, ch. 2). From it dates the founding of the Christian Church. In the church calendar Pentecost is alternatively called Whitsunday.

pen'u·ry. Extreme poverty (Prov. 14:23; Luke 21:4).

per'fume. A substance producing a pleasing odor, usually an extract of the scent of such spices as aloes, cassia, cinnamon, myrrh, frankincense and spikenard, which were raised in the Jordan Valley or imported from Arabia and the east. The aromatic matter was separated by boiling and the ex-tract was carried as scent in perfume bottles suspended from the girdle, or was mixed with oil and used as an ointment (S. of Sol. 1:3; Isa. 3:20; John 12:3). Frequently sev-eral spices were compounded (Ex. 30:23-24). Perfumery was applied to the person to counteract body odors, to gar-ments and furniture (Ps. 45:8; Prov. 7:17; S. of Sol. 4:11). It was used in the Temple ser-vice (Ex. 30:22-38) and was placed on dead bodies (II Chron. 16:14; John 19:39-40).

pes'ti·lence. A fatal contagious disease; a plague; often associated with famine and the sword as symbols of punishment for dis-obedience to God (Jer. 27:13; Ezek. 6:11). Pestilence often follows war, crop destruc-tion, the siege of cities and lack of sanitary facilities.

pes'tle. A tool used to pound or grind sub-stances in a mortar (Prov. 27:22).

Pe'ter. Also called Simon, Simeon and Ce-phas ("a rock"), he is always named first in the lists of apostles;

chosen and sent out (Matt. 4:18; 10:2; Mark 1:16; 3:16, etc.)

PESTLE AND MORTAR

fails test of faith (Matt. 14:28-31)
present at Transfiguration (Matt., ch. 17;
    Mark, ch. 9; Luke 9:28-36)
denies Christ 3 times (Matt. 26:69-75;
    Mark 14:66-72; Luke 22:54-62; John
    18:15-27)
encourages apostles; explains gift of
    tongues (Acts 1:13-22; 2:14-40; see
    TONGUES, GIFT OF)
heals lame man (Acts 3:1-4:22)
rebukes Ananias (Acts, ch. 5)
shares vision with Cornelius (Acts
    10:1-11:18)
freed from prison by angel (Acts, ch. 12)
debates on circumcision (Acts 15:1-21;
    cf. Gal., ch. 2)
his martyr's death foretold (John 21:19).
Authentic history adds little to what the
N.T. tells us about the life of Peter. He
probably went to Rome near the end of his
career, and probably suffered martyrdom
there in A.D. 64 or 67. Tradition holds that
he was buried under what is now the altar
of St. Peter's Basilica in Rome.
Phar'aoh. The title of the rulers of Egypt until
the sixth century B.C.; it is the Hebrew form
of an Egyptian term meaning "great
house." The title was sometimes prefixed to
the personal name of the ruler, as in Pharaoh-nechoh (II Kings 23:29), but it was
usually used alone, as a proper name (Gen.
12:15; I Kings 3:1; Jer. 37:11). Of the Pha-

raohs mentioned in the Bible, several, among whom are the Pharaohs of Abraham and Joseph, cannot be identified, and the Pharaohs of the oppression and the Exodus are uncertain because the dates of these events are uncertain.

Phar′i·see. A member of one of the 3 chief Jewish parties, the others being the Sadducees and Essenes. The origin of the Pharisees goes back to the period before the Maccabean war (began 166 B.C.), in a reaction against the inroads made by Hellenistic culture among Jews, to the point where many of the people adopted Greek customs and fell away from the practice of their own religion. Those Jews who regarded Greek practices with abhorrence and their spread with alarm were urged to strict and open conformity to the Mosaic law, and so the party of the Pharisees was born. To the written law the Pharisees added, as having equal binding force, oral expositions of the Mosaic law, esp. those by the great teaching rabbis. From its beginning as a patriotic and idealistic reaction against religious and cultural deterioration, by the time of Jesus the Pharisees were showing the inherent weaknesses of a concept of religion that makes religion consist in conformity to the law and that promises God's grace only to the doers of the law. The Pharisees' religion had become external. The disposition of the heart was less vital than the outward act. The proper interpretation of the law and its application even to the minute details of ordinary life had become a matter of grave consequence. It had made the Pharisees a cunning body of men. While they believed in an after-life, that men are rewarded or punished in the future life according as they have lived in this life, and in the coming of a Messiah—and were more liberal in their ideas than the Sadducees—they refused to allow Jesus claim of Messiahship (John 9:16), and also disagreed with many of his teachings. Jesus in turn upbraided the Pharisees for hypocrisy, pride, covetousness and impenitence (Matt. 5:20; 16:6, 11-12; 23:1-39). The Pharisees' insistence on full adherence to the law in all its details was the heart of their differences with Jesus. They took a prominent part in plotting his death (Mark 3:6; John 11:47-57). Yet they always numbered in their ranks individuals of perfect sincerity and the highest character. Paul in his young manhood was a Pharisee (Acts 23:6; 26:5-7; Phil. 3:5). His teacher, Gamaliel, was of the same sect. The word "Pharisee" means "separated." See also SADDUCEES.

Phi·le'mon. A convert of Paul.

Phil'ip. 1. One of the 12 (Matt. 10:3; Mark 3:18; Acts 1:13; etc.); he brings Nathanael to Jesus (John 1:43-48) and is present at the miracle of loaves and fishes (6:5-6). 2. The evangelist, chosen as a deacon (Acts 6:5); see also Acts 8:5-40; 21:8-9. 3. A son of Herod the Great and husband of Herodias (Matt. 14:3; Mark 6:17; Luke 3:1, 19). See TETRARCH.

Phi·lis'tines. Apparently the Philistines came from Crete soon after 1200 B.C., and settled on the s.e. coast of the Mediterranean. They were one of the "Peoples of the Sea," invading peoples of Greek background who moved e. by sea in a period of turmoil in Greece and Anatolia. Ramses III of Egypt (1195-1164 B.C.) prevented them from invading his country. Their chief cities, governed as city-states allied to one another, were Gaza, Ashkelon, Ashdod, Ekron and Gath. In the course of time they probably adopted the religion and culture of the Canaanites. They seemingly dropped their language and spoke a Semitic dialect; their gods have Semitic names, and Samson and David had no trouble conversing with them. After the Israelites settled in the Promised Land, the tribe of Judah had initial successes against the Philistines (Judg.

1:18). This began a 250-year-period of wars between the two peoples. The Philistines had a great advantage in that they knew how to make iron tools and weapons (I Sam. 13:19-21), just coming into use. Saul and David had various encounters with them, but at length, to escape Saul, David twice sought refuge in their country (I Sam. 21:10-15; chs. 27-29). The Philistines penetrated to the heart of Canaan when they defeated Saul on Mt. Gilboa (I Sam. 28:4; 29:11; 31:1-13). David, when king, repelled invasions and also fought them in their own country (II Sam. 3:18; 5:17-25, etc.). After his death the Philistines are less frequently mentioned, as if their power were waning. In the N.T. they are not mentioned at all; perhaps ultimately they merged into the Jewish nation.

Phin′e·has. 1. Grandson of Aaron. An everlasting priesthood was promised him and his descendants (Num. 25:1-18; Ps. 106:30); his line held that office until Jerusalem was destroyed in A.D. 70. 2. The younger of Eli's 2 degenerate sons (I Sam. 2:22-4:11).

Phoe·ni′cians. Occupants of a narrow strip of territory between the Mediterranean Sea and the crest of the parallel Lebanon Mountain range. In the O.T. Phoenicia extended about 14 miles s. of Tyre; in the time of Christ its limit was 16 miles s. of Mt. Carmel. The origins of the Phoenicians are obscure, but apparently they were basically Semites (they spoke a Semitic language) with a much later infusion of Greek elements from the Aegean Sea area. Their chief cities were Tyre and Sidon. Their territory had good natural harbors, and Mt. Lebanon provided them with unlimited hardwood timber for shipbuilding, and they became the most skillful navigators known to antiquity. They not only traded with distant countries, but colonized locations favorable for commerce, such as Carthage on the n. African coast, near modern Tunis, and Cadiz, Spain. Hemmed in by aggressive peoples, they turned to trade and the sea. Hiram, king of Tyre, the chief Phoenician city-state, was friendly with David (II Sam. 5:11; I Kings 5:1; I Chron. 14:1) and Solomon (I Kings 9:10-14; II Chron. 2:3-16). Another Hiram, a metalsmith, cast pillars for the Temple (I Kings 7:13-14, 40, 45). A princess of Tyre, Jezebel, became Ahab's queen. The Phoenicians' taste was not for war, but for manufacture, commerce, sea voyages, colonization. They produced purple dyes, metal products and glassware. Their merchants were princes (Isa. 23:8). The friendship with the Hebrews was broken later and never rebuilt. The prophets from Jeremiah on predicted Tyre's fall, which Alexander accomplished in 332 B.C. by building a mole from the mainland out to the island city. But the city regained its importance. Jesus once visited the coasts of Tyre and Sidon (Matt. 15:21-28; Mark 7:24-31).

phy·lac'ter·ies. Small leather cases holding slips of parchment inscribed with 4 Scriptural passages (Ex. 13:1-10; 13:11-16; Deut. 6:4-9; 11:13-22). They were worn on the forehead or on the arm (Matt. 23:5), by every male Jew during the time of morning prayer, except on the Sabbath and festivals. See also FRONTLET.

pi'geon. See DOVE.

Pi'late, Pon'tius. The Roman prefect of Judea A.D. 26-36, appointed by Tiberius (Luke 3:1). He is best known for his sentencing of Jesus to death by crucifixion. The historians Josephus and Philo record 5 other incidents in Pilate's career which evidence, on the one side, Pilate's insensitivity to Jewish sensibilities and his readiness to use more force than was required; and on the other side, the touchiness of Jews over matters of Roman symbols brought into Jerusalem that would be hard for a Roman administrator of a conquered province to understand. Pilate was ultimately sent to Rome to answer to the emperor for his conduct in breaking up a gathering at the foot of Mt. Gerizim of Samaritan religious fanatics who were also armed, in the course of which many were killed or executed later. But Tiberius died before Pilate arrived, and the new emperor, Caligula, seems to have quashed Pilate's case as he did with other carry-over cases from the previous regime. That Pilate committed suicide is sheer legend. He simply slipped out of history.

plague. 1. A deadly contagious disease (Mark 3:10; 5:29); often applied to leprosy (Lev. 13:3-6). 2. Anything that afflicts or punishes; in God's hands, an instrument for the punishment of evildoers (Ex. 9:14; Num. 11:33; II Chron. 21:14), esp. any of the 10 disasters He inflicted upon the Egyptians (Ex. 7:14-12:30).

plait'ing. Weaving the hair into braids, fashionable among Roman women, frowned upon by Christians (I Peter 3:3).

plane tree. See CHESTNUT.

Ple'ia·des. A cluster of stars in the constellation Taurus (the Bull), six of which are visible to the naked eye and represent, according to Greek mythology, the 6 daughters of Atlas (the seventh one being lost), placed in the heavens by Zeus (Job 9:9; 38:31).

plow'share. The cutting edge of a plow (Isa. 2:4). Early plowshares were of wood; the Philistines may have introduced iron ones (I Sam. 13:20).

plum'met. A cord suspending a stone or metal weight, used in determining whether a wall is vertical; used figuratively by God in measuring the uprightness of His people (II Kings 21:13; Isa. 28:17). Also "plumbline" (Amos 7:7-8).

pods. See HUSK.

Pol'lux. See CASTOR AND POLLUX.

pome'gran·ate. A tree, 12-15 ft. tall; its flowers generally have scarlet petals. The fruit is about the size of an orange, and has a hard, red rind, filled with numerous seeds enveloped in bright red pulp, refreshing to the taste. The pomegranate is wild in n. Africa and w. Asia, and possibly in Gilead. It was largely cultivated in Palestine in biblical times (Num. 13:23; 20:5; Deut. 8:8; I Sam. 14:2; S. of Sol. 4:3, 13; 6:7, 11; 8:2; Joel 1:12;

POMEGRANATE

Hag. 2:19). The juice of the fruit made a pleasant drink. Figures of the pomegranate were used for decoration in buildings (I Kings 7:18) and on ceremonial clothing (Ex. 28:34).

por′cu·pine. See HEDGEHOG.

por′phy·ry. An Egyptian rock consisting of feldspar crystals embedded in a compact dark red or purple groundmass (Esth. 1:6, RSV).

post. A runner or messenger (II Chron. 30:6).

Pot′i·phar. Pharaoh's captain, who bought Joseph (Gen., ch. 39).

pot′sherd. A piece of broken pottery (Job 2:8); used as a symbol of dryness (Ps. 22:15) and of utter worthlessness (Isa. 45:9).

pot′tage. A kind of stew or thick soup made with or without meat, having lentils as the principal ingredient (Gen. 25:29–30; II Kings 4:38).

pot′ters′ field. See ACELDAMA.

prae·to′ri·um. The official residence of a provincial governor. In the N.T.: 1. The palace occupied by Pontius Pilate at Jerusalem, where his judgment seat was erected (Mark 16:15). 2. Herod's palace (Acts 23:35, RSV). 3. The praetorian guard (Phil. 1:13, RSV) which guarded the imperial palace; the KJV simply says "palace" here.

pray'er. Humble and earnest communion with God for the purpose of seeking some blessing, for confessing sin or for acknowledging mercies received. Prayers are made from various bodily positions including kneeling (Acts 9:40), lying with the face downward (Matt. 26:39), standing (Matt. 6:5), and raising one's hands (Ps. 28:2). The effectiveness of prayer, however, is determined only by the gracious will of God and by a person's sincerity and faith, his spirit of devotion to God, his sense of repentance and his willingness to submit to God's will.

pre·des'ti·nate. To establish or arrange beforehand whatever comes to pass; to foreordain. The noun "predestination" means God's determination for the salvation of man, whereby, without cancelling human freedom and responsibility, He by His own will ordains in eternity the salvation of the elect (Rom. 8:29-30; Eph. 1:5, 11).

pre'fect. See PROCURATOR.

prep'a·ra'tion, day of. Friday, the day before the Sabbath (Mark 15:42; John 19:31). The preparation for the Sabbath of the Passover was the eve of a particularly high day.

pres'by·ter'y. The group, or body, of elders in a local Christian church (I Tim. 4:14).

priest. In the world of the O.T., a priest is an authorized minister of a deity who, on behalf of the community, officiates at the altar and in other rites. The essential idea of a priest was that he performs sacrificial, ritualistic and mediatorial functions; and in this sense he represents the people before God, while a prophet generally is an intermediary in the opposite direction—between God and man. The priests formed a distinct class in all nations of the O.T. (Gen. 47:22;

Ex. 2:16; I Sam. 6:2; Acts 14:13). When the Hebrew nation was organized at Sinai, a sanctuary and service were projected. Priests were needed for the altar. Aaron and his sons were appointed to that office, and the priesthood was made hereditary in the family and restricted to it (Ex. 28:1; 40:12-15; Num. 16:40; ch. 17; 18:1-8). All the "sons of Aaron" were priests unless debarred by legal disabilities. The duties of the priests were mainly 3: to minister at the sanctuary before the Lord; to teach the people the law of God, and to inquire for them the divine will by Urim and Thummim (Ex. 28:30 and Ezra 2:63; Num. 16:40; 18:5; II Chron. 15:3; Jer. 18:18; Ezek. 7:26; Micah 3:11). Before the establishment of the priesthood, or in the absence of any priest, the natural head of a body of people acted as priest. See also HIGH PRIEST; LEVITES.

prince. A person of chief rank or authority in any official relation: as the leader of a nation (I Kings 14:7), a governor over a province (Dan. 3:2), head of a tribe (Num. 1:16) or of a tribal family (Num. 25:14), etc. Beelzebub is called prince of the demons (Matt. 9:34). The Messiah is called the Prince of Peace (Isa. 9:6). Jesus is called the Prince (or Author) of life (Acts 3:15); Prince and Saviour (Acts 5:31); prince of kings on earth (Rev. 1:5).

prin′ci·pal′i·ties. This is the plural form of a word designating the organized powers of angels (Rom. 8:38; Eph. 3:10; Col. 1:16).

Pris′ca, Pris·cil′la. Wife of Aquila (Rom. 16:3; II Tim. 4:19). See also AQUILA.

pro·con′sul. See DEPUTY.

proc′u·ra′tor. The agent of a Roman emperor, who resided in an "imperial," not a "senatorial" province. However, the Roman representative in Judea until the time of Emperor Claudius was a "prefect" not a "procurator," as proven by the engraved stone of Pontius Pilate found at Caesarea, in which he calls himself "prefect." Felix and Festus were appointed by Claudius and Nero respectively, and were in fact "procurators." The governor of Judea was backed up by soldiers except for matters on which the Jewish council or Sanhedrin had power.

pro·fane'. *v.* To treat any sacred person or thing (the holiness of God, the sanctuary, a priest, the Sabbath, etc.) as if it were not holy. To bring any holy thing into contact with ritual uncleanness was to profane it. Idolatry (Ezek. 20:39), child sacrifice (Lev. 18:21), immorality (Lev. 19:11-12) were major forms of profanation of holiness. *adj.* Applied to a person who shows disregard or contempt for sacred things, and to things that are unhallowed or ritually unclean.

proph'et. A person who speaks for God and makes known His will. The prophet was a person qualified by God to be His spokesman to men (Deut. 18:18). Beginning with Samuel, and with renewed force several centuries later, the prophet became a constant presence in the national life, an ambassador of God to Israel, an authoritative preacher of righteousness, an interpreter of past and present history on its moral side, an admonisher of the consequences which God the Judge has annexed to conduct, a forewarner of the certainty of the divine judgment on sin, and a fosterer of fidelity toward God. The prophets were taught of the Spirit of God (I Kings 22:24; Mic. 3:8). The instruction was ordinarily imparted by dreams, visions and inward suggestions recognized by the prophets as not of themselves. The prophets did not exercise the prophetic power at all times, but when God told them to speak. The call of the prophets came directly from God (Amos 7:15). Spiritually the prophets were prepared to receive divine communications. They were holy men, dedicated to God's service, men of habitual prayer (like Samuel, I Sam. 7:5;

8:6, etc.), who gave themselves to quiet con-
templation to wait for revelation (Isa. 21:8;
Hab. 2:1). Prophecy included the predic-
tion of future events (Isa. 38:5-6; Jer. 20:6;
Amos 1:5; Micah 4:10), but the more important function was to deal with the present and the past, and to instruct men in
God's ways (Isa. 41:26; 42:9; 46:9). The
prophet speaks for, or on behalf of, another;
he is the spokesman, the mouthpiece, of
God. He is a forthteller rather than a fore-
teller. The office of prophet seems to have
disappeared with the death of Malachi. At
the approach and Advent of Christ the
tongue of prophecy was again loosed (Luke
1:67; 2:26-38). In the church of the N.T.
also there were prophets (I Cor. 12:28), specially illumined expounders of God's revelation. See also SEER.

pro·pi′ti·a′tion. This word, and its near-syn-
onym, "expiation," means the extinguishing
of guilt by suffering a penalty or offering a
sacrifice as an equivalent. The idea is this:
sin places a barrier between God and man,
and it is necessary that the human guilt be
removed. It is God who sent forth His Son
to be the expiation of sin. Through the
death of Christ sins are expiated or an-
nulled, and fellowship can be and is restored (Rom. 3:25; I John 2:3; 4:10). The
shed blood of Jesus can be thought of as the
means by which sin is covered, just as the
blood sacrifices in the O.T. were referred to
as covering for sin, thus effecting an atonement, a reconciliation (Lev. 14:18; 17:11).
See also ATONEMENT; RECONCILIATION; SIN
OFFERING.

pros′e·lyte. In the N.T., a convert to Judaism.
Among pagans the monotheism and ethical
ideas of Judaism were very attractive. A
proselyte may have been either a non-Jew-
ish resident of Israel or a foreigner in his
own land. There were probably 2 classes of
converts: 1. those who accepted most of the

customs but refused to accept circumcision,
and therefore were not fully identified with
the Jews; and 2. those who subscribed to all
the Mosaic laws (Matt. 23:15; Acts 2:10;
6:5; 13:43).

prov'en·der. Food for livestock.

pro'verb. 1. A short saying that strikingly expresses some simple truth or familiar experience (Ezek. 16:44; Luke 4:23). The book
of Proverbs is thought of as a guide to practical wisdom and successful living. 2. An
enigmatical saying (John 16:25, 29).

prun'ing·hook. A tool with a curved blade at
one end of a wooden handle, used for pruning grapevines.

psalm. A religious poem specially employed
in the public worship of God; a hymn of
praise and worship.

psalm'ist. A writer or composer of psalms.

psal'ter·y. A harp. The number of strings in
the common instrument is unknown, but in
a special variety there were 10 (Ps. 33:2). It
could be carried about while played (I Sam.
10:5).

pub'li·can. A collector of public revenues,
tolls, etc.; a tax collector. The Roman system of collecting taxes in the provinces was
to put up to auction the privilege of farming
the public revenues. Those who bid at the
auction were necessarily wealthy, for they
undertook to pay a given sum to the government. In some cases they in turn sold the
right of farming portions of the revenue to
subcontractors; in others they engaged
agents under their immediate supervision to
do the actual work of collecting the taxes.
This "publican" had to make good any defi-
cit in the collections, and he could of course
pocket all the taxes in excess of the pur-
chase price. (The people employed to do
the actual collecting are also called "publicans," but "tax collectors" in modern translations.) The system encouraged greed and
extortion. Jews who participated in it were
despised by their fellow citizens: they were

playing the Romans' game as well as engaging in virtual robbery. They were not admitted into society; in fact, it was considered disreputable for anyone to be their friend and associate. Hence the charge against Jesus that he ate with publicans and sinners (Matt. 9:10-13) and was even their friend (11:19).

Pul. See TIGLATH-PILESER.

pulse. This is a rarely used word today for the edible seeds of any legume such as peas or beans. "Vegetables" generally may be understood (Dan. 1:12, 16).

Pur. To "cast Pur" (Esth. 3:7) is to cast a lot, as a way to determine something. See LOT.

Pu'rim. A Jewish festival commemorating the deliverance of the Jews by Esther from a general massacre inspired by Haman (Esth. 9:21-32), celebrated on the 14th and 15th days of the month of Adar. Haman cast lots (*purim*) as a way of deciding which day he should put into effect the king's decree calling for the extermination of the Jews.

pur'ple. Purple was a costly dye obtained from the fluid of a marine mollusk secreted by a gland in the neck. Most of it came from Tyre. Much labor was required to collect it in quantity and the price was high. The dye was applied to the yarn, not the woven cloth. Purple clothing was costly and therefore was the privilege of the rich exclusively. Purple was the color of kings (Judg. 8:26).

purs'lane. An annual herb with fleshy leaves, this is a common salad plant in Palestine and considered good for health.

pu'tre·fy'ing sores. Lesions of the skin and tissue so bad that they give off the foul-smelling odor of decomposing flesh.

py'garg. The name of a "clean" animal (Deut. 14:5); the pygarg of the ancients was the white-rumped antelope. The RSV calls it an ibex.

Q

quail. A bird that the Israelites had for food in abundance twice during their journeyings near Sinai (Ex. 16:12-13; Num. 11:31-34).

QUAIL

Each time it was spring. The migratory quail of Europe arrives in Palestine from the south in immense numbers in March. If the birds become exhausted from a long flight against the wind, the whole flock may fall to the ground, where the birds lie stunned. In this condition they can be captured by hand in great quantities. This quail is about 7½ inches long.

qua·ter'ni·on. This was a guard consisting of 4 soldiers. The 4 quarternions assigned to Peter (Acts 12:4) each had the duty for one night watch of 3 hours.

queen of heav'en. A goddess of fertility known throughout the ancient Near East and worshiped esp. by women (Jer. 7:18; 44:15-30). She appears to have been the Assyro-Babylonian Ishtar and was of the same type as the Canaanite Asherah and Astarte. The cult may have been introduced in the time of Manasseh (II Kings 21:1-18); it was suppressed by Josiah (23:4-14) and apparently reappeared under Jehoiakim (23:36-24:7). See ASHERAH.

queen of the south. The Queen of Sheba (in

Arabia, s. of Israel).

quick'sands. A sandbank that moves, quick being used in the sense of living. The quicksand of Acts 27:17 was probably the shallow, sandy gulf called Greater Syrtis, now called the Gulf of Sidra, on the n. coast of Africa, s. of Sicily.

quince. See APPLE.

R

Rab'bi. Literally, "my master," "my teacher." One learned in the Jewish law, a teacher of it. It was widely used as a title of respect applied by pupils to teacher or learned layman, without suggesting that the title represents an official ordaining or appointment as it does today. "Rabboni" is an Aramaic variation of Hebrew "rabbi." John uses them interchangeably (1:38; 20:16).

Ra·ca'. An expression of contempt; the meaning is uncertain, perhaps empty, good-for-nothing (Matt. 5:22).

Ra'chel. Daughter of Laban, she was the favorite wife of Jacob and the mother of Joseph and Benjamin (Gen., chs. 29–31; 35:16–20; 48:7). In Jer. 31:15 and Matt. 2:18, she is said to be heard "weeping for her children."

rain. The climate of Palestine is characterized by a winter period of rain and a rainless summer. The former (early) rain may be placed in October; the main rain in January and the latter (later) rain in April.

rai'sin. See VINE.

ram'part. A fortification encircling some cities outside the principal wall, often an embankment constructed from earth made available from the digging of a moat. Sometimes "rampart" is used of fortifications in general (Nahum 3:8).

ram's horn. The curved, hollow horn of a ram, used as a signaling trumpet (Josh. 6:4–6, 8, 13). Called *shophar*, it is still blown on the

Jewish New Year and the Day of Atonement.

RAM'S HORN

rase. To level with the ground; demolish (Ps. 137:7).

ra'ven. A bird, black in color, feeding on all sorts of food, even carrion, and hence "unclean" (Lev. 11:15). The bird referred to in Scripture is undoubtedly the common raven, found in every part of Palestine. It is about 26 inches long. Noah sent one forth (Gen. 8:7). It frequents valleys (Prov. 30:17) and makes its nest in solitary places (Isa. 34:11).

rav'en, rav'in. To prey or plunder; to devour greedily (Gen. 49:27; Ezek. 22:25, 27).

rav'en·ing. n. Greed (Luke 11:39). adj. Greedily looking for prey (Ps. 22:13; Matt. 7:15).

rav'en·ous. Eager for food; greedy.

Re·bek'ah. Wife of Isaac and mother of twin sons, Esau and Jacob. The story of her deception in favor of Jacob is told in Gen., chs. 24-27; see also 49:31.

Rech'a·bites. A branch or tribe of Kenites. Unlike most Kenites, who lived s. of Judah or in Midian, they dwelt among the Israelites. Their chief, Jonadab, son of Rechab, commanded them to abstain from wine and intoxicating liquor, not to live in houses or plant or own vineyards, but to dwell in tents (Jer. 35:6). The object of these rules was the preservation of primitive simplicity of manners.

rec'on·cil·i·a'tion. The restoration of harmony,

friendship and fellowship between estranged persons. In the O.T. the word refers
to God's "covering" or "removal" of sin,
particularly by the blood of the sacrifice
(Lev. 8:15; Ezek. 45:15). In the N.T. the
word is used esp. of God's gracious action
through Christ to restore persons, who by
sinning had become estranged from God, to
a relationship of peace with God. The atoning death of Christ reveals fully God's
changeless love for sinful man and constitutes an irrefutable appeal to man to aban-
don his hostility and be reconciled to God
(II Cor. 5:14–21; Col. 1:19–23). See also
ATONEMENT; PROPITIATION.

rec′ord. A witness (Phil. 1:8).

re·cord′er. An official of high rank in the Hebrew government from the time of David
onward (II Sam. 8:16; I Kings 4:3; II Kings
18:18, 37; II Chron. 34:8). His official duty
was to record decrees and judgments of the
king as well as important events, and to ad-
vise the king in respect to these records.

Re·deem′er. One who redeems or sets free.
Redemption is a release effected by the payment of a ransom price from some bondage,
restriction or taboo (Ex. 13:15; Num. 3:49).
For example, a man who on account of
debt sold himself into slavery could be "redeemed" by a kinsman (Lev. 25:47–49). In
the story of Ruth, Boaz became her "redeemer" (Ruth 4:1–6). "Redemption" came
to mean "deliverance," as of God's people
from Egypt (Deut. 7:8) and from sin (Isa.
44:22). God is called a Redeemer (Job
19:25; Ps. 19:14; Isa. 49:26; 59:20; 63:16; Jer.
50:34). In the N.T. redemption refers to
Christ's giving of his life to deliver men
from the bondage of sin (Titus 2:14), the
law (Gal. 4:5) and death (Rom. 8:23). The
death of Christ is the price paid for man's
redemption. It is closely associated with
forgiveness, since man receives forgiveness
through the redemptive price of Christ's
death (Eph. 1:7; Col. 1:14). Christ thus be-

comes mankind's Redeemer.

re·dound'. To flow back as a consequence (Ezek. 39:13, RSV); in II Cor. 4:15 (KJV), to increase the thanksgiving to the glory of God.

reed. 1. Any tall, broad-leaved grass growing in a wet place, esp. along the Nile River. It grew to 10 feet high. It is easily shaken by the wind (I Kings 14:15) and fragile when leaned on (II Kings 18:21; Isa. 36:6; Ezek. 20:6-7). 2. A stalk of this grass used as a measuring rod; it came to denote 6 cubits (Ezek. 40:5; 41:8), or about 9 feet. See MEA-SURES.

re·fin'er. A craftsman who makes ("refines") pure metal by melting the ore and removing the impurities, alloys, sediment, etc. (Mal. 3:2-3).

ref'uge, cit'y of. See CITY OF REFUGE.

re·gen'er·a'tion. This word refers to a decisively new stage in the life of a redeemed person (Titus 3:5; see REDEEMER). It signifies a complete renewal (II Cor. 5:17), or a rebirth in which there is union with Christ by faith and baptism into him (Rom. 6:3-11; Gal. 3:27; Col. 2:11-13). This renewal is effected by the Holy Spirit.

Re'ho·bo'am. Son of Solomon (I Kings 11:43); made king (I Kings 12:1; II Chron. 10:1)

10 tribes revolt (I Kings 12:3-20; cf. II Chron. 10:3-19)

Shemaiah forbids war; Rehoboam fortifies cities (I Kings 12:21-24; II Chron. 11:1-12)

Shishak's invasion and plunder (I Kings 14:21-28; II Chron. 11:13-17; 12:1-12)

Rehoboam's descendants (II Chron. 11:18-23)

his death (I Kings 14:31; II Chron. 12:16).

See JEROBOAM; KINGS, TABLE OF.

re·lease', year of. The year of jubilee (Deut. 15:9). See JUBILEE.

Rem'phan, Re'phan. A god who has a star associated with him, and who was worshiped by the Israelites in the wilderness (Acts 7:43); probably the Babylonian equivalent of the Roman god Saturn.

re·pent'ance. A decisive change of attitude brought about by a deep feeling of sorrow over one's sins, causing one to turn to God and to accept His will (II Cor. 7:9-10). In the O.T. esp. the concepts of returning to God and repenting are closely related (Isa. 10:22; Jer. 3:7; Hos. 5:4; 6:1; 7:10; 14:2). Repentance as the first step toward salvation involves more than a feeling of sorrow for one's sins; it requires the recognition of the evil of sin, an inward feeling of abhorrence for sin bound up in a decision to forsake it. Repentance to Christians is inseparable from faith and is a condition for forgiveness and salvation; without becoming aware of one's sin and turning wholeheartedly from it toward God (repenting), one has not entered the Christian life (Matt. 3:2, 8; II Peter 3:9).

rep'ro·bate. *n.* A worthless person (Ps. 15:4; II Cor. 13:5-7). *adj.* Disapproved, unworthy, unfit, of poor quality (Jer. 6:30). A reprobate person is rejected by God because he is unable to stand the test of faith (Rom. 1:28; II Tim. 3:8; Titus 1:16).

re·spect' of per'sons. A showing favor or partiality toward someone because of his wealth, social position, etc. Both O.T. and N.T. argue its invalidity (Lev. 19:32; Eph. 6:9). Jesus showed no partiality (Luke 20:21), and God is no respecter of persons (Acts 10:34; Rom. 2:11).

res'ur·rec'tion. A rising from the dead; coming back to life; specifically: 1. the rising of Jesus from the dead after his death and burial; the restoration of his physical life and the reunion of his body with his spirit, brought about by the power of God (Acts 1:22; 2:31); 2. the rising of all the dead at the last judgment (Matt. 22:29, 32). Paul speaks of it as taking place in stages, with the believers coming first (I Cor. 15:18-23). Put another way, the Resurrection of Jesus Christ is the promise and assurance of the resurrection of believers and of eternal blessedness with him and the Father (Rom. 6:3-11; I Cor., ch. 15).

Re·turn′ of Christ. See SECOND COMING.

Reu′ben. 1. Oldest son of Jacob and Leah (Gen. 29:33; 35:23), he forfeited his birthright (I Chron. 5:1). For his story, see Gen., chs. 30; 35; 37; 42; 49. 2. The tribe of Reuben's descendants, divided into the families of his 4 sons (Num. 26:5-11), and their territory. After the Israelites' defeat of kings Sihon and Og, the tribes of Reuben, Gad and half Manasseh settled e. of the Jordan (Josh. 12:4-6). The combined tribes overcame the Hagarites (I Chron. 5:18-22), but many of their towns were later taken by the Moabites (Isa., ch. 15).

Reu′el. See JETHRO.

rev′e·la′tion. A revelation is an act of revealing, the disclosure to others of something previously unknown to them. It is also the thing that is revealed. In the Bible the word is used of God's disclosure of Himself and His will to man. He does this so that man may become aware of His reality and His love, and of the fact that He seeks man's salvation from sin (Eph. 3:3).

re·vile′. To use abusive or contemptuous language (Ex. 22:28; Mark 15:32).

Rho′da. A servant girl who left Peter standing at the gate (Acts 12:13-16).

righ′teous·ness. In the O.T. righteousness is a word connected with a relationship, whether between man and man or man and God. The righteous man is the one who fulfills the demands of that relationship, whether that of king to his people, a father to his family, an individual to God, etc. Man may vary in his righteousness, but God's righteousness endures, always intervening for man, forgiving him and offering

ways of salvation. In the N.T. God mani-
fests His righteousness in His dealings with
sinful men by His gracious action through
Christ to justify and save all who respond in
faith to His redeeming work. Accordingly
the term righteousness is applied to man's
condition, not only to signify his conformity
to God's will in thought, word and deed
(Matt. 5:6, 20), but esp. to designate the
state of those who, having responded in
faith to the redeeming work of God through
Christ, are accepted and approved by God
(Rom. 5:17; 10:3, 10).

Rim'mon. A Syrian god, with a temple probably at Damascus (II Kings 5:18). He was
identical with Hadad, worshiped by Assyrians as the god of storm, rain and thunder.

rock badg'er. See CONEY.

rod. 1. A straight, slender shoot or stem of a
bush or tree (Gen. 30:37). 2. An offshoot or
branch of a family or tribe (Isa. 11:1; Ps.
74:2; Jer. 10:6). 3. The crook or staff of a
shepherd (Ps. 23:4). 4. A stick or switch for
beating as a punishment (Ex. 21:20) or for
threshing (Isa. 28:27). 5. A symbol of office,
rank, power or authority (Ps. 2:9; Jer.
48:17). 6. Power or authority, as a means of
exercising discipline (Job 9:34), or offering
protection and guidance (Micah 7:14). 7.
"Pass under the rod": shepherds counted
and checked the condition of their sheep by
making them file under a staff, in a narrow
passage (Lev. 27:32). God is said to do this
of men in Ezek. 20:37.

roe, roe'buck. See DEER.

rose. The "rose of Sharon" is a wild, bulbous
plant, a member of the narcissus family,
with beautiful white flowers, common in
the Plain of Sharon in springtime (S. of Sol.
2:1). The Hebrew word translated "rose" in
Isa. 35:1 of the KJV is translated "crocus"
in the RSV. But true roses were certainly
known late in O.T. times.

ru'by, ru'bies. The true or Oriental ruby, rich
red in color, is a crystallized variety of co-

rundum not known in the Near East until
the third century B.C. Some therefore think
that the Hebrew word found in Job 28:18;
Prov. 3:15; 8:11; 20:15; 31:10; Lam. 4:7
would be better translated "coral" or
"pearls."

rud'dy. The underlying Hebrew word means
"to be red," and is a compliment to male
good looks. A ruddy complexion may have
been attractive to Hebrews as lighter than
the usual dark, swarthy complexions of the
Near East, but some suggest that "red-
haired" is meant, esp. in I Sam. 16:12 and
17:42.

rue. A strong-smelling perennial plant of
which the Pharisees, careful about minute
points, were scrupulously accurate in paying tithes (Luke 11:42). Had it been wild it
would not have been titheable. It was cultivated for use as a condiment; as a medicine
for rheumatism, earache and stomachache;
and as a good-luck charm.

rush. Rushes, bulrushes (papyrus), reeds and
flags are much the same (Job 8:11). All are
tall, broad-leaved grasses that grow in wet
places.

Ruth. A widow from Moab, the story of her
loyalty and devotion is told in the book
bearing her name.

rye, rie. See SPELT.

S

sa·bach'tha·ni. See ELOI.

Sab'a·oth. Hosts or armies. The Lord of Saba-
oth is the same as the Lord of Hosts. See
HOSTS, LORD OF.

Sab'bath. 1. The seventh day of the Hebrew
week, set aside by the fourth commandment
for rest and worship (Ex. 16:23; Lev. 23:3).
It lasted from sunset Friday to sunset Saturday. The institution of the Sabbath is traditionally associated with the Creation (Gen.
2:2-3). The first occurrence of the name

Sabbath is in Ex. 16:23. The Mosaic law
consistently emphasizes the holiness of the
Sabbath and the obligation upon Israel to
observe it as a Sabbath to God. In the Tabernacle and Temple worship, additional
sacrifices were offered on a Sabbath, and a
considerable body of laws forbidding certain activities was developed, closely controlling the activities of individuals. In the
time of our Lord the Pharisees applied the
laws of Sabbath to the most trivial acts, and
forbade in the process many acts of necessity and mercy. This brought on controver-
sies with Jesus (Matt. 12:9-13; Luke
13:10-17; Mark 2:23-28). The day for synagogue worship was the seventh day of the
week, Saturday (Acts 13:14). The young
Christian Church held assemblages for
worship on the first day of the week, the
day on which Christ rose from the dead
(Acts 2:1). It was designated "the Lord's
day" in Rev. 1:10. 2. The Sabbath of the
land was a year in which the land of Canaan had a solemn rest. It came around
once every 7 years. In it the ground was not
sown or reaped, nor the vineyard pruned,
nor its fruits gathered in. The spontaneous
growth of field and orchard was free to all.
Hebrew slaves and debtors were freed (Ex.
23:10-11; Lev. 25:3-7; Deut. 15:1-8). See
also JUBILEE.

Sab'bath, cov'ert for. The meaning of the Hebrew phrase so translated (II Kings 16:18)
is uncertain. Perhaps we should understand
"covering of the seat" (in the house of the
Lord)—some kind of canopied seat as one
sees in the choir stall of a cathedral.

Sab'bath day's jour'ney. The distance that a
person was permitted to travel on the Sabbath, as established by the legislation of the
scribes (Acts 1:12). This was set at 2,000
cubits (3,000 feet by Greek measure, 3,600
by Roman) on the basis of Num. 35:5 and
Josh. 3:4, which interpreted the original in-

junction not to leave the camp on the Sabbath (Ex. 16:29).

Sab·bat'i·cal year. See JUBILEE; SABBATH (2).

Sa·be'ans. The people of Sheba in s.w. Arabia (Isa. 45:14). See SHEBA.

sack'but. This was some kind of early English wind instrument, like a trombone, which did not exist in O.T. times in Israel. The instrument referred to in Dan., ch. 3 was a stringed instrument. The RSV calls this a trigon, a triangular lyre or harp.

sack'cloth. A coarse cloth, of a dark color, usually made of goat's hair (Rev. 6:12). It was worn customarily by mourners (II Sam. 3:31; II Kings 19:1-2); often, if not habitually, by prophets (Isa. 20:2; Rev. 11:3), and by captives (I Kings 20:31). The garment of sackcloth may have resembled a sack, sacks being made from the same material (Gen. 42:25; Josh. 9:4), with openings for the neck and arms and a slit down the front. Gen. 37:34; I Kings 20:31 and II Sam. 3:31 suggest that it was also used as a loincloth. It was generally worn next to the skin (I Kings 21:27; II Kings 6:30; Job 16:15; Isa. 32:11).

sac'ri·fice. 1. An offering to God or a god for purposes of gaining favor, avoiding disaster or showing one's honor and respect (Gen. 31:54; Lev. 7:12; II Kings 5:17). In more general terms O.T. sacrifice may be regarded as an external expression of man's response to the grace of God, and as a visible form of prayer offered to God. The act of sacrifice brought before the altar symbolized an intercommunication between God and His worshiper. See also OFFERINGS. 2. The ceremony in which the offering was prepared, brought to the altar and consumed (Ezra 9:5; Dan. 8:11).

Sad'du·cees. A Jewish party, opponents of the Pharisees. They were comparatively few in numbers, but were educated, wealthy and of good position. It is generally believed that the name comes from Zadok, high

priest in David's time, in whose family the
high priesthood remained until the second
century B.C., and whose descendants and
partisans were Zadokites or Sadducees. The
Sadducees, unlike the Pharisees, limited
their creed to the doctrines that they found
in the sacred written law; they held that
written law alone was binding and held to
the letter of Scripture. In distinction from
the Pharisees: 1. They denied the resurrection of the body, did not believe in penalties
and rewards in the next world, and main-
tained that the soul dies with the body. 2.
They did not believe in angels and spirits. 3.
They contended for the freedom of the will
in the fashion of the Greeks, thereby de-
parting from the clear teaching of the Mosaic law which they professed to believe
(Gen. 3:17; 4:7; 6:5-7). As early as the time
of Ezra the family of the high priest was
worldly and, unconsciously perhaps, began
to place political above religious considerations. The Zadokites-Sadducees in the second century were ready to neglect Jewish
customs and traditions, and favor Greek
culture and influence. By the time of the
Romans and Herod the Great, the collabo-
rating Sadducees had regained the high
priesthood, and the conduct of political affairs in Palestine was largely in their hands
by means of the ruling council, the Sanhedrin (Acts 5:17). The Sadducees joined the
Pharisees in harassing Jesus (Matt. 16:1-4),
and Joseph Caiaphas, Sadducee and high
priest, proposed the death of Jesus (John
11:49-53; 18:14) and was deeply responsible
for the judicial murder of the innocent prisoner. See also COUNCIL; HIGH PRIEST;
PHARISEES; ZADOK.

saf'fron. A plant of the crocus family and its
product, a spice extracted from its flower
(S. of Sol. 4:14). Clothing and rooms were
sprinkled with water scented with saffron.
Olive oil perfumed with it was used as an
ointment. Food was spiced with it. It was

also used in medicine.

saint. 1. A person who has dedicated himself and is faithful to God; a holy person (I Sam. 2:9; II Chron. 6:41; Ps. 31:23). 2. One who belongs exclusively to God through faith in His son (Rom. 1:7; I Cor. 16:1; Eph. 1:4). See also COMMUNION OF SAINTS.

Sa·lo′me. 1. Wife of Zebedee and mother of James and John (cf. Matt. 27:56 with Mark 15:40; 16:1). 2. Herodias' daughter (see HERODIAS).

Salt Sea. The Dead Sea (Gen. 14:3; Num. 34:12; Josh. 3:16). Also called the sea of the Arabah or Plain (Deut. 3:17; Josh. 3:16). It lies 1,292 feet lower than sea level, and its waters are much saltier than the ocean, by about 4 times. Eggs will float on its surface. There is no outlet to the sea, so the mineral salts brought to it by the Jordan and various tributaries remain and accumulate, year by year.

Sa·mar′i·tan. In the only appearance of this word in the O.T. (II Kings 17:29), it means an individual belonging to the old kingdom of Northern Israel. In later Hebrew literature it signifies an inhabitant of the district of Samaria in central Palestine, a region s.w. of the Sea of Galilee in Jesus' time (Luke 17:11, 16). The Samaritans were neither of pure Hebrew blood nor of uncontaminated worship. Those Hebrews who had not been carried off into captivity by Sargon in 722-721 B.C. became rebellious. Sargon therefore began a systematic course for their denationalization: he transplanted colonists from other regions of his vast empire, defeated enemies, and these intermarried with the remaining Israelites and continued to practice idolatry in their new home. Upon the Jews' return from exile, the Samaritans first sought to help them rebuild the Temple. When this offer was rejected by Zerubbabel, Jeshua and their associates, the Samaritans made no further efforts at conciliation but did their best, with other adversaries, to prevent the completion of the work (Ezra 4:1-10). They also opposed the later rebuilding of the walls of Jerusalem (Neh. 4:1-23). The Samaritans finally built their own temple on Mt. Gerizim. The hostility between the two groups (John 4:9) was so intense by Jesus' time that he used a Samaritan as the subject of a parable to show neighborliness and benevolence in action.

Sam'son. A member of the tribe of Dan, his great strength failed him when he broke his vows. His deeds and his betrayal by Delilah are described in Judg., chs. 13-16.

Sam'u•el. The first great Hebrew prophet after Moses and the last of the judges;

> born in answer to Hannah's prayer (I Sam., ch. 1)
>
> Eli's successor as priest (I Sam., chs. 2-3)
>
> judges Israelites (I Sam., ch. 7)
>
> his sons unworthy (I Sam. 8:1-5)
>
> anoints Saul when Israel demands a king (I Sam. 8:6-10:25)
>
> reproves people and king for sins (I Sam., chs. 12-13; 15)
>
> anoints the young David as king (I Sam., ch. 16; see also 19:18-22)
>
> dies; his spirit comes to Saul (I Sam. 25:1; 28:3-20).
>
> See also DAVID; ELI; PROPHET; SAUL.

sanc'tu•ar'y. A holy place set aside for the worship of God. The term may be applied to the Tabernacle (Ex. 25:8) or the Temple in Jerusalem and its precincts (I Chron. 22:19). The word is also applied, more narrowly, to the Most Holy Place, or the Holy of Holies, in the Tabernacle and Temple (Lev. 4:6). See MOST HOLY PLACE.

San'he•drin. The name generally given by historians to the highest Jewish assembly for government in the time of our Lord. See COUNCIL; SADDUCEES.

Sap•phi'ra. Wife of Ananias (Acts 5:1).

sap'phire. A precious stone, the lapis lazuli of the ancients, of rich azure color, the color of the sky on a clear day (Ex. 24:10).

Sar'ah. Also called Sarai. Wife of Abram (Abraham) (Gen. 11:31), she became the mother of Isaac at an advanced age. See Gen., chs. 12; 17; 20; 23.

sar'di·us. A red variety of chalcedony, darker than the carnelian, and a precious stone (Rev. 4:3). It was found near Sardis in w. Asia Minor, whence comes its name.

sar·do'nyx. A kind of onyx marked by parallel layers of sardius and of mineral of another color (Rev. 21:20). It was much used in cameos and signets.

Sar'gon II. A king of Assyria 722-705 B.C. (Isa. 20:1), successor to his brother Shalmaneser V. Samaria fell to him and he took more than 27,000 captives, transplanting other colonists into their lands. He built a vast and elaborate palace at a new capital 10 miles n. of Nineveh. See ASSYRIA.

Sa'tan. The Hebrew word means "obstructor" or "adversary." In the book of Job, however, "the adversary" is translated as though it were a proper name: Satan. He is said to be "among the sons of God," that is, supernatural beings, angels, subordinate to God, not opposed to Him. In I Chron. 21:1 "a satan" is called "Satan," who incited David to make a census in Israel. In the N.T. he is for the first time in Scripture clearly identified with the devil (Matt. 4:1, 10-11; Mark 1:13) and equated with Beelzebub (Matt. 12:24-27; Mark 3:22-26; Luke 11:15-20). The existence of a personal hostile power, whether called Satan or by any other name, is taken for granted in the N.T. He is the tempter, aiming to undo the work of God (Mark 4:15), seeking to persuade men to sin, desirous of leading them to renounce God (Matt. 4:9-10). He is held responsible for certain types of physical sickness (Luke 13:16). He is, however, under the control of God. But he is the demon of this world, in N.T. doctrine, who has access to the hearts of men, deceives them, and re-

ceives their witting or unwitting obedience
(Acts 5:3; 26:18; II Cor. 4:4; II Thess. 2:9;
Rev. 12:9). He is the ruler of a kingdom
(Matt. 12:24, 26; Luke 11:18; Rev. 12:7, 9).
Jesus, however, saw the overthrow of Sa-
tan's power (Luke 10:18). In Revelation,
the day when Satan will be thrown down in
two stages is described (12:9; 20:1-3, 7-10).

sa'trap. 1. The governor of a province in ancient Persia. 2. Hence, a petty prince acting
under a superior or any person acting in a
responsible administrative position.

sa'tyr. In Greek mythology a satyr was a
woodland deity, an attendant on Bacchus,
the god of wine and revelry, represented
with long, pointed ears, snub nose and a
goat's tail, later with goat's legs. He was
supposed to possess a half-brutal and lustful
nature. But in Isa. 13:21 and 24:14 the word
is applied to a goatlike demon which supposedly lived in the desert.

Saul. 1. First king of Israel. Although warned
of the consequences, the people demanded
a king, and Saul was chosen (I Sam., chs.
8-9);

> anointed by Samuel and made king (I
> Sam., chs. 10; 11)
>
> disobeys God; his curse falls upon Jona-
> than; Saul rejected as king (I Sam., chs.
> 13; 14; 15)
>
> evil spirit upon him allayed by David (I
> Sam. 16:14-23)
>
> jealousy and pursuit of David (I Sam.,
> chs. 17-28)
>
> consults witch of Endor (I Sam. 28:7-25)
>
> dies after battle of Gilboa (I Sam.
> 31:1-13; I Chron., ch. 10)
>
> his descendants (I Chron. 8:33).

See also DAVID; ISH-BOSHETH; SAMUEL.

2. Saul of Tarsus was the name by which
Paul was first known. See PAUL.

sa'vour. *n.* Scent, fragrance or breath; esp. in
Lev. and Num. "sweet savour" from a sacrifice. It means much the same as "burnt

offering" or "offering by fire," because these latter caused the "sweet savour" (Num. 28:2). *v.* To enjoy with appreciation (Matt. 16:23; Mark 8:33). American spelling of this word is *savor*.

scab'bard. A sheath or case to hold the blade of a sword, dagger, etc. (Jer. 47:6).

scar'let. A bright, rich crimson is meant (Lev. 14:4), not the hue of recent origin known as scarlet. The coloring matter was obtained, by methods early known, from an insect about the size of a pea that abounds on the prickly oak tree in Palestine. The female alone yields the coloring matter.

scent'ed wood. See THYINE WOOD.

schism. A split, a division, caused by unresolved differences of opinion.

school'mas'ter. The Greek word translated "schoolmaster" means "one who leads a boy," not a teacher but a trusted slave, a custodian, to whose care the children were committed. He was responsible for their safety, led them to and from school, etc. At age 16 a boy outgrew the need of such a custodian. He no longer needed to be protected from physical evil or bad company. Paul compared the Jewish law to such a custodian, one that led us to Christ, prepared us to accept him as our Redeemer, etc. (Gal. 3:24; cf. Rom. 3:19-21; 4:15; 7:7-25).

scor'pi·on. Akin to the great spiders, this

SCORPION

small, 6-inch invertebrate animal has 8 jointed legs and a tail armed with a sting that inflicts great pain (Rev. 9:5. 10). It has a pair of claws like the lobster. It seizes its beetle and locust victims with its claws and stings them to death. It abounds in Palestine, and is common in the wilderness s. of Judah (Deut. 8:15). Rehoboam's "scorpions" (I Kings 12:11) were probably whips armed with sharp points to make the lash more painful.

scourge. 1. A whip of cords or strips of leather, fastened to a handle, used for flogging (John 2:15). 2. Any means of inflicting severe punishment, suffering or vengeance (Isa. 10:26; 28:15). 3. As a verb, to whip, to flog severely (Matt. 27:26; Mark 15:15; Acts 22:25).

scribe. 1. A secretary; a government clerk (II Kings 12:10; Ezra 4:8); a person who could take dictation (Jer. 36:4, 18, 32). 2. One who copies the law and other parts of the Scriptures (Jer. 8:8). The most noted of the earlier scribes of this kind was the priest Ezra, a scribe skilled in the law of Moses and who had set his heart to teach statutes and judgments in Israel (Ezra 7:6, 10). He is the prototype of the N.T. scribes, who were professional interpreters of the law, the legal experts among the Pharisees (Matt. 5:20; 12:38; 15:1; 23:2, 13-29; Mark 2:16; 7:1, 5; Acts 23:9). They devoted themselves (a) to the study and interpretation of the law, which was both civil and religious, and to determining its application to the details of daily life. The decisions of the great scribes became the oral law or tradition; (b) to the study of the Scriptures generally in regard to historical and doctrinal matters; (c) to teaching, each noted scribe having a company of disciples about him. At the time of Christ the scribes had attained top-ranking influence among the people. The Sanhedrin counted many of them among its members (Matt. 16:21; 26:3). Though there

were among them some who believed in
Christ's teaching (Matt. 8:19), the majority
of them were hopelessly prejudiced against
him. They murmured at or found fault with
much that he and his disciples said or did
(Matt. 21:15), and they had a large share in
the responsibility for his death. See PHARI-
SEES.

scrip'ture. 1. A writing; any story or other
matter committed to writing (Dan. 10:21).
2. The term is applied in the N.T. esp. to
the sacred writings of the Hebrews, viewed
either collectively or individually, or even a
single passage or quotation from them, as in
Mark 12:10; Luke 4:21; John 19:37. When
this collection of sacred documents is
thought of as forming one book, the singular word, "the scripture," is used (John
7:42; Gal. 3:22). More frequently the many
documents by many authors are in mind
and the plural form is used, "the scriptures"
(Matt. 21:42; Luke 24:27; Rom. 1:2; II Tim.
3:15-17). 3. N.T. books gradually became
"scriptures" and a part of canonical "scripture."

scum. An unclean or impure quality; uncleanness. Some translators prefer "rust" in these
verses (Ezek. 24:6, 11-12).

scur'vy. A skin disease characterized by dry,
scaly coating (Lev. 21:20; 22:22).

sea gull. An indefinite term, broad enough to
include gulls, terns and petrels, all of which
abound on the shore and lakes of Palestine.

se'ah. A unit of dry measure, equivalent to 1.4
U.S. pecks. In the Bible it is simply called a
"measure." See MEASURES.

seal. 1. A design, initial or other mark placed
on something, as a letter or document to
prove its authenticity, on a manufactured
item for identification, etc. A signet ring or
cylinder engraved with such a seal was a
necessary part of the belongings of every
man of property, since a seal took the place
of a signature in an age when few could
write or read (I Kings 21:8). 2. Something

that confirms or authenticates, as circumcision was the seal of righteousness of Abraham (Rom. 4:11). 3. Any outward indication or sign of an inward condition or relation, as of God's approval (II Tim. 2:19) or promise (I Cor. 4:2; II Cor. 1:22).

sear. To wither or scorch; to cauterize (I Tim. 4:2).

Sec'ond Com'ing. Also called the Second Advent or the Return of Christ. This refers to his coming in divine majesty and judgment at the end of the age to complete the defeat of evil (I Cor. 15:24), to judge all men (Acts 7:31; II Cor. 5:10), and to give the blessing of complete salvation to his faithful followers (Heb. 9:28). Just how this great event will manifest itself and how it will affect mankind are questions about which significant differences among various Christian groups have arisen.

sec'ond death. The state of final damnation and punishment to which the wicked are condemned at the last judgment (Rev. 2:11; 20:14; 21:8).

Se'cond Quar'ter. See COLLEGE.

sec're·tar'y. See SCRIBE.

seer. The basic qualifications of "seer" and "prophet" seem identical. Both exercised the function of "seeing" (through prophetic vision) and of "speaking forth." The word "seer" seems to be applied to earlier prophets, like Samuel, Gad and Iddo, and then to have been replaced by "prophet." See PROPHET.

seethe. To boil or stew (Ex. 16:23).

seine. A large fishing net, with sinkers on one end and floats on the other. It hangs vertically in the water, and when its ends are brought together or drawn ashore encloses the fish (Hab. 1:15, RSV).

se'lah. A word occurring 71 times in the Psalms and in Hab. 3:3, 9, 13. It is universally agreed that this word is a liturgical or musical direction of some sort, but the exact meaning has not been determined.

The most widely accepted theory is that the word indicates a pause or rest for the voices, while the accompanying instruments continue to play, thus being heard with full effect during the vocal interlude.

sel'vedge. A specially woven edge that prevents cloth or fabric from raveling (Ex. 26:4; 36:11).

Se'mites. Descendants of Shem (Gen. 5:32). Semitic languages are found all over the ancient Near East, which makes it difficult to locate the original home of the Semites. A commonly held theory is that they came originally from n. Arabia and moved in every direction throughout the Fertile Crescent. The Semitic family today embraces Jews and Arabs living in Turkey, Syria, Lebanon, Iraq, Jordan, Arabia and n. Africa. Semites are not a race; they are a group of people speaking languages which have much in common. From Semites have come 3 world religions: Judaism, Christianity and Islam.

Sen·nach'er·ib. King of Assyria, he overcame many towns of Judah, took thousands of captives, collected tribute from King Hezekiah and besieged Jerusalem. But the plague smote his armies and he returned to Nineveh, his capital. After a long reign, during which he totally destroyed the city of Babylon, he was killed by 2 of his sons, and a third, Esar-haddon, came to the throne. See II Kings 18:13-19:36; II Chron., ch. 32; Isa., chs. 36; 37; also ASSYRIA; NISROCH.

sep'a·rate place. The unoccupied yard next to the Temple (Ezek. 41:12-14).

sep'ul·chre. A vault for burial; a tomb. It was usually a natural cave, enlarged and adapted for burial purposes, or one cut out of the soft rock mostly found in Palestine. The opening was closed off with a stone (I Kings 13:31; Matt. 27:60), to exclude jackals and other animals that prey upon dead bodies. Sepulchres were deliberately separated from human habitation, generally outside the town, and the entrances were often whitewashed, not only for cleanliness but also so that they might be seen clearly and not touched, for the touch brought ritual defilement. The whitewashed sepulchre is the basis of Jesus' comparison of "whited sepulchres," which had the outward appearance of purity but the inner reality of death and rottenness.

ser'a·phim. (Seraphim is the plural form of seraph; seraphims, in the KJV, is incorrect.) Heavenly beings who stood before the enthroned Lord when He appeared in a vision to Isaiah (6:2, 6). Scripture gives no further information about them. In Jewish tradition they are an order of angels; with the cherubim they make up the celestial choir.

Ser'gi·us Pau'lus. See PAUL.

ser'pent. Another word for snake. Serpents are mentioned often in the O.T., under many names—viper, adder, asp, etc. It is impossible to identify these precisely, or to match them up with the 30-odd varieties known in modern Palestine. The serpent of the temptation (Gen. 3:1, 14) was a snake "more subtle than any beast of the field," and afterwards cursed above all of them. In the usual theological interpretation, the Devil was in this serpent. See ASP, VIPER.

ser'vi·tor. A person who serves another; a servant or attendant (II Kings 4:43).

ser'vi·tude. The condition of slavery or political subjection to a foreign state (Neh. 5:18, RSV).

set'tle. Either of 2 lower edges of the altar in the Temple (Ezek. 43:14, 17).

sha'dow of death. A region of deep darkness and gloom (Ps. 23:4; Isa. 9:2; Matt. 4:16).

Shad'rach. See ABEDNEGO.

Shal'lum. A name of numerous men in the O.T., the most significant being: 1. A king of Israel who ruled only 1 month (II Kings 15:8–15); he murdered his predecessor,

Zechariah. 2. Another name for Jehoahaz (son of Josiah), king of Judah. See KINGS, TABLE OF. 3. The chief gatekeeper of the sanctuary (I Chron. 9:17-19; Ezra 2:42).

Shal'man·e'ser. The name of several Assyrian kings. Shalmaneser III was the first of his line to battle the Israelites, and he defeated the league formed to oppose him. Shalmaneser V besieged Samaria and took Hoshea, the last king of Israel, a prisoner (II Kings 17:1-6; 18:9-10). See ASSYRIA; CAPTIVITY; HOSHEA.

shear'ing house. The Hebrew word literally translated means "house of shearing," a barn where shepherds sheared their flocks. The word may, however, be a place name, "Beth-eked," a place on the road between Jezreel and Samaria where shepherds gathered to water their flocks at the several cisterns.

She'ba, Queen of. The story of this wealthy monarch's visit to Solomon is told in I Kings, ch. 10 and I Chron., ch. 9. Cf. Matt. 12:42.

sheep. The sheep of Palestine are usually white (Ps. 147:16; Isa. 1:18; Ezek. 27:18). The broad-tailed sheep is the more common of 2 varieties raised there, and has been bred since early ages in Arabia and Palestine. Sheep were herded by the Hebrew patriarchs (Gen. 12:16) and continuously by their descendants down into N.T. times (Luke 2:8). Major pasturelands were the Wilderness of Judea, the plateau of Moab, the borders of Palestine generally, and the country around Haran. But sheep in flocks of modest size were common everywhere. The sheep was a "clean" animal; its flesh was much eaten (I Sam. 14:32; 25:18; II Sam. 17:29; I Kings 4:23), and the rich milk of the ewes was drunk (Deut. 32:14; Isa. 7:21-22; I Cor. 9:7). The skin served as rude clothing (Heb. 11:37) and was sometimes used in covering tents (Ex. 26:14). Cloth was woven (Lev. 13:47-48;

Job 31:20; Prov. 27:26; Ezek. 34:3) from the wool, which was thus a valuable commodity and was rendered as tribute (II Kings 3:4). Sheepshearing was a time of festivity (Gen. 38:12; I Sam. 25:4; II Sam. 13:23). Sheep were much used in the sacrifice system (Ex. 20:24; Num. 22:40; John 2:14). The sheep was known for its affection (II Sam. 12:3), docility (John 10:3-4), meekness and submissiveness (Isa. 53:7; Jer. 11:19), helplessness when left to itself (Micah 5:8; Matt. 10:16), and its need of guidance (Num. 27:17; Ezek. 34:5; Matt. 9:36; 26:31). In the O.T., God is pictured as a shepherd (Ps. 23:1) or as sending a shepherd (Jer. 23:3-4). In the N.T., Jesus Christ is the shepherd of the flock.

sheep'fold. An enclosed yard for sheep (Num. 32:16; Judg. 5:16).

shek'el. 1. A weight used for metals (Gen. 24:22; I Sam. 17:5, 7). Payments were made in weighed-out metals, usually silver, expressed in shekels. See WEIGHTS. Coinage was not known in Palestine until the Persian period, and no Jewish silver coins were struck prior to A.D. 66.

shek'el of the sanc'tu·ar'y. The weight known as the shekel varied somewhat from country to country. The Phoenician shekel was regarded by the Hebrew authorities as the standard. In paying his Temple tax of one-half shekel, the Hebrew adult male had to pay in silver metal enough to counterbalance a one-half shekel weight on the other side of the scale, this half-shekel being of authentic Phoenician (not Babylonian) variety. The "shekel of the sanctuary" may at times have been heavier than the shekel of the trade markets.

Shem. Probably the firstborn son of Noah, blessed by his father (Gen. 5:32; 9:18-26). For his descendants, see Gen. 10:21-31; 11:10; I Chron. 1:17. From his line came the chosen people. See SEMITES.

She·ma′iah. This is a very common name in the O.T. Most notable are: 1. A prophet during Rehoboam's reign (I Kings 12:22-24; II Chron. 11:1-4; 12:5-15). 2. A false prophet who complained against Jeremiah (Jer. 29:24-32). 3. A false prophet who plotted against Nehemiah (Neh. 6:10-13).

shem′i·nith. The meaning of this instruction concerning the type or kind of performance to be given (Ps. 6; 12) is unknown.

She′ol. See HELL.

sherd. A broken piece of pottery (Isa. 30:14; Ezek. 23:34).

sher′iff. The word "sheriff" denotes a king's officer over a shire (county) in England. In ancient Babylonia some other kind of magistrate or officer is no doubt intended in Dan. 3:2-3.

shew′bread, show′bread. The Hebrew expression means literally "bread of the Presence (of God)." It consisted of 12 loaves of bread, laid in 2 rows, displayed on a table in the holy place before the Lord continually. The bread was changed every Sabbath, and the old loaves were eaten by the priests in the holy place (Ex. 25:30; Lev. 24:5-9; I Sam. 21:6; Matt. 12:4). The 12 loaves represented the 12 tribes of Israel. These loaves set in the presence of the Lord probably signified the constant communion of His people with Him in those things which His bounty provided and they enjoyed in His presence and used in His service.

Shib′bo·leth. The test word used by the Gileadites to identify fleeing Ephraimites who in their own speech could not pronounce *sh* at the beginning of a word (Judg. 12:6). "Shibboleth" has entered the English language, and is used to mean a test word or the watchword or saying characteristic of a party or sect.

Shig·ga′ion. A musical term of very uncertain meaning (Ps. 7, title); perhaps the idea of a wild and enthusiastic ode or song is intended.

Shig·i·o'noth. Plural of Shiggaion (Hab. 3:1).

Shim'e·i. Among the many bearing this name in the O.T., the most prominent is a member of Saul's family who insulted David (II Sam. 16:5–14; 19:16–23), and was later put to death by Solomon (I Kings, ch. 2).

ship'mas·ter. The captain (Rev. 18:17).

shit'tah tree, shit'tim wood. The tree is mentioned only once in the KJV (Isa. 41:19), its wood (shittim) 26 times, esp. Ex. 25:5–28; 26:15–37). The tree meant was the acacia, which grew 15–25 feet high in the Wilderness of Sinai and all along the Jordan Valley. The wood is hard and close-grained. The Egyptians used it in boat-building.

SHITTAH

sho'phar. See RAM'S HORN; TRUMPET.

sho·shan'nim. This word, meaning "lilies," that appears in the titles of Psalms 45, 69, 80 and in its singular form (shushan) in Ps. 60, seems to represent a direction to the singers to sing the words of these Psalms to a well-known tune of the period, "Lilies."

show'bread. See SHEWBREAD.

shu'shan. See SHOSHANNIM.

sig'net. A ring or seal (Dan. 6:17; Ex. 28:11; Jer. 22:24), esp. one used in place of a signature in marking documents official. It was engraved in metal, a precious stone or gold, and pressed down on soft, plastic material such as wax. See SEAL.

Si'hon. A king of the Amorites who was defeated by Israel and his territory divided (Num. 21:21-35; 32:33-38). See REUBEN.

Si'las. A companion of Paul (Acts 15:22; 16:19; 17:4; II Cor. 1:19; I Peter 5:12). In the Epistles he is always called Silvanus.

Sil'va·nus. See SILAS.

Sim'e·on. 1. Second son of Jacob and Leah (Gen. 29:33; 35:23), his story is found in Gen. 34:25-31; 42:24; 49:5-7. 2. The tribe of Simeon, founded by 5 of his 6 sons (Gen. 46:10; I Chron. 4:24). Their territory lay in the extreme s. of Canaan, w. of the Dead Sea, in the midst of the inheritance of Judah, and included the town of Beer-sheba (Josh. 19:1-9). When Moses blessed the tribes he did not mention Simeon explicitly (Deut., ch. 33), which may mean that they had become a part of the tribe of Judah. The tradition of 12 tribes was retained in Rev. 7:5-8. 3. A man to whom it was predicted that he should not die until he had seen Christ (Luke 2:25-35). 4. Simeon Niger, a prophet (Acts 13:1). 5. Simon Peter (Acts 15:14).

si·mil'i·tude. 1. Form, image or likeness (Ps. 106:20; Rom. 5:14). 2. A parable (Hos. 12:10). See PARABLE.

Si'mon. 1. Simon Peter (see PETER). 2. Simon Zelotes (the Zealot), one of the 12 apostles (Matt. 10:4; Mark 3:18; Luke 6:15; Acts 1:13). 3. A brother of the Lord (Matt. 13:55); see BRETHREN OF THE LORD. 4. A Pharisee at whose house Jesus once ate (Luke 7:36-50). 5. A householder in Bethany (Matt. 26:6-13; Mark 14:3-9; John 12:1-8). 6. Simon the Cyrenian (Matt. 27:32). 7. Simon Magus (the magician), who tried to buy the gift of God (Acts 8:9-24). 8. A tanner at Joppa with whom Peter lodged

(Acts 9:43; 10:6, 17, 32).

sin. A willful transgression of the law of God
(I John 3:4); want of conformity to His will.
Sin consists in both overt evil deeds and the
attitudes and disposition of the heart (Mark
7:20-23; Prov. 4:23). The sin of Adam and
Eve is thought to have had a unique significance for the entire human race (Rom.
5:12-14; I Cor. 15:21-22); the term "original
sin" is, however, not used in Scripture; it
means that since the Fall all persons are
born with the tendency to sin. The "unpardonable sin" is blasphemy against the Holy
Spirit (Matt. 12:31-32; Mark 3:28-29; Luke
12:10); such a sinner remains obstinate in
his wickedness, rejects God and His goodness, and completely reverses the facts of
God's moral order by adopting evil and
calling it good.

sin'ew. A tendon; a specialized kind of con-
nective tissue by which muscles are at-
tached to bones (Gen. 32:32; Job 10:11; Isa.
48:4).

sin offer-ing. A sacrificial offering made for
the purpose of gaining forgiveness for sin.
The ritual called for the individual to place
his hand on the head of the animal offered—a bullock, a male or female goat, a
female lamb, a dove or a pigeon might be
used—designating it as his substitute. Next
came the slaying of the animal by the offerer himself, who thus symbolically accepted
the punishment due for his sin. (In later
times the priests slew the animals.) Following this the priest sprinkled or smeared the
blood on the altar and poured it out at the
base. In specified cases a part was put on
the offerer, or it was sprinkled before the
veil of the sanctuary (Lev. 4:6), or carried
into the Holy Place (Lev. 6:30; 16:14). Finally came the burning of the sacrifice, the
whole of it or its fat only, on the altar of
burnt offering, whereby its essence and flavor ascended to God. A special sin offering
was made for all the people each year on

the Day of Atonement. See also OFFERINGS; SACRIFICE.

Sis'er·a. Commander of the defeated Canaanite army, he was killed by Jael while he slept (Judg., chs. 4; 5; I Sam. 12:9; Ps. 83:9).

skull, the place of a. See CALVARY.

slaugh'ter, val'ley of. See TOPHET.

slime. 1. A mineral pitch, a form of bitumen, semi-liquid or solid, found at or near the Dead Sea. It made a kind of cement (Gen. 11:3). See also MORTAR. 2. In Job 6:6 of the RSV, "slime" is a simile for something tasteless.

snail. Two different Hebrew words are translated "snail" in the KJV, but what mollusk is intended by either word is very uncertain.

snuff. v. 1. To express contempt by sniffing (Mal. 1:13). 2. To breathe heavily; to pant (Jer. 2:24; 14:6). n. The charred end of a wick (see SNUFFDISHES; SNUFFERS).

snuff'dish'es. Trays for removing the charred remains of wicks of candles (Ex. 25:38; Num. 4:9). See SNUFFERS.

snuff'ers. Part of the equipment of the golden lampstand of Tabernacle and Temple; "tongs of bronze or gold" for pruning off charred ends of wicks may be understood (I Kings 7:50; II Chron. 4:22).

sock'ets. Hollow receptacles, made of stone or occasionally metal (I Kings 7:50; II Chron. 4:22) for holding in place and upright the pivots on which swinging doors were hung.

so'der·ing, sol'der·ing. The joining of metal surfaces or parts with a melted metal alloy which hardens when it cools (Isa. 41:7).

sod'om·ite. A person guilty of sodomy, the unnatural vice of Sodom (Gen. 19:5); a male person who engages in sexual relations with another male, a practice strictly prohibited among the Hebrews (Deut. 23:17), but apparently sometimes found (I Kings 14:24; 15:12; 22:46; II Kings 23:7).

so'journ. v. To live somewhere temporarily (Gen. 26:3; Judg. 19:16). n. A brief or temporary stay, often said of the time spent by the tribes of Jacob (Israel) in Egypt.

so'journ·er. A person who visits another land temporarily; a stranger, a foreigner (Gen. 23:4; Lev. 25:23).

sol'der·ing. See SODERING, SOLDERING.

sol'emn as·sem'bly. A religious gathering of the community of Israel for a solemn occasion, either on a stated day (Deut. 16:8) or for an exceptional reason (Joel 1:14).

so·lem'ni·ty. A regular, usually yearly, ceremony, feast, etc. (Deut. 31:10; Ezek. 45:17).

Sol'o·mon. Son of David and Bath-sheba; king of Israel; also called Jedidiah (II Sam. 12:24-25; I Chron. 3:5; 22:9);

Adonijah seizes kingdom (I Kings 1:5)

Solomon acquires throne (I Kings 1:11-40)

Adonijah and Joab put to death and old scores settled (I Kings, ch. 2)

Solomon's wisdom (I Kings, chs. 3; 4; II Chron. 1:7-12)

makes league with King Hiram; they build and dedicate Temple (I Kings, chs. 5-8; II Chron., chs. 2-6)

Solomon's covenant with God (I Kings, ch. 9; II Chron., ch. 7)

Queen of Sheba's visit (I Kings, ch. 10; II Chron., ch. 9; cf. Matt. 12:42)

Solomon fails to keep covenant; his adversaries and death (I Kings, ch. 11; II Chron. 9:31; Neh. 13:26).

After Solomon's death (c. 922 B.C.), 10 of the 12 tribes revolted against King Rehoboam and formed the Northern Kingdom (Israel) under Jeroboam I. This was the beginning of the Divided Kingdom. See KINGS, TABLE OF; TEMPLE.

Sol'o·mon's porch. A splendid colonnade or portico on the e. side of the Temple area, probably built in N.T. times by Herod the Great and named after the king who built the first Temple (John 10:23; Acts 3:11; 5:12). See also TEMPLE.

Son of God. A title of the Messiah (Ps. 2:7; John 1:49); in its deepest sense expressive of the mysterious relation existing between the eternal Father and the eternal Son. In the N.T. the designation is used about 45 times, all but once denoting unmistakably our Lord (Matt. 4:3; Mark 1:1, etc.). As Son of God, Christ is God with all the infinite perfections of the divine essence (John 1:1-14; 10:30-38; Phil. 2:6), and is equal with God (John 5:17-25). He is subordinate in mode of subsistence and operation; that is, he is of the Father, is sent by the Father, and the Father operates through him (John 3:16-17; 8:42; Gal. 4:4; Heb. 1:2). Accordingly the word "Son" is not a term of office but of nature. He has the same nature, a fact that includes equality with God. See also SONS OF GOD.

son of man. 1. A man; a human being, possessed of humanity in distinction from divinity (Num. 23:19; Job 25:6; Ps. 8:4; Isa. 51:12). The expression stresses the gulf between the glory of God and the weakness of man. 2. Son of man, Jesus Christ; a title adopted for himself by Jesus, evidently with reference to the vision of Daniel (7:13-14, 27), and as a means of identifying himself as God's messenger who, on a mission from heaven, was to receive a universal and lasting dominion. He chose a title which, by reason of its several possible interpretations, until fully defined by Jesus himself, could not be used against him by his foes. He is recorded as having applied it to himself 78 times. It is also used of him by Stephen (Acts 7:56). Son of man and Son of God are united in the same person; see Matt. 16:13, 16-17.

sons of God. 1. Men as the creation of God (Luke 3:38). 2. The offspring of godlike beings and earth women (Gen. 6:4). 3. Angels (Job 1:6; 2:1). 4. In the N.T. the phrase indicates the believer's relationship to God through adoption (Rom. 8:14; Phil. 2:15). The teachings of Jesus disclose that God's purpose was to bring men into a conscious filial relationship with Himself and consequently into brotherhood with one another. See also ADOPTION; SON OF GOD.

sooth'say·er. A person who predicts or pretends to foretell the future by means of signs found in nature or dreams (Josh. 13:22). The pagan custom was forbidden in Israel (Deut. 18:14; Isa. 2:6; Micah 5:12), but was practiced in the time of King Manasseh (II Kings 21:6). See DIVINATION.

sor'cer·er. A person who attempts to gain power or information in any manner, esp. from evil spirits (Ex. 7:11), for divining the future; another English word for a magician or wizard. They were strictly forbidden (Ex. 22:18; Lev. 20:27). See DIVINATION; WIZARD.

sor'cer·ess. A female sorcerer (Deut. 18:10–12; Isa. 57:3).

sor'cer·y, sor'cer·ies. The practice of a sorcerer, esp. the type of black magic in which spells are cast, charms are used and potions are brewed for a harmful or sinister purpose (Isa. 47:9; Acts 8:9, 11).

South'ern King'dom. See JUDAH.

span. About 9 inches; see MEASURES.

spar'row. There is a very common Palestine house sparrow that nests in towns and villages in spring and frequents olive groves and farms in summer. The rock sparrow lives in holes in mountainsides or walls of cisterns, where it is often caught by the natives. Other sparrows have been identified. In the N.T. the "sparrows" of Matt. 10:29; Luke 12:6 represent an object of very little worth.

spelt. An inferior kind of wheat, the chaff of which sticks to the grain. It was sown in Egypt, springing up after the barley. In Ezek. 4:9 of the KJV it is called "fitches" and is the "rie" of Ex. 9:32 and Isa. 28:25. Rye is not grown in Egypt or Palestine, requiring northern climates.

spi'der. The number of species in Palestine amounts to 600 or 700.

spike'nard. A fragrant plant (S. of Sol. 4:13-14) from which an aromatic ointment was made. It is called "nard" in the RSV. It came from India, where it was early used by Hindus as a perfume and medicine, and the long journey to Palestine assured its preciousness. The alabaster jar of it (Mark 14:3, 5) was worth 300 denarii, the value of 300 days' labor on the part of a common workman.

Spir'it, Ho'ly. See HOLY SPIRIT.

spoil. *n.* Goods, territory, taken by force, as in warfare; plunder, booty (Gen. 49:27); also *spoils* (Josh. 7:21). *v.*: 1. To seize (goods) by force (Hos. 13:15; Matt. 12:29). 2. To strip (a person) of goods, money, etc. by force (Isa. 11:14; Ezek. 39:10). 3. To rob; to pillage; to plunder (II Chron. 14:14). 4. To destroy; to devastate or ruin (Jer. 10:20; Hos. 10:14).

spoil'er. A person or thing that spoils, robs or plunders (Judg. 2:14; I Sam. 13:17) or that ruins and destroys (Isa. 16:4; Jer. 6:26).

stac'te. A sweet spice, used for incense (Ex. 30:34). It is believed that the Hebrew word refers to the gum of the storax tree, or else of the opobalsamum.

sta'di•a. See MEASURES.

stan'dard bear'er. The man assigned to carry the flag or banner of an army or people; he was considered a symbol of their strength and unity (Isa. 10:18).

star'gaz•er. A person who claims to foretell the future by studying the movements of stars (Isa. 47:13).

stat'ute. An established rule or law, esp. a rule of conduct usually developing out of custom and formulated into a law declaring what is right (I Kings 3:3; Jer. 44:23).

stead. 1. The place or position of a person or thing (Gen. 30:2; II Sam. 16:8; I Kings 1:35). 2. Behalf; interest (II Cor. 5:20; Philemon 13).

steel. "Bronze" is probably meant, for steel-making was unknown in Bible lands.

Ste′phen. The first Christian martyr, he was falsely accused of blasphemy and stoned to death. The persecution which followed forced many Christians to flee, thus spreading the gospel rather than eliminating its teachings (Acts, chs. 6–7; 8:1; 9:1).

steppe. A large tract of arid land (I Chron. 6:78; Job 39:6, RSV). See also WILDERNESS.

ste′ward. 1. A person put in charge of the affairs of a large household (Gen. 15:2; I Kings 16:9). 2. A minister as the caretaker of the church of God (I Cor. 4:1; Titus 1:7).

stiff‑necked′. Stubborn, obstinate (Ex. 32:9).

stocks. An instrument of punishment consisting of a heavy wooden frame with holes for locking in an offender's ankles and often his wrists and neck (Jer. 2:2–3; 29:26). The "stocks" of Hos. 4:12 were wooden idols and not the above-described fastening device.

Sto′ics, Sto′icks. Members of a Greek school or sect of philosophy which Paul encountered at Athens (Acts 17:18), founded c. 300 B.C. The important quality of Stoics in contrast to Epicureans was their moral earnestness. They declared that an act was good or evil in itself, and that pleasure should never be made the end, the purpose, of an action. To Stoics, the highest good was virtue, which was based on knowledge and the conformity of one's conduct with the law of the universe. See also EPICUREANS.

stom′ach·er. A rich, ornamental robe (Isa. 3:24), worn over the upper portion of the body by a man or woman.

stork. A long-legged wading bird, related to the herons, a stork stands about 4 feet high, with white plumage and glossy black wings. It was "unclean" (Lev. 11:19; Deut. 14:18); dwelt in fir trees (Ps. 104:17); and was migratory (Jer. 8:7). It feeds on fish, frogs and small reptiles.

STORK

strait. *n.* Difficulty, distress (I Sam. 13:6). *adj.* Restricted, narrow, confined (II Kings 6:1); also strict or rigid (Acts 26:5).

strait'en. 1. To bring into difficulty, distress, etc. (Jer. 19:9). 2. To restrict or confine; to hamper (II Cor. 6:12). 3. To make impatient (Micah 2:7).

strait'ly. In a strict or rigid way, allowing for no deviation (Matt. 9:30; Ex. 13:19); also tightly (Josh. 6:1).

strange fire. Burning incense which was not made of the proper ingredients or made in some way contrary to the law (Lev. 10:1; Num. 3:4); "unholy fire."

stran'ger. In the Mosaic law a stranger meant a person not of Israelite descent, dwelling with the Hebrews, as distinguished from a foreigner temporarily visiting the land (Ex. 20:10; Lev. 16:29; 17:8; II Sam. 1:13; Ezek. 14:7). The stranger was not a full citizen, yet he had recognized rights and duties. His rights were guarded by the law (Ex. 22:21; 23:9), and the prohibitions that rested on an Israelite rested on him (Ex. 12:19; Lev. 16:29; 17:10; 18:26; 20:2; 24:26). He was not obligated to all the religious duties of the Israelites. In the N.T. the word means simply one who is unknown (Luke 17:16, 18; John 10:5; Acts 2:10).

stripe. A stroke or blow (Ex. 21:25). See also

SCOURGE.

stub´ble. The short stalks of grain left standing after harvesting (Ex. 5:12). Because it burned readily and was blown about easily, it became a symbol for anything that lacked stability or lasted for only a short time (Isa. 33:11; 40:24; 47:14).

su·born´. To obtain through bribery or other illegal methods (Acts 6:11).

sub´urbs. Open land lying outside a city, used for pasturing animals (Lev. 25:34; Num. 35:3, 7; Josh. 14:4).

Suc´coth-be´noth. The Hebrew word here transliterated "Succoth-benoth" has been distorted, for it means "tents of young women," which makes no sense here. Probably Marduk, the god of Babylon, and his consort Sarpanitu, combined into one god, are being referred to in II Kings 17:30. See BEL.

suc´cour. To aid, help or give assistance to in time of need or distress (II Sam. 8:5; 18:3; Heb. 2:18).

sun´der. To break apart, separate or split (Job 14:17, KJV). The phrase "in sunder" (Ps. 107:16; Isa. 45:2, KJV; Job 8:14, RSV) means "into parts (or pieces)."

sup´pli·ant. A person who makes a humble plea (Zeph. 3:10).

sup´pli·ca´tion. A humble request or prayer addressed to God (Acts 1:24; Eph. 6:18).

sure´ty. A person who makes himself responsible for the obligations of another (Gen. 43:9; Prov. 22:26–27). In commercial transactions a surety was often required to be found before credit was given. Jesus became the surety for the performance of the promises of God (Heb. 7:22). The expression, "of a surety," means certainly, surely.

sur´feit. Excess; overindulgence.

sur´feit·ing. Nausea and discomfort resulting from any kind of overindulgence.

swad´dling band, swad´dling cloths, clothes. A band or clothes wrapped around an infant (Job 38:9; Luke 2:7).

swal'low. One kind of swallow (*Hirundo transitiva*) resides in Palestine the year round. The European barn swallow is a part-time resident, from March to late fall. Swallows nested in the Temple area (Ps. 84:3) and were found in company with other small birds (Prov. 26:2). They are famous for their graceful flight.

swan. The graceful swan is rarely found in Palestine; some therefore believe that another water bird was meant, perhaps the ibis or the coot.

swarm'ing thing. The RSV interpretation in some instances (Gen. 7:21; Lev. 5:2; 11:29, 41-46) of the "creeping thing" of the KJV. See CREEPING THING.

swathed. Wrapped or swaddled as with a band or bandage.

sweet cane. A species of reed, probably imported, from which was obtained an aromatic oil used in holy oils and perfumes. See Isa. 43:24; Jer. 6:20; also CALAMUS.

swine. The swine or pig was an "unclean" animal, unfit for use in any kind of sacrifice (Lev. 11:7; Deut. 14:8). It was also considered taboo or unclean by Phoenicians, Egyptians and Ethiopians. The use of its flesh in hot countries was supposed to cause skin diseases. To the Jews, swine's flesh was abominable and the pig was the symbol of filth and coarseness (Prov. 11:22; Matt. 7:6; II Peter 2:22). To feed swine was the lowest kind of work a Jew could sink to (Luke 15:15). In Decapolis, a region colonized by Greeks, swine was highly esteemed as meat. Jesus encountered a herd of swine there (Mark 5:11-13).

syc'a·mine tree. The Greek N.T. calls the mulberry tree *sykaminos*. From this Greek name comes "sycamine" (Luke 17:6).

syc'a·more, syc'o·more. A fig tree, abundant in the lowlands of Judah (I Kings 10:27; I Chron. 27:28; II Chron. 1:15; 9:27). It grew in the Jordan Valley (Luke 19:4), and its timber was much used (Isa. 9:10). It grows to 50 feet high. The fruit, inferior to the common fig, grows in clusters on twigs that spring directly from the trunk and larger branches (Amos 7:14), and cannot be eaten until it has been punctured and the insect that infests it has been allowed to escape.

syn'a·gogue. A building or place used by Jews for worship and religious study (Luke 4:16; 7:5). The origin of the synagogue probably lies in the time of the Babylonian captivity when the Jews had lost their worship in the Temple and the conditions in the Exile called for new forms of worship and religious instruction to prevent assimilation into Babylonian culture. Meetings began to take place each Sabbath in which the learned men would explain the law to members of the congregation. The affairs of the synagogue after the Exile were under the general direction of the elders; there was a ruler of the synagogue, probably elected by the congregation, who had responsibility for the building and property and general supervision of public worship (Luke 13:14), including the appointing of persons to read the Scripture and the inviting of strangers to address the congregation (Acts 13:15); this explains how Jesus was able to teach in synagogues (Matt. 13:54). The word "synagogue" is also applied to the assembly of Jews that met and worshiped in a synagogue (Mark 1:23; Luke 4:20).

T

ta'ber·na'cle. 1. A temporary shelter, as a tent, hut or booth (Ps. 76:2; Isa. 4:6). 2. The movable sanctuary in the form of a tent. It was regarded as the Lord's dwelling place (Ex. 25:9; 26:1), the "house of the Lord" (Ex. 34:26; Josh. 6:24) and the place where He met His people. It was thus the holiest place on earth and the focus of Hebrew life. It also housed the Ark of the Covenant and the tables of the law. When erected, the Tabernacle formed a rectangle 30 cubits long by 10 broad (approx. 45 feet by 15). The interior was divided into 2 apartments by 4 pillars sunk in bases of silver and hung with a veil (Ex. 26:31-32, 37). The outer room was called the sanctuary or holy place, which was approx. 30 feet by 20; the inner was the Most Holy Place, measuring 15 feet in every direction. The Tabernacle stood in a courtyard, about 150 feet by 75, surrounded by an enclosing fence 7½ feet high.

When the people broke camp, the Levites took down the structure and put it together again at the new camping ground (Ex. 40:34-38). During the conquest of Canaan the Ark remained in the camp at Gilgal. After the settlement of the Israelites, Joshua set up the Tabernacle at Shiloh, where it remained during the period of the Judges (Josh. 18:1), until the Philistines destroyed the town (c. 1050 B.C.) and captured the Ark. When the Ark was returned to Jerusalem, David built a new tabernacle for it.

The Tabernacle was the model used by Solomon in the construction of the Temple; in the case of the Most Holy Place, the dimensions of the one in the Temple were twice those of the Tabernacle. It is also called "tabernacle of the congregation" (Ex.

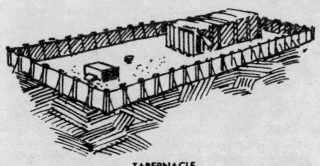

TABERNACLE

29:42), "tabernacle of witness" (Num. 17:7) and "tent of testimony" (Num. 9:15). 3. In the N.T., "tabernacle" is used figuratively for the human body (II Cor. 5:4) and for heaven (Heb. 9:11). See also ALTAR; MOST HOLY PLACE.

Ta′ber·na′cles, Feast of. The last of the 3 great annual festivals at which (originally) every man of Israel was required to appear before the Lord at the sanctuary, and the second of the harvest festivals (Deut. 16:16; II Chron. 8:12-13). It took its name from the custom of dwelling in booths during its celebration (Lev. 23:40-42), which after the establishment of the sanctuary at Jerusalem were erected in the open places of the city, on rooftops, and in open country outside the city walls. It was an 8-day festival, starting on the 15th day of the 7th month, 5 days after the Day of Atonement. This was the time of the year when all products from the fields, olive-yards and vineyards had just been gathered; hence the name "Feast of Ingathering" under which it began (Ex. 23:16; 34:22; Lev. 23:39; Deut. 16:13-15). The booths, made from the boughs of trees, were a reminder of life on the march through the wilderness and of God's protection during that period. Hence came still another name, "Feast of Booths." See also BOOTH. Jews who were unable to attend the celebration at Jerusalem because of the distance from their home kept the festival at the synagogue of the town where they lived, without of course the offering of sacrifices which were restricted to the Temple. See also PASSOVER; WEEKS, FEAST OF.

Tab′i·tha. See DORCAS.

tab′ret. A small kind of drum, with 2 membranes, beaten by hand, used in secular music, probably with jingling pieces of metal around it, like a tambourine (I Sam. 10:5; 18:6; Isa. 24:8). The timbrel seems to have been the same instrument.

tal′ent. A weight used both for ordinary com-

modities and for the precious metals. It was
the standard large weight, but it varied from
time to time and from country to country.
In most Bible passages it may be figured at
approx. 75 pounds. Naturally the talent as a
money unit was not coined. A talent of silver would in N.T. times have been worth
6,000 drachmas, perhaps $1,200 in U.S.
money of the present day. See also
WEIGHTS.

Tal'i·tha cu'mi. An Aramaic expression:
"Maiden, arise" (Mark 5:21).

tam'a·risk. See MANNA.

tam'bou·rine'. See TABRET.

Tam'muz. The Babylonian and Assyrian god
of the pasture and patron of flocks and their
keepers. His supposed annual death and
resurrection symbolized the winter and
spring cycle (Ezek. 8:14); he allegedly died
and retired to the underworld as the vegetation died in the fall, and was revived and
brought back to life in the spring. The
Babylonians named the fourth month of
their calendar after him and the Jews also
adopted the name for their fourth month
(June–July) in their post-Exile calendar.

tare. A weed. The specific weed referred to by
Jesus is doubtless the bearded darnel,
which grows in grainfields and is difficult to
distinguish from wheat until it heads, near
harvest time (Matt. 13:25–29, 36).

tares. A true "tare," a member of the vetch
family, would be easily distinguishable
from the wheat in Jesus' parable (Matt.
13:25–30). But another weed, the bearded
darnel, fits perfectly: it is almost indistin-
guishable from wheat while both are only
in blade, but can be separated without difficulty when both come into ear.

task'mas·ter. A person who assigns tasks to
others (Ex. 1:11).

teil tree. The linden (Isa. 6:13). The RSV
reads "terebinth"—the turpentine tree,
which is native to Palestine. See also OAK.

tem'per·ance. The state or quality of being

moderate in indulging the appetites; self-restraint in conduct, expression and desire or passion (Acts 24:25; Gal. 5:23; II Peter 1:6).

tem′ple. 1. A building for the worship of a god or gods (I Chron. 10:10; Joel 3:5; Acts 19:27); also called "house" (Judg. 9:46; I Sam. 5:2). 2. The Temple in Jerusalem, any of the 3 successive buildings erected on the same site. The first one was built by Solomon (I Kings, chs. 5-8) about 1000 B.C. and was destroyed by the Babylonians in 586 B.C. The temple of Ezekiel (Ezek., chs. 40-47) was an ideal structure envisioned by him to be built in Jerusalem when ideal conditions for it arrived. It was never built.

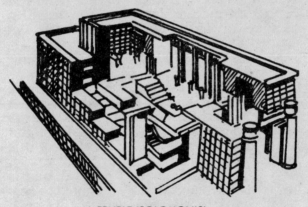

TEMPLE (SOLOMON'S)

The second Temple, therefore, was begun in about 536 B.C.; work was then dropped until Zerubbabel took it up again about 520 B.C. and finished it in 515. It was projected on a smaller and much less magnificent scale than Solomon's Temple. The third was the Temple undertaken in about 20 B.C. by Herod the Great, who assembled the materials before taking down the old structure. The main edifice was built in 18 months, but the entire complex of courts and outlying buildings was not completed until about A.D. 62. Except at the n.w. cor-

ner, where stood the Tower of Antonia
housing Roman soldiers, this Temple was
bordered on all sides by magnificent covered colonnades or cloisters. The colonnade
on the e. side was regarded as a remnant of
the first Temple and was called Solomon's
Porch (John 10:23; Acts 3:11). It was in this
court that the money-changers set up their
tables (Matt. 22:12; John 2:14). The entire
sacred area was surrounded by massive
walls, pierced by gates. During the siege of
Jerusalem by the Romans in A.D. 70, the
Temple area, used as a fortress by the Jews,
was twice burned, and afterward the Romans threw down the walls. In A.D. 136 the
Roman emperor Hadrian built a temple to
Jupiter on the site. In 691 a Mohammedan
mosque, called the Dome of the Rock, was
erected there, where it still stands. See AL-
TAR; MONEY-CHANGERS; MOST HOLY PLACE;
TABERNACLE.

tempt. In the Bible the use of this word is
consistently to test, to put to the proof. It
may be either the testing of a man or a nation, or also a man's testing of God. But
while God has cause to test out men, it is
never for evil. For a man to tempt or test
God is presumptuous and disloyal, and is
always condemned. Satan attempted to persuade Jesus to test God by, for example,
leaping off the pinnacle.

temp·ta'tion. 1. A test or a trial to prove the
value or ascertain the nature of something
(Deut. 4:34; 7:19; 29:3). 2. An attempt to
persuade a person to commit sin or to submit to some kind of evil enticement (James
1:12).

Ten Com·mand'ments. A comprehensive for-
mulation of the basic laws that govern
man's relation to God and to his fellow
men; also called the Decalogue. They became the fundamental laws of the Hebrew
state. They were revealed by God at Sinai,
and written on two tables of stone (Ex.
31:18). These 10 laws appear in two forms:

the older form, Ex. 20:1-17, and the later version, Deut. 5:6-21. See also LAW.

ten'on. A projecting part cut on the end of a piece of wood for insertion into a corresponding hole (a "mortise") in another piece to make a joint (Ex. 26:17; 36:22).

tent of the con·gre·ga'tion, tent of meet'ing. See TESTIMONY.

ter'a·phim. Idols, probably in human form, representing household gods. They varied in size from those small enough to be easily carried in hasty flight and hidden in a saddle of a camel (Gen. 31:19, 30, 34) to one apparently large enough to represent a man (I Sam. 19:13). They were probably regarded as bringers of good luck, and were consulted with respect to the advisability of proposed actions, as a form of divination.

ter'e·binth. See OAK; TEIL TREE.

tes'ta·ment. 1. A binding and solemn agreement; a covenant (Matt. 26:28; Mark 14:24). The Old Testament is that division of the Bible centered on the covenant between God and the Hebrew people, originating with Abraham and reinforced with the Exodus. The New Testament offers the new covenant which God established with man through Jesus Christ. 2. A will; a document in which a person (called the testator) expresses his wishes concerning the disposal of his property after death (Heb. 9:17). See also COVENANT.

tes'ti·mo·ny. A solemn declaration or affirmation given by a witness or witnesses in a legal situation. In the O.T. the following special uses of the word are found: 1. The "testimonies" of God are especially the Decalogue (Ten Commandments) and the entire book of the law (Deut. 4:45; 6:17, 20; Ps. 25:10), the first 5 books of the O.T. 2. The "tables of the testimony" are the 2 tables of the law (Ex. 31:18). 3. The Ark of the Covenant is often called the "Ark of the Testimony" (Ex. 25:22; 26:33-34; Num. 4:5, etc.). 4. The tent of the congregation (Ex.

40:34-35, KJV; "tent of meeting," RSV) is
also called the "tent of the testimony"
(Num. 9:15; 17:7-8).

te'trarch. One who rules over a one-fourth
part of a kingdom or province. Eventually
the Romans used the word loosely as a con-
venient title for a prince with a small territory whom they were unwilling to dignify
with the authority and rank of a king. Herod Antipas and Philip each received approximately one-fourth of the kingdom of
Herod the Great, and so "tetrarch" was the
appropriate title for them, even in the original sense (Matt. 14:1; Luke 3:1, 19).

Thad·dae'us. See JUDAS (1).

thank of'fer·ing. See PEACE OFFERING.

Theu'das. The leader of a band of rebels (Acts
5:36).

Thom'as. One of the 12 apostles (Matt. 10:3;
Mark 3:18; Acts 1:13, etc.), also called in
Greek Didymus (both names mean "twin");
determined to share Jesus' peril (John
11:16)
queries Jesus about his departure (John
14:1-6)
expresses doubt about Resurrection
(John 20:24-29)
present at Sea of Galilee appearance
(John 21:1-8).

thorn. 1. Any of various small trees, shrubs or
weeds, abundant in Palestine, bearing short,
hard, leafless stems that come to a sharp
point; often planted as hedges (Hos. 2:6) or
dried and used as fuel (Ps. 58:9). 2. One of
these short, pointed stems. Used figuratively (often with "thistle," Gen. 3:18; Hos.
10:8) for the worthlessness of the people (II
Sam. 23:6); as instruments of punishment
(Judg. 8:7, 16); for distress and desolation
(Isa. 7:23, 25); and to depict God's wrathful
judgment (Ps. 118:12). 3. The "thorn" of
Job 41:2 is translated "hook" in the RSV;
God is teasing Job with the things he cannot do but God can do. 4. The "thorn in the

flesh" of Paul (II Cor. 12:7) may have been some physical affliction, pain or ailment which had come upon him. A "thorn in the eye" (or "side") was a persistent cause of annoyance or irritation (Num. 33:55; Josh. 23:13).

thorns and this'tles. Both terms are generic rather than specific. Thorny weeds, bushes and trees of various kinds are abundant in Palestine. About their only useful function was as hedges. Thistles are equally numerous in variety, and are found in fields and waste places; some grow so thick and have such vicious spines as to make passage on foot impossible. What Paul's "thorn in the flesh" was (II Cor. 12:7) is uncertain, perhaps a physical ailment of a recurring nature.

thresh'ing·floor. A place where the process of separating grain from the straw was performed in volume. It was generally common to a whole village, but may have had a private owner (II Sam. 24:16). If possible it was the surface of a flat rock on the top of a hill exposed to any wind that blew, which would carry off the light chaff. Otherwise an artificial floor (Jer. 51:33) was laid out and soon assumed a circular shape about 50 feet in diameter and became firm and hard under the tread of oxen, which were driven round and round to trample out the kernels, or made to drag over the separated sheaves a weighted sled provided with sharp metal discs which rolled over the straw to loosen the grain. The winnowing was done by tossing the threshed grain high in the air with shovel or fork; the chaff was blown off by a breeze, while the clean, heavier grain fell to the ground.

Thum'mim. See Urim and Thummim.

thy'ine wood. A large tree of the cypress family. In Rev. 18:12 it is listed among the luxurious items of merchandise in Babylon. In the RSV it is referred to as "scented wood."

Ti·be'ri·as, Sea of. See GALILEE, SEA OF.

Tig'lath-pi·le'ser III. King of Assyria (745-727 B.C.), also called Pul and Tilgath-pilneser. Deporting many captives from the Northern Kingdom, thus breaking down national ties, and collecting tribute from kings Menahem and Ahaz (II Kings 15:19; 16:7-8; I Chron. 5:26; II Chron. 28:16-21), he reduced all the petty kingdoms of Palestine and Syria to vassal states and brought the Assyrian empire to a power formerly unknown. See ASSYRIA; CAPTIVITY.

till'er. One who tills the ground; a plowman (Gen. 4:2).

tim'brel. See TABRET.

Ti·mo'the·us. See TIMOTHY.

Tim'o·thy. An assistant of Paul, usually referred to as Timotheus, his early life and works are described in Acts 16:1-3; 17:14-15; 19:22; 20:4, and he is often mentioned in the Epistles (e.g. I Cor. 4:17).

Tir·sha'tha. The Persian title of the governor of Judah under the Persians. It was borne by Zerubbabel (Ezra 2:63) and Nehemiah (Neh. 8:9).

tithe. A tenth part of one's income consecrated to God. Contrary to the custom in Egypt and elsewhere, where the tithe was a tax, the tithe among the Hebrews was primarily a prescribed gift for religious purposes. Deut. 12:5-6, 11 suggests that tithing was directed to the sanctuary, with Levites receiving it every third year. In Num. 18:21, 24, the Levites are specified as the recipients of all tithes in return for the service they rendered at the sanctuary and as compensation to them for their lack of landed possessions. Probably changes in the regulations were perforce introduced to meet changed situations or local customs. All the fruits of ground and cattle were subject to tithing (Lev. 27:30-32), but the tithe of grain and fruit need not be paid in kind: the owner might redeem it by purchasing it at 20% more than its market value. In times of religious decline the people neglected to pay tithes (II Chron. 31:4-12; Mal. 3:7-12). The second Temple was provided with storehouses (Neh. 13:10-14) and Levites gathered tithes into the towns and tithed them for the sanctuary (Neh. 10:37-38). The payment of tithes continued (Luke 11:42; 18:12) despite the burden of Roman taxes, but changes had occurred. The tithes went to the priests and Levites, and were regarded as their due. For Jesus' comment on the tithing of the Pharisees, see Matt. 23:23.

tit'tle. A point or small sign used to distinguish one letter of the Hebrew alphabet from another, notably *beth* from *kaph* and *resh* from *daleth.* Hence, a minute requirement of the law (Matt. 5:18).

Ti'tus. A young companion of Paul (Gal. 2:1-3), sent to Corinth to correct certain abuses (II Cor. 2:12-13; 7:6, 13-14; 8:6; 12:18) and later to Dalmatia (II Tim. 4:10).

toils. Any snare or trap like a mesh, network or enclosure (Prov. 5:22, RSV).

tongue. 1. The tongue of a human (Judg. 7:5) or animal (Ps. 68:23). 2. In a figurative sense, speech or language (Gen. 10:5), or the people speaking it (Isa. 66:18). 3. A human being, esp. in terms of the ideas expressed in speech (Isa. 45:23; 54:17). 4. A manner or style of speaking (Prov. 12:18; Hos. 7:16).

tongues, gift of. A spiritual gift mentioned many times in the N.T., particularly in Acts and in the Epistles of Paul (Acts 2:1-13; 10:44-46; 19:6; I Cor., ch. 12; 14:14-17). The gift appeared as the disciples were assembled in the upper room on the day of Pentecost, and as the Holy Spirit descended upon them (Acts 2:4). Many Jews from other lands, in Jerusalem for the festival, were astonished to hear the disciples speaking in the various languages or dialects represented in the audience (Acts 2:5-13). Some scholars are of the opinion that the phenomena described in Acts 2:1–13 were similar to those in I Cor. 12:10, 30; 14:13–16, 27–28, and were unintelligible ecstatic utterances. However, it has been pointed out that the manifestations in Acts may have been a temporary, irresistible experience, while at Corinth it appears to have been a continuing experience under the control of the speaker, and it was necessary to have an interpreter (I Cor. 14:5, 13, 27). The nature and significance of this gift are variously interpreted today, a time of great increase in "speaking in tongues."

ton'sure. 1. Act of clipping the hair or shaving the crown of the head. 2. The shorn crown or patch.

to'paz. A precious stone, yellow to orange in color, found in Ethiopia (Job 28:19) and on an island in the Red Sea. The topaz of the ancients was probably a variety of corundum.

To'phet, To'pheth. A place in the valley of Hinnom where the people of Jerusalem in the times of Isaiah and Jeremiah on occasion burned their sons and daughters in the fire (Jer. 7:31) as offerings to the Ammonite god Molech (II Kings 23:10). Jeremiah prophesied that God's punishment for the people's sins would cause so many deaths that the name Topheth ("place of burning") would disappear by being used to bury corpses—the ultimate defilement, to a Jew—and the place would be known thereafter as the "valley of slaughter" (Jer. 7:32–33; 19:6). See MOLECH.

To'rah. See LAW.

tor-men'tors. The Greek word so translated in Matt. 18:34 of the KJV was "torturers"; the RSV here uses "jailers." No doubt they made the debtor's life miserable by chains and other forms of torture until his debts were paid and he was released.

tor'toise. Lev. 11:29 is the only occurrence of this word in the KJV. The RSV says "lizard."

tow. The coarse and broken fibers of hemp, flax, etc., ready for spinning; it burns readily (Judg. 16:9; Isa. 1:31; 43:17).

traf'fic, traf'fick. Trade; buying and selling (I Kings 10:15); a "trafficker" was a merchant or trader (Isa. 23:8).

Trans·fig'u·ra'tion. The glorified change in the appearance of Jesus on the mountain (unnamed) in the presence of 3 of his disciples (Matt. 17:1-8; Mark 9:2-8), having the effect of impressing them with his divine nature and convincing them that he was sent by God the Father.

trans·gres'sion. The breaking of a law or commandment; the most profound word for "sin" in the O.T. To transgress is to rebel, to revolt against God. It is a willful disobedience (Ex. 34:7; I Sam. 14:33; Ps. 59:5; Isa. 43:27). To transgress and transgression may also be applied to acts against men (I Kings 12:19; Amos 1:3).

trans·late'. 1. To bear or change from one place or condition to another (II Sam. 3:10). 2. To remove to heaven, originally implying without death (Heb. 11:5). "Translation" is the act of such removal.

trav'ail. *v.* To labor hard; to suffer the pangs of childbirth (Gen. 35:16). *n.* Heavy labor; agony (Isa. 53:11).

tree of knowl'edge, of life. In these two trees ancient pre-Israelite material stemming from Babylon has been transformed into symbols of the relation between God and man. Adam and Eve were forbidden to eat of the tree of knowledge; they disobeyed the command of God and were expelled from the garden (Gen. 2:9; 3:3-7). "Knowledge" has been interpreted as secular knowledge, moral judgment, sexual knowledge, universal or divine knowledge, and those "secret things which belong only to God" (Deut. 29:29). No one of the interpretations is certain or satisfies everything involved in the symbolism. The "tree of life" (Gen. 2:9; 3:22, 24) represents a means of obtaining immortality. The life intended for man was a harmonious existence with God; through disobedience, man lost this full life (Gen. 2:17; 3:7-19). See FALL. The "tree of life" symbol occurs in Rev. 2:7 and 22:2, 14, 19, where its use enriches the final vision of John as to man's life with God.

tres'pass. A lapse into sin, a word applied to an individual sinful act rather than to a condition of sinfulness. It is more commonly used in the N.T. than in the O.T.

tres'pass offer·ing. An offering that was primarily a fine imposed on a person who had done damage to a neighbor's property or committed other civil offenses (Lev. 5:16, 19; 7:1-7, 14; Num. 5:7-8). See GUILT OFFERING. Special trespass offerings were made in the cleansing ceremonies of lepers (Lev. 14:12) and defiled Nazarites (Num. 6:12).

tri·bu'nal. The seat of a judge. See also JUDGMENT SEAT.

trib'une. In Roman history, a military commander, at first appointed by the consuls, later elected by an assembly of the people. Tribunes could inflict punishment, even death, and their persons were sacrosanct. They gradually became political leaders. (Acts 21:31-37; 22:24-29; 23:10-22; 24:22, RSV).

trib'u·tar'y. A person compelled to work at forced labor (Deut. 20:11; Judg. 1:30, 33, 35).

trib'ute. 1. Money, goods or services exacted by a nation or king from foreign subjects (Deut. 20:11; Judg. 1:28). 2. The didrachma, or half-shekel, individual tax levied to cover the expenses of the Temple worship (Matt. 17:24). This was the successor of the half-shekel atonement payment imposed on Hebrew males 20 years and over (Ex. 30:11-16). Each year collectors of the tax traveled from town to town to raise the tribute money; Jews living outside Palestine paid theirs at tax houses set up in each Jewish center abroad.

tri'gon. A triangular lyre or harp.

Troph'i·mus. A Gentile thought to have been brought illegally into the Temple, causing Paul's arrest (Acts 20:4; 21:29). See also II Tim. 4:20.

trum'pet. 1. A wind instrument, made of the horn of an animal or in imitation of it (Josh. 6:4-5). The Hebrew word is *shophar*. The sound of the shophar was audible at a great distance (Ex. 19:16, 19). It stimulated shouting (II Sam. 6:15); trumpet blasts and shouting felled Jericho's walls (Josh. 6:1-20). It was used to assemble an army (Judg. 3:27); to sound the attack (Job 39:24); to signal the end of a pursuit (II Sam. 2:28); to proclaim the accession of a king (15:10). The ram's horn trumpet or shophar was ill-suited to be played with harps and pipes in an orchestra; it was a signaling instrument. 2. The trumpet evolved for Temple use was a straight, narrow, silver wind instrument about 18 inches long. Somewhat thicker than a flute, it ended in the form of a bell. Trumpets were used by priests to announce festivals, and were rarely blown by laymen. They were used in pairs from the beginning, either in unison or antiphonally, and trumpet-signals began every Temple event, sacrifice or ceremony. 120 were blown in unison at the dedication of the Temple (II Chron. 5:12-13). Priests may have blown them at the coronation of Joash (Jehoash) (II Kings 11:14).

Trum'pets, Feast of. A festival celebrated on the occasion of the seventh new moon of the year. This fell on the first day of the month Tishri (Lev. 23:24-25; Num. 29:1-6).

Tu'bal-cain'. The first of the metalworkers (Gen. 4:22).

tu'mors. Swellings. The RSV uses this word instead of the "emerods" of the KJV. See EMERODS.

tur'tle, tur'tle·dove. A species of dove, gentle

and harmless, an apt symbol of a defenseless and innocent people (Ps. 74:19). The most common species migrated s. at the approach of winter (Jer. 8:7); its return heralded spring (S. of Sol. 2:12). Easily trapped, it was readily obtainable by the poor and much used in sacrificial worship (Lev. 1:14; 5:7; 12:6, 8; 15:14, 29-30; Num. 6:10-11).

Twin Broth'ers. See CASTOR AND POLLUX.

Tych'i·cus. A messenger of Paul (Acts 20:4; Eph. 6:21; Col. 4:7; II Tim. 4:12; Titus 3:12).

U

un·cir'cum·cised. 1. Not circumcised; hence not of the Israelites; heathen (Gen. 17:14; Judg. 14:3). 2. Morally impure; unclean (Lev. 26:41; Jer. 6:10).

un·clean an'i·mals. A distinction between "clean" and "unclean" meats was made by ancient peoples. Some animals were seen as fit for food and sacrifice, others were not. The distinction was based on the suitableness of the flesh for food, on the habits of the animals, on national customs and on an unexplainable national abhorrence to certain animals, such as the serpent. Unclean animals are classified for Israel in Lev., ch. 11 and Deut., ch. 14. These were unclean and forbidden under any circumstances.

un·clean'ness. The law distinguished between "clean" and "holy" (Lev. 10:10); for example, animals are clean or unclean, not holy or unholy. Uncleanness was a ceremonial problem; it was not the same as moral defilement. It excluded men from the sanctuary (Lev. 7:20-21) and from fellowship with other Israelites until the rules for purification had been met, but not from communion with God in prayer. Ceremonial defilement was acquired by contact with a human corpse (Num. 19:11-22); leprosy in man, clothing or building (Lev., chs. 13; 14);

natural and morbid issues from the generative organs (Lev., chs. 12; 15); and eating the flesh of an unclean animal (Lev., ch. 11). See also UNCLEAN ANIMALS.

un'clean spir'it. An evil spirit that took hold of and controlled a person, thereafter described as a demoniac. Such a person was not thought to be wicked but was considered ceremonially unclean and contact with him was forbidden (Matt. 10:1; Mark 3:11; Luke 4:36).

un·ho'ly fire. See STRANGE FIRE.

u'ni·corn. Literally, a 1-horned animal. It existed only in Greek mythology. Legends about the unicorn were popular in the Middle Ages and the animal appears frequently in medieval paintings and tapestries. The translators should have said "wild ox" or perhaps "antelope" wherever "unicorn" appears (Job 39:9-10).

un'known god. The Greeks had so many gods that often they did not know which one they should pray to; so they would build an altar to a god or gods whose names they did not know, in the hope that in this way they would avoid offending or unintentionally neglecting the god from whom some benefit had been received (Acts 17:23).

un·leav'ened bread. Bread or cakes made from unfermented dough, i.e., without yeast. It was associated esp. with the 7-day Feast of Unleavened Bread, connected with the Passover celebration (Ex. 23:15; Deut. 16:16), during which only unleavened bread was permitted. It was eaten with bitter herbs (Ex. 12:8; Num. 9:11), reminding the Hebrews of the haste of their flight from Egypt, the hardships of the wilderness wanderings and of God's protection of them. See PASSOVER.

un·sa'vour·y. 1. Without savour, flavor; tasteless (Job 6:6). 2. Disagreeable; stubborn (II Sam. 22:27).

un·tem'pered mor'tar. The intent of these words (Ezek. 13:10, 11, 14, 15) is to describe

a claylike coating, weak and insipid, super-
ficial; something such as whitewash that
covers up, but provides no strength or re-
sistance to rains.

un·wit'ting·ly. Without knowing (Lev. 22:14).

up'per room. A room in the upper part of a
house, or built on the flat roof, used in summer because it was cooler and to entertain
guests. Such a room was the scene of the
Last Supper (Mark 14:15; Luke 22:12).
Also called "upper chamber" (II Kings 1:2;
Acts 9:37).

U·ri'ah. Bath-sheba's husband, whom David
sent to his death (II Sam., ch. 11). In Matt.
1:16 he is called Urias.

U·ri'jah. Among other O.T. men: 1. A prophet
put to death by King Jehoiakim of Judah
(Jer. 26:20-23); 2. A high priest in Ahaz'
reign (II Kings 16:10-16).

U'rim and Thum'mim. Certain unknown and
unidentifiable objects worn in the breastplate of the high priest and apparently serving as a device for determining the will of
God in doubtful cases (Ex. 28:30; Lev. 8:8).
This method was not used for inquiring the
divine will concerning private matters, but
was employed only in behalf of the nation;
hence the required place for the Urim and
Thummim was in the breastplate of judgment which bore the names of the 12 tribes
of Israel on 12 precious stones. With them
the will and desire of the Lord were learned
(Num. 27:21; Judg. 1:1; 20:18, 23, 27-28; I
Sam. 10:22; 14:36-42, etc.). There is no reference to their use after the reign of David.
Different explanations of what the Urim
and Thummim were and how they were
used have been offered. One is that they
were 2 appendages of the ephod and were
detachable. They were used as the lot, cast
like dice, and by their fall somehow revealed the divine will. Some have supposed
that they were flat stones, white on one side
and black on the other. If both fell white
side up, the answer was in the affirmative; if

both fell black, then negative. If one of each turned up, no reply had been given to the question.

u'su·ry. 1. The art or practice of lending money or goods at interest. The word did not suggest an excessive or unlawfully high rate of interest as it does today (Prov. 28:8; Jer. 15:10). According to their law the Israelites were not permitted to lend money or goods to their fellow Israelites at an interest rate of any kind; however, they were allowed to charge interest from foreigners (Deut. 23:19-20). The practice of lending money was primarily for the relief of the poor, who borrowed out of necessity (Lev. 25:36-37). 2. The interest paid on a loan. By the time of Jesus the lending of money had become recognized as a legitimate business practice (Matt. 25:27; Luke 19:23).

ut'ter. To speak or make known (Job 8:10).

Uz'zah. A man struck dead for touching the Ark (II Sam. 6:3-11; I Chron. 13:7-14).

Uz·zi'ah. (Also called Azariah.) King of Judah, son of Amaziah, in the time of Isaiah, Hosea and Amos (II Kings 14:21; ch. 15; Isa. 1:1; Hosea 1:1). There was a well-remembered earthquake in his reign (Amos 1:1; Zech. 14:5). He was stricken with leprosy after a successful reign and his son Jotham became regent-ruler (II Chron. 26:16-21). See KINGS, TABLE OF.

V

vac'il·late. To waver or hesitate; to be variable in one's emotions or judgments (II Cor. 1:17, RSV).

vag'a·bond. A wanderer (Gen. 4:12, KJV; Prov. 6:11, RSV).

vail, veil. 1. A garment worn by women. The Hebrew words all translated "veil" in the KJV include what seem to have been stoles (Isa. 3:23; S. of Sol. 5:7), hoods (Ex. 34:33-35; II Cor. 3:13-16), scarves or shawls (Gen. 24:65). kerchiefs to cover the

head (Ezek. 13:18), as well as face veils
(Gen. 38:14, 19; S. of Sol. 4:1, 3; Isa. 47:2).
It was not the custom for Hebrew women,
as with women in most Muslim communi-
ties, to go always veiled about the face. 2.
The veil that hung at the entrance to the
Holy of Holies, separating it from the holy
place. It is described in Lev. 16:2, 15; 21:23.

vain. Having no real value or significance;
worthless, empty, foolish, unreliable, as
transient as vapor (II Kings 18:20; Jer. 10:3;
Col. 2:8). To take God "in vain" is to treat
Him without respect, or profanely. Applied
to man's labors, "in vain" means without
results, fruitlessly (Lev. 26:16; Job 9:29).

vain·glo'ry. Excessive pride; extreme self-sat-
isfaction (Gal. 5:26; Phil. 2:3, KJV; Ezek.
7:20, RSV).

vale. A valley (Gen. 37:14; Deut. 1:7, KJV; Ps.
60:6; 108:7, RSV).

val'ley of vi'sion. A phrase used by Isaiah in
an ominous prophecy (22:1, 5), probably al-
luding to the idolatrous practice of divination, foretelling the future, that was carried
on at certain places in the Valley of Hinnom outside Jerusalem.

van'i·ty. 1. Any thing or act that is worthless,
empty, or futile (II Kings 17:15; Isa. 44:9;
Jer. 14:22). 2. The quality or fact of being
worthless, empty, etc.; futility (Eccles. 1:2;
2:1; Job 7:3; Jer. 10:15). 3. Foolishness (II
Peter 2:18).

va'por, va'pour. 1. A steamlike mist (Jer.
10:13; 51:16; Acts 2:19). 2. A cloud (Ps.
135:15). 3. Anything insubstantial (James
4:14). 4. Stormy weather (Job 36:33; Ps.
148:8).

Vash'ni. In I Chron. 6:28 the name Joel seems
to have been left out, and "vashni," meaning "the second," should apply to Abiah.
Cf. I Sam. 8:2.

Vash'ti. Xerxes' first queen (Esth. 1:9-2:4).

vaunt. To brag or boast (Judg. 7:2).

ven'ture, at a. At random; by mere chance (I
Kings 22:34).

ver·mil′ion. A bright red pigment, obtained from red ocher, widely used in painting the interiors of edifices (Jer. 22:14) and wooden objects.

vest′ments. The special ceremonial garments worn by Hebrew priests (Ezra 3:10) or worshipers of Baal (II Kings 10:22).

ves′ture. A garment or garments (Ps. 22:18), KJV; Gen. 49:11, RSV).

vex. To trouble or afflict (Matt. 15:22, KJV). "Vexation" (Job 5:2, etc., RSV) is often translated "grief" or "sorrow" in the KJV.

vi′al. 1. A container, a small piece of pottery; a juglet, used primarily for perfumes or oils (I Sam. 10:1). 2. A shallow cup or bowl (Rev. 5:8; 15:7; 16:2-4).

vile. Highly objectionable; of poor quality (Jer. 29:17).

vil′lan·y, vil′lain·y. Crime; depraved acts, evildoing. In Isa. 32:6 and Jer. 29:23, the Hebrew word suggests instead "folly."

vine. Any plant with a long, slender, prostrate or climbing stem, with tendrils, as a gourd (II Kings 4:39). The word usually denotes the common or grape vine. In regions that received enough rain, the soil and climate of Palestine were favorable to its culture. The vineyard was frequently on a hillside (Isa. 5:1). It was surrounded by a hedge or stone wall to keep out destructive animals (Num. 22:24; Ps. 80:8-13; Prov. 24:30-31). A booth or tower was erected for the watchman, a press was constructed, and a vat was hewn in the rock; all of these required upkeep (Isa. 1:8; 5:1-8; Matt. 21:33-41). The grapes ordinarily grown were red. They began to ripen in August. The dried grapes, or raisins, were preserved in clusters or pressed into cakes and were esteemed as food. The grapes were also eaten fresh or the juice was expressed and was drunk fresh or fermented. The gathering and wine-making season (Sept. to early Oct.) was a season of festivity (Judg. 9:27; Isa. 16:10; Jer. 25:30; 48:33). The image of

the vine lent itself to figures of speech by
the poets of Israel (Ps. 80:8) and by our
Lord (John 15:1-6).

vine·dress'er. One who cultivates vines,
prunes them, etc.

vin'e·gar. See GALL.

vine of Sod'om. The plant so called in Deut.
32:32 may be a trailing plant found in the
Dead Sea valley with a beautiful fruit
which resembles an orange but which when
fully ripe is merely a quantity of powder
and seeds inside its rind. It is a bitter and
drastic cathartic. But the language may be
figurative.

vi'per. Any of a family of poisonous snakes.
The viper is mentioned in Job 20:16; Isa.
30:6; 59:5. The poisonous reptile encountered by Paul on the island of Malta (Acts
28:3) was probably the common viper,
found all around the Mediterranean. The
horned viper is known to attack even
horses (Gen. 49:17). See also ASP; SERPENT.

vis'age. The face, usually the human face;
hence, appearance aspect (Lam. 4:8).

vi'sion. Something seen by other than normal
sight. In the Bible no sharp line is discernible between visions and dreams; the one
shades into the other. They were for the
most part private; they were apprehended
by the individual prophet, but not by his
companions. With the possible exception of
the diviner Balaam (Num. 24:34), visions
were granted to holy men only, men who
were surrendered to God's service, men between whom and their divine Sovereign
there "had arisen an understanding." These
visions were clearly distinguished by those
who saw them from ordinary dreams, and
were recognized as proceeding from God.
The visions recorded in the Bible stand
alone, in the history of religions, for purity
and righteousness. They always have a
clearly discernible moral and instructive
content. They belonged to an age of revelation, and came to men who in different

ways proved themselves to be vehicles of revelation.

vi'sion, val'ley of. See VALLEY OF VISION.

vis'it·a'tion. A reward or punishment brought upon people as a result of their behavior, through an act of God (Jer. 10:15; Hos. 9:7; Luke 19:44).

void. Containing nothing; empty; vacant (Gen. 1:2).

vo'tive of'fer·ing. See PEACE OFFERING.

vow. A solemn promise or pledge made to God, dedicating oneself to an act, service or way of life, usually made with the hope of receiving some benefit or favor. Vows were assumed voluntarily, but once made were regarded as compulsory (Num. 30:2; Deut. 23:21-23). In a few instances the Nazarite vows were prescribed by parents: Samson, Samuel, John the Baptist. Vows were taken by persons of every nation (Jonah 1:16) and not by Jews only. The first vow recorded in Scripture, and a typical case, is that of Jacob at Bethel (Gen. 28:18-22). See also OATH.

vow of'fer·ing. A variety of the peace offering, it could be presented upon making the vow or afterward, upon the granting of the person's request (Lev. 7:16-17; 22:21; ch. 27; Num. 6:21; 15:3-13; Deut. 23:21-23).

vul'ture. A bird of prey which has a head thinly covered with feathers or naked and which feeds largely on carrion, causing it to be considered "unclean." The vulture generally called the griffon (about 4 feet high) is so common in Palestine that it is impossible to look up in any part of the country and not see some of them soaring about, often at great heights. The ravines of the country hold great colonies of their eyries. A "gier eagle" (Lev. 11:18, KJV) is probably the Egyptian vulture, a smaller species common in Palestine in the warmer months. "Gier" means "vulture."

W

wa'fer. A thin, flat, crisp cake made of flour, sometimes flavored with honey (Ex. 16:31), but more often made of unleavened flour rubbed with oil. Wafers were used in connection with cereal offerings (Lev. 2:4), thank offerings (Lev. 7:12), and with the consecration of priests (Ex. 29:2, 23; Lev. 8:26).

wal'low. To roll about in (Jer. 48:26).

wars of the Lord, book of the. A last book mentioned in Num. 21:14, and from which direct quotation is made in the second half of v. 14 and in v. 15, and possibly also in vv. 17-18. It was apparently a collection of ancient Israelite poetry about the wars fought at the time of the conquest of the Promised Land.

watch'es of the night. See NIGHT WATCHES.

wa'ter of sep'a·ra'tion. Water used in the cleansing ceremony of a person who has become ceremonially unclean. The water is mixed with the ashes of the sacrifice and sprinkled on the person with a hyssop branch, symbolically removing the impurity (Num. 19:9, 13, 20; 31:23).

wave of'fer·ing. The exact nature and manner of this ritual act of offering agricultural produce before the altar are unclear. What was being offered to the Lord was apparently "waved" by the priests toward the altar, that is, toward the Lord, and then waved away. It was perhaps returned to the offerer for use again in parts of the more important sacrifices; but more likely wave offerings were handed over to the priests for the support of themselves and their families. See Ex. 29:24-25; Lev. 7:28-34; also OFFERINGS.

wax. To grow gradually larger, stronger (II Sam. 3:1; II Chron. 13:21; Rev. 18:3, KJV; Deut. 32:15, RSV). "Waxen" (Gen. 19:13, KJV) means "grown."

way'far·ing. Traveling, esp. on foot (Isa. 33:8).

way'mark. A guidepost (Jer. 31:21).

wed'lock. The marriage vows (Ezek. 16:38).

Weeks, Feast of. The second of the 3 annual festivals at which every male Israelite was required to appear before the Lord at the sanctuary (Ex. 34:22-23; II Chron. 8:12-13). It was so called because it was celebrated 7 complete weeks after the consecration of the harvest season, on the fiftieth day after the waving of the sheaf. This gave rise to the name Pentecost, or Fiftieth Day (Acts 2:1). It celebrated the close of the grain harvest. See also PASSOVER; TABERNACLES, FEAST OF.

Weights. The Hebrews used scales and weights (Lev. 19:36), and they weighed money—gold and silver in bars, bracelets, rings and other uncoined forms—as well as other commodities. The Hebrew denominations were: talent, mina (or maneh), shekel, gerah and bekah (half-shekel). Exact weights are necessary in the economic life of a nation (Deut. 25:13-16; Prov. 11:1). The inscriptions or marks on some weights found are doubtless more or less a guarantee of the exactness of the weight. Hebrew weights were of stone. From the varying weights of stones of the same denomination found by archaeologists, we infer that there were different local standards in Palestine, varying throughout the country, all subject to fluctuation from year to year or decade to decade. In Babylon and Assyria, 60 shekels made a mina; in Palestine a mina consisted of 50 shekels, except in Ezek. 45:12 where the addition gives a total of 60 to the mina. Various values may be determined for the weight of a shekel, ranging from 0.371 oz. avoirdupois to 0.432 oz., simply on the basis of shekel stone weights found in one excavated city, Lachish. For want of more exact knowledge, the shekel for practical purposes may be considered as 0.404

oz., avoirdupois. The several O.T. weights, then, have the following relationships and approximate weights avoirdupois:

gerah (1/20 shekel)	about 0.87 grains
1/3 shekel	about 0.135 ounce
bekah (1/2 shekel)	about 0.202 ounce
shekel	about 0.404 ounce
mina (50 shekels)	about 1.25 pounds
talent (3,000 shekels)	about 75.0 pounds

wen. An open sore, characterized by a discharge of pus (Lev. 22:22).

whale. In the Bible the word translated "whale" means any great animal of the sea or very large fish. But whales and dolphins were native to the Mediterranean, and many biblical people must have seen them.

wheat. A grain cultivated in all Bible lands from a very early period. In Palestine wheat was sown in November or December, after the rains began. The harvest was in April, May or June, depending on the locality, the soil and the weather at the time. The ordinary bread of the Hebrews was made of wheat flour (Ex. 29:2). Ears of grain were also roasted and eaten, and the grain, bruised and crushed, was also used as food. A grain of wheat as a symbol was used by our Lord (John 12:24) and by Paul (I Cor. 15:35-44). Egypt was the granary of the Mediterranean region, and vast quantities were shipped annually to Rome from Alexandria (Acts 27:6, 38). In some Bible verses where "corn" is used "wheat" should be understood. See CORN.

whelp. The young of a dog or a beast of prey. In Scripture it is used only with the young of a lion (Gen. 49:9; Jer. 51:38; Nahum 2:11-13).

whis′per·er. A talebearer or gossip (Prov. 16:28).

whit′ed sep′ul·chre. See SEPULCHRE.

Whit′sun′day. See PENTECOST.

wild beasts of the islands. See HYENA.

wil′der·ness. A place or region uncultivated

and uninhabited by people; it may be mountainous or flat, wooded or barren. The Wilderness of Judea is a barren, arid region in s. Palestine along the w. side of the Dead Sea; it is characterized by limestone cliffs. The land is capable of supporting vegetation; if sufficient water could be brought to it, it could be made fertile and productive. The vast Wilderness of the Wandering is the triangular area bordered by the Mediterranean Sea, the s. border of Palestine, the gorge of the Arabah, the Gulf of Akabah, the Gulf of Suez and the Bitter Lakes. The region is barren and the great nations of antiquity accordingly left it virtually to itself. The vast sandy region paralleling the Mediterranean in a broad band was the Wilderness of Shur. In the north-central portion of the inverted triangle, mostly sterile tableland 2,000–2,500 feet high, was the Wilderness of Paran (Num. 10:11–12; 13:25; I Sam. 25:1), in which the Israelites wandered, seeking water and food, for 38 years. That portion of it lying between Horeb and Kadesh was remembered by them as "that great and terrible wilderness" (Deut. 1:19). The Wilderness of Zin lay just s. of Beersheba and extended to Kadesh, on the edge of Paran, where there was water for man and beast and some herbage. The Wilderness of Sin is in the s. portion, the tip, of the triangle. Out of the wilderness experience a nation, Israel, was formed. In figurative language any place of misery and desolation was called a wilderness (Deut. 32:10; Ps. 107:40).

wil'low tree. Any tree of the genus *Salix* which includes willows as known in the U.S. (e.g. weeping willow) and poplars (Ezek. 17:5).

will wor'ship. Probably an ascetic practice, some rigor of devotion to create "an appearance of wisdom," but ineffective in controlling human behavior (Col. 2:23).

wine. Wine is made from grapes. The ripe

clusters were gathered in baskets (Jer. 6:9), carried to the press and thrown into it. The press was a shallow vat, with holes in the bottom, leading to a lower vat, often excavated in the rock. The grapes were crushed by treading (Neh. 13:15; Job 24:11). From the upper vat the juice trickled into the lower vat. From this receptacle the juice was put in wineskins (Matt. 9:17), or in large earthenware jars, where it was allowed to ferment. When the fermentation had proceeded far enough, the wine was drawn off into other vessels (Jer. 48:11-12). The juice of the grape when pressed out was used in various conditions: as sweet wine, or "must," fresh from the press; as wine, produced by the fermentation process; and as vinegar which resulted when the fermentation was let go unchecked to a final state. Wine differed from "strong drink" (Isa. 28:7; Luke 1:15), which was made from fruits other than grapes (e.g. dates) or from grain (e.g. barley), allowed to ferment. Wine was in common use: bread and wine signified the staples of life (Ps. 104:14-15; Prov. 4:17). Wine was offered as an ordinary hospitality (Gen. 14:18) and was served at festivities (Job 1:13; John 2:3). But the danger of excess was clearly discerned by the Hebrews, and the sinfulness of drunkenness was earnestly taught (I Sam. 1:14-16; Isa. 5:11-17; I Cor. 5:11; Gal. 5:21; Eph. 5:18; I Peter 4:3).

wine'bib·ber. One who drinks wine to excess (Prov. 23:20).

wine'skin. See BOTTLE.

win'now·ing. See THRESHINGFLOOR.

witch. A man or woman regarded as possessing evil powers (Deut. 18:10).

wit'ness. 1. Something providing or serving as evidence. In O.T. times writing was not common, so some other physical evidence was needed to prove that a business transaction had taken place with the consent of both parties: as by erecting a heap of stones as a memorial (Gen. 31:46-52), or by calling in men to witness the event (Gen. 23:10-18; Ruth 4:9), or by having someone draw up a deed or letter of divorce (Deut. 24:1, 3; Jer. 32:10). The concurrent testimony of at least 2 witnesses to give a first-hand account was required to establish guilt of a capital crime (Num. 35:30; Deut. 17:6; Heb. 10:28). The witness, before testifying, was adjured to tell the truth and conceal nothing; and then it was a sin to withhold evidence in his possession (Lev. 5:1; Prov. 29:24). False witness-bearing was forbidden in the Ten Commandments (Ex. 20:16). God was sometimes asked to act as a witness (Judg. 11:10; John 8:17-18; Rom. 1:9). In the N.T. especially, a witness is a person who attests to his belief in God and to his faith (Luke 24:48; Heb. 12:1; also Isa. 43:9).

wiz′ard. A sorcerer, esp. one thought to be capable of calling up the spirit of a dead person, which then temporarily inhabited the body of the sorcerer, supposedly, and spoke through the sorcerer of future happenings or of secrets of an unseen world. The Canaanites consulted wizards (Deut. 18:9-12); so did the Egyptians (Isa. 19:3); but for a Hebrew to go to such a person defiled him: a dead body was unclean, and so was the dead person's spirit. Consulting wizards was also an act of apostasy from God (Lev. 19:31; 20:6; Isa. 8:19). The offense of wizardry was punishable by death (Lev. 20:27). Saul enforced the law but later violated it himself (I Sam. 28:3, 7). Josiah also enforced it (II Kings 23:24), while Manasseh violated it shamelessly (21:6). See NECROMANCER.

wolf. The wolf of Palestine is a variety of the European species. Owing to the ease with which food is obtained and the mildness of the winter, these wolves do not hunt in packs but prowl alone. The wolf is carnivorous, wild and fierce (Isa. 11:6; Hab. 1:8), kills sheep (John 10:12) and is accustomed to hide by day and seek its prey in the evening (Zeph. 3:3).

wont. Accustomed (II Sam. 20:18).

worm'wood. A plant ranked with gall, having a very bitter juice (Prov. 5:4). In Amos 6:12 (RSV) it is a symbol of injustice.

wroth. Angry; wrathful (Isa. 28:21).

X-Y-Z

Xer'xes. See AHASUERUS.

yearn. To be filled with desire; to be uneasy with longing and anxiety (Gen. 43:30).

yoke'fel·low. A close comrade or companion (Phil. 4:3).

Yom Kip'pur. See ATONEMENT, DAY OF.

Zab'u·lon. See ZEBULUN.

Zac·chae'us. A wealthy publican, later converted, who climbed a tree to see Jesus (Luke 19:2).

Zach'a·ri'ah. See ZECHARIAH (2).

Zach'a·ri'as. 1. Father of John the Baptist, he lost his speech when a son was promised and regained it when the child was born (Luke, ch. 1). 2. A man murdered between the sanctuary and the altar (Matt. 23:35; Luke 11:51). Both these men are called Zechariah in the RSV.

Za'dok. A descendant of Eleazar (I Chron. 24:3), he was high priest with Abiathar until the joint priesthood came to an end. Because he remained faithful to David and Solomon, the office was restored to the line of Eleazar (II Sam. 15:29; I Kings 1:8, 39; 2:35). See ABIATHAR; HIGH PRIEST; SADDU-CEES.

Zea'lot. A member of a Jewish patriotic party organized in order to resist Roman aggression.

Zeb'e·dee. The father of James and John (Matt. 4:21-22; Mark 1:19-20).

Zeb'u·lun. 1. Jacob's tenth son, the sixth by Leah (Gen. 30:19-20; 35:23). 2. The descendants of Zebulun, also called Zebulunites (Deut. 33:18; Num. 26:27), and their territory, which lay to the w. of the Sea of Galilee and included Bethlehem (Josh. 19:10-16). 50,000 warriors of the tribe went with other tribes to make David king (I Chron. 12:33, 40). In Rev. 7:8 the tribe is called Zabulon.

Zech'a·ri'ah. This name is applied to more than 30 men in the O.T. Most notable: 1. A prophet stoned to death (II Chron. 24:20-21), possibly the same as Zacharias (2). 2. A king of Israel, son of Jeroboam II (called Zachariah in II Kings 14:29; 15:8-11; 18:2, KJV). See KINGS, TABLE OF. 3. Member of a priestly family and author of the book bearing his name. The RSV also uses this spelling for the father of John the Baptist and another N.T. man. See ZACHARIAS.

Zed'e·ki'ah. The name given by Nebuchadnezzar to Mattaniah, one of Josiah's sons, on appointing him vassal-king of Judah in place of his nephew, Jehoiachin. He was the last king of Judah. The story of his ultimate and disastrous rebellion against Nebuchadnezzar is told in II Kings 24:17-25:7; II Chron. 36:10-21; Jer., chs. 21; 27; 29; 37; 39; 51; 52. See KINGS, TABLE OF.

Ze·lo'tes. See ZEALOT.

Zeph'a·ni'ah. Among others, 1. A priest who carried messages between Jeremiah and Zedekiah (Jer. 21:1; 27:3; 52:24-27); 2. The prophet.

Ze·rub'ba·bel. Governor of Judah (c. 520-515 B.C.), his influence in rebuilding the Temple led to its being known as Zerubbabel's Temple. He was the representative of the Davidic monarchy, and a Messianic hope appears to have been centered upon him (Hag., chs. 1; 2; cf. Ezra 3:1-4:3; Zech. 4:6-10). In Matt. 1:12-13 (KJV) he is called Zorobabel. See also SAMARITAN; TEMPLE.

Zeus. See JUPITER.

Zim'ri. A military officer under Elah, king of Israel, whom he assassinated. Zimri ruled for one week (I Kings 16:8-20). See KINGS, TABLE OF.

Zip-po'rah. A daughter of the priest Jethro and wife of Moses (Ex. 2:21; 4:20; 18:1-6).

Zo-rob'a-bel. See ZERUBBABEL.

THE PARABLES OF CHRIST

	MATTHEW	MARK	LUKE	JOHN
The Mote and the Beam in the Eye	——	——	6,41-42	——
Builders upon the Rock and the Sand	7,24-27	——	6,47-49	——
The Two Forgiven Debtors	——	——	7,40-50	——
The Sower	13,3-9, 18-23	4,3-9, 14-20	8,5-8, 11-15	——
Seed Sown and Bearing Fruit		4,26-29	——	——
The Wheat and the Tares	13,24-30, 37-43	——	——	——
The Grain of Mustard Seed	13,31-32	4,30-32	13,18-19	——
Leaven in the Meal	13,33	——	13,20-21	——
Hidden Treasure	13,44	——	——	——
The Pearl of Great Price	13,45-46	——	——	——
The Net	13,47-50	——	——	——
The Householder	13,52	——	——	——
A Parable of the Lost Sheep	18,12-14	——	——	——
The Unforgiving Servant	18,23-35	——	——	——